War and Remembrance in the Twen

No scholarly consensus exists about how the terms 'memory' and 'collective memory' may most fruitfully inform historical study. Hence there is still much room for reflection and clarification in this branch of cultural history. How war has been remembered collectively is the central question in this volume. War in the twentieth century is a vivid and traumatic phenomenon which left behind it survivors who engage time and time again in acts of remembrance. Thus this volume, which contains essays by outstanding scholars of twentieth-century history, focuses on the issues raised by the shadow of war in this century. Drawing on material from countries in Europe, and from Israel and the United States, the contributors have adopted a 'social agency' approach which highlights the behaviour, not of whole societies or of ruling groups alone, but of the individuals who do the work of remembrance, who feel they have a duty to remember, and who want to preserve a piece of the past. More specifically, the traumatic collective memory resulting from the horors of the First World War, the Spanish Civil War, the Second World War, and the Algerian War is examined through studies of public forms of remembrance, such as museums and exhibitions, literature and film, thus demonstrating that a popular kind of collective memory is still very much alive.

JAY WINTER is a Reader in Modern History at the University of Cambridge and Fellow of Pembroke College, Cambridge. His recent publications include *Sites of memory, sites of mourning* (1995) and, with Jean-Louis Robert, *Capital cities at war: Paris, London, Berlin, 1914–1919* (1997). He is winner of an Emmy for Outstanding TV Series 1997.

EMMANUEL SIVAN is Professor of History at the Hebrew University of Jerusalem, and is a world authority on Islamic history. His publications include *Radical Islam* (1990), *The 1948 generation* (in Hebrew, 1991) and *Mythes Politiques Arabes* (1995).

Studies in the Social and Cultural History of Modern Warfare

General Editor
Jay Winter *Pembroke College, Cambridge*

Advisory Editors
Omer Bartov *Brown University*
Carol Gluck *Columbia University*
David M. Kennedy *Stanford University*
Paul Kennedy *Yale University*
Antoine Prost *Université de Paris-Sorbonne*
Emmanuel Sivan *The Hebrew University of Jerusalem*
Robert Wohl *University of California, Los Angeles*

In recent years the field of modern history has been enriched by the exploration of two parallel histories. These are the social and cultural history of armed conflict, and the impact of military events on social and cultural history.

Studies in the Social and Cultural History of Modern Warfare presents the fruits of this growing area of research, reflecting both the colonization of military history by cultural historians and the reciprocal interest of military historians in social and cultural history, to the benefit of both. The series offers the latest scholarship in European and non-European events from the 1850s to the present day.

For a list of titles in the series, please see end of book.

War and Remembrance in the Twentieth Century

Edited by

Jay Winter and Emmanuel Sivan

CAMBRIDGE
UNIVERSITY PRESS

PUBLISHED BY THE PRESS SYNDICATE OF THE UNIVERSITY OF CAMBRIDGE
The Pitt Building, Trumpington Street, Cambridge CB2 1RP, United Kingdom

CAMBRIDGE UNIVERSITY PRESS
The Edinburgh Building, Cambridge CB2 2RU, United Kingdom
http://www.cup.cam.ac.uk
40 West 20th Street, New York, NY 10011–4211, USA   http://www.cup.org
10 Stamford Road, Oakleigh, Melbourne 3166, Australia

© Jay Winter and Emmanuel Sivan   1999

First published 1999
First paperback edition 2000

Printed in the United Kingdom at the University Press, Cambridge

Typeset in Plantin 10/12 pt. [CE]

A catalogue record for this book is available from the British Library

Library of Congress cataloguing in publication data
War and remembrance in the twentieth century / edited by Jay Winter
and Emmanuel Sivan.
    p.   cm. (Studies in the social and cultural history of modern warfare: 5)
ISBN 0 521 64035 0 (hardcover)
1. History, Modern – 20th century.   2. Memory.
3. War and society.   4. Civilization, Modern – 20th century.
I. Winter, J. M.   II. Sivan, Emmanuel.   III. Series.
D421.W36   1999
909.82 – dc21   98–24909   CIP

ISBN 0 521 64035 0 hardback
ISBN 0 521 79436 6 paperback

Contents

Preface

There is a rough common denominator in this book, fashioned through discussion among contributors. We all refer in different ways to what may be termed a 'social agency' approach, which highlights the behaviour not of whole societies or of ruling groups alone, but rather of those groups and individuals, frequently but not always obscure, who do the work of remembrance. This interpretation is set out by the editors in the first chapter, in which many of the conceptual problems in the study of 'collective memory' are addressed. We hasten to add that the contributors to this volume have adopted very different approaches to the problem of 'social agency', collective memory, and victimhood. These differences are discussed in the introduction. Our intention is simply to introduce a rich field of historical inquiry – that of collective memory – and to clarify its topography by reference to the experience of war in this century. No orthodoxy arises here, though a number of questions in common recur throughout this volume.

Thanks are due to many people and groups whose support and assistance we are happy to acknowledge. A grant from the Harry Frank Guggenheim Foundation made this collective investigation possible. The encouragement, support, and critical participation of Karen Colvard and James Hester of the Foundation were of the greatest importance. They joined the contributors and a number of other scholars at two fruitful meetings in 1995 and 1996 at Pembroke College, Cambridge and Chinchón, Spain, where these questions were formulated and some approaches to them thrashed out. We are particularly grateful to the staff of these institutions for providing a congenial environment in which these difficult issues were discussed, and for the help of the following scholars who also contributed to the evolution of this project: Susan Bayly, Elisabeth Domansky, Lauri Harkness, Ira Katznelson, Dori Laub, Jayne Leonard, Tony Robben, Steve Southwick, and Arthur Waldron.

Emmanuel Sivan
Jay Winter

Introduction

This book arose from the sense of unease the editors have felt over a number of years about weaknesses in the huge and rapidly growing historical literature on the subject of 'collective memory'. It seems as if everyone is talking about this subject. The terms 'memory' and 'collective memory' appear with such frequency and ease that readers may be under the impression that there is a scholarly consensus about what these terms mean and how they may be used effectively in historical study.

Nothing could be further from the truth. There is much discussion, but very little agreement, as to whether or not there are meaningful links between individual cognitive psychological processes and the cultural representations and gestures of groups. How groups 'remember' – or even if they 'remember' – cannot be extrapolated simply from evidence on the ways individuals store and retrieve information or images. Furthermore, the word 'memory' has profoundly different shades of meaning in different languages. It should not be surprising, therefore, that historians frequently talk at cross purposes or in complete ignorance of each other's position in this field.

A good example of the ambiguity of much writing on collective memory is the work of Pierre Nora, the organizer and inspiration behind an influential, seven-volume collection of essays on sites of collective memory, *Les lieux de mémoire*, published between 1984 and 1992. His programmatic essay presents his point of view on collective memory in emphatic terms. 'Memory is constantly on our lips', he writes, 'because it no longer exists.' Or rather it no longer exists in the midst of life.[1] Since 'society has banished ritual', and thereby 'renounced memory',[2] everyone cries out for artificial or symbolic substitutes for what less rapidly changing societies have taken for granted. What we have is

---

[1] Pierre Nora (ed.) *Realms of memory. The construction of the French past. I. Conflicts and divisions*, trans. by Arthur Goldhammer (New York: Columbia University Press, 1996), p. 1.

[2] Ibid., p. 6.

second-order memory: we collect, organize, exhibit, catalogue, but observe the form and not the substance of memory: 'The trace negates the sacred but retains its aura.'[3]

These sites, and their study by historians, reproduce what literature once did, and now – in Nora's view – no longer can accomplish. Hence the exploration of these artefacts and phenomena helps to refill 'our depleted fund of collective memory'. Thus a new kind of 'History offers profundity to an epoch devoid of it, true stories to an epoch devoid of real novels.' 'Memory', he concludes, 'has been promoted to the center of history: thus do we mourn the loss of literature.'[4]

When Nora argues that society has banished ritual, or claims that it has no further use for the sacred,[5] and that literature is dead, he displays the weakest links in his position. Anybody observing the difficulties attendant on the assimilation of Muslims into French society would scoff at such claims. The sacred hasn't vanished, though few would seek it primarily in the institutional life of churches and synagogues.

Furthermore, if the claim is that society has banished ritual, and not that French society has banished ritual, we need to pose the question of the strength of the claim in other than French contexts. The parochial character of Nora's argument raises doubts as to its relevance outside France. It is true that historical legitimacy has been contested terrain since the revolution of 1789, and, ever since, polemicists have ransacked the symbolic vocabulary and imagery of French history to espouse one cause and deride others. But the same is true of German history, and more recently, of Russian history. What is missing here is an account of precisely what is French about the exercise Nora conducts.

The Frenchness of the position is its particular kind of cultural pessimism. Again there are equivalents across the Rhine and elsewhere, but French pessimism has its own distinctive flavour. Where else would intelligent commentators equate the decline in the birth rate and the drop in the number of people speaking the French language with the decline of Western civilization itself? Are these the unspoken assumptions of a world of French intellectuals who take themselves just a bit too seriously?

The insularity of the claims made by Nora has another source. The French government spends more on museums and cultural activities per capita and as a share of the national budget than does any other Western country. Why? Is it because the sacred is dead and we need a set of symbolic substitutes? The explanation may be more mundane. History sells: it is a popular and money-making trade because it locates family

---

[3] Ibid. p. 9.   [4] Ibid. p. 20.   [5] Ibid. p. 7.

stories in bigger, more universal, narratives. The government invests in this part of the service sector because it pays to do so.

The huge growth of museums at the end of the twentieth century is also a reflection of another facet of the 'memory business': the contemporary link between grandparents and grandchildren. This link has spawned a huge market for museums and literature about this turbulent century. Yes, literature: the same literature which Nora considers dead. Examples abound: like Jean Rouaud's *Champs d'honneur* winner of the Prix Goncourt in 1991,[6] or Sebastien Japrisot's moving *Un long dimanche de fiançaille*,[7] or Pat Barker's fictional trilogy on the Great War,[8] or Sebastian Faulks's powerful *Birdsong*.[9] Today's grandparents were children after the 1914–18 war, and their stories – family stories – are now embedded in history, and fiction, and exhibitions, and museums, and pilgrimage, in all the stuff of ritual Nora considers as signs of a loss of 'true' collective memory. The linkage between the young and the old – now extended substantially with the life span – is so central to the concept of memory that it is surprising that Nora doesn't simply urge us to leave our libraries and just look around, at our own families. A vital, palpable, popular kind of collective memory is, then, alive. Its obituary, written by Nora, is premature and misleading.

Given the difficulties and ambiguities raised by a work of a major historian like Pierre Nora, it is evident that that there is much room for reflection and clarification in this branch of cultural history. This book is a preliminary step towards that end. It focuses on one particular set of problems in the field of 'collective memory', namely, the issues raised by the shadow of war in this century.

How war has been remembered collectively is the central question in this volume. We investigate this issue in the twentieth-century context, when the reach of war – geographically and socially – has extended far beyond that of earlier, non-industrial conflicts. Most of the chapters are about European experience, though some American and Israeli evidence is examined too. We have chosen war in this century as a vivid, indeed a traumatic phenomenon, which has left in its wake survivors who engage time and again in acts of remembrance. The voluminous records they have left enable us to put to the test the ambiguities and inner tensions of our general subject: the contour and character of 'collective memory'.

A word or two about coverage is essential. Our aim is to address a set

---

[6] Jean Rouaud, *Champs d'honneur* (Paris: Editions de Minuit, 1990).
[7] Sebastien Japrisot, *Un long dimanche de fiançailles: roman* (Paris: Denoël, 1991).
[8] Pat Barker, *Regeneration* (New York: Viking, 1991); *The eye in the door* (New York: Viking, 1993); *The ghost road* (New York: Viking, 1995).
[9] Sebastian Faulks, *Birdsong* (London: Hutchinson, 1993).

of questions about the nature of 'collective memory' in the context of twentieth-century warfare. We do not, indeed could not, survey more than a handful of cases drawn from the documentary history of this century. We discuss issues related to the First World War, to the Spanish Civil War, to the Second World War, to the Algerian War, and to the shadows left by each of these conflicts in Europe, the United States, and the Middle East. In one volume, little more is possible. If time and space permitted, it would be valuable to examine other instances, covering the globe from China to Armenia to Rwanda to Argentina. Our field of inquiry is limited, and extra-European historians and social scientists have much to add.

There is one set of problems, specifically European, which we do not treat directly, not because it is undocumented or unimportant, but because it is such a special case that it threatens to overshadow all other cases. There is now a huge literature on Germany and the Holocaust, and on German approaches to remembering their war between 1939 and 1945 and on the crimes committed during it.[10] Such commentaries collide with a problem so complex that we believe it is unacceptable simply to lump together the Holocaust and the experience of war in this century. For the history of the Death Camps is the history of industrial murder, remote from war of the kind we consider in chapters on Europe in 1914 to 1918, on Spain in 1936 to 1939, on Algeria in 1954 to 1962, in the Middle East, and so on. We discuss the problem of mass death in Russia in the First World War, in the Civil War, in the Gulag, and in the Second World War, but here too we are remote from the history of the 'Final Solution'.

There is a special danger here. Locating Germany and the Holocaust within the framework we set out is, on the face of it, a challenging assignment. But to do so *here* risks 'historicizing' the Holocaust, making it one more chapter in the history of warfare, akin to the American treatment of Indians or the Japanese rape of Nanking. There are different and violently expressed views on this issue. We would prefer to leave the subject to a separate volume, since its inclusion presents one set of risks, while its exclusion presents another.

---

[10] Some recent examples are: Ian Buruma, *Wages of guilt. Memories of war in Germany and Japan* (London: Jonathan Cape, 1994); Anson Rabinbach and Jack Zipes (eds.), *Germans and Jews since the Holocaust. The changing situation in West Germany* (London: Holmes & Meier, 1987); Norbert Kampe, 'Normalizing the Holocaust: the recent historians' debate in the Federal Republic of Germany', *Holocaust and Genocide Studies*, 2, 1 (1987), pp. 61–80; Mannfred Henningsen, 'The politics of memory: Holocaust and legitimacy in post-Nazi Germany', *Holocaust and Genocide Studies*, 4, 1 (1989), pp. 15–26; Wolfgang Benz, 'Auschwitz and the Germans: the remembrance of the Genocide', *Holocaust and Genocide Studies*, 8, 1 (1994), pp. 25–40.

We have not ignored these issues entirely. Three of our authors have addressed them: directly, in the chapter on French survivor-'witnesses'; tangentially, in the chapter on German and Italian post-1945 films; and indirectly in the discussion of Walter Benjamin's ambiguous treatment of the 'healing' effects of remembrance; he died, of course, before Auschwitz, but his ideas have a disturbing relevance to the overall subject. Remembrance as a means to healing, Benjamin held, may perpetrate injustice, by covering up crimes and thereby protecting their perpetrators. But those ultimately responsible for his death and those of millions of other Jews in Europe were guilty of a crime so enormous as to demand separate discussion, inquiry, and reflection, and not to be treated as one story among many. If this book stimulates such research, and if the framework of theories of 'collective memory' and 'social agency' proves useful in that inquiry, then the editors and all the contributors will have realized one of the aims of this book.

1   Setting the framework

Jay Winter and Emmanuel Sivan

Collective remembrance

Collective remembrance is public recollection. It is the act of gathering bits and pieces of the past, and joining them together in public. The 'public' is the group that produces, expresses, and consumes it. What they create is not a cluster of individual memories; the whole is greater than the sum of the parts. Collective memory is constructed through the action of groups and individuals in the light of day. Passive memory – understood as the personal recollections of a silent individual – is not collective memory, though the way we talk about our own memories is socially bounded. When people enter the public domain, and comment about the past – their own personal past, their family past, their national past, and so on – they bring with them images and gestures derived from their broader social experience. As Maurice Halbwachs put it, their memory is 'socially framed'.[1] When people come together to remember, they enter a domain beyond that of individual memory.

The upheavals of this century have tended to separate individual memories from politically and socially sanctioned official versions of the past. All political leaders massage the past for their own benefit, but over the last ninety years many of those in power have done more: they have massacred it. Milan Kundera tells the story of a photograph of the political leadership of the Czech socialist republic in 1948. One man in the photo was later purged. That individual had been removed from the photograph; all that remained was his hat, in the hands of a surviving colleague.[2] The snapshot – an image of a past event – had been

---

[1] Maurice Halbwachs, *On collective memory*, trans. by Lewis A. Coser (Chicago: University of Chicago Press, 1992). For recent elaborations, see Iwona Irwin-Zarecki, *Frames of remembrance: the dynamics of collective memory* (New Brunswick: Transaction, 1994); and Peter Burke, 'History as social memory,' in *Memory: history, culture and the mind*, edited by Thomas Butler (Oxford: Basil Blackwell, 1990), pp. 97–113.

[2] Milan Kundera, *The book of laughter and forgetting* (Harmondsworth: Penguin, 1980), p. 3.

reconfigured; those who 'remembered' that the hat had once had a man under it, had to think again.

In many other ways, private and public modes of remembering were severed in the Soviet period. The lies and distortions were terribly visible.[3] To be sure, there were counter-trends. In some authoritarian societies, popular theatre and ceremony played a critical role, especially in bringing women's voices into the chorus of public comment on the past. Because memory can be gendered, women's testimony arises in different places than that of men.[4] But this distinction should not be drawn too sharply. The poetry that Nadezdha Mandelstam memorized, written by her husband Osip Mandelstam, was their joint and precious possession. She stayed alive, she said, to ensure that his voice was not silenced.[5] Others were not so fortunate.

The circulation of fiction was similarly significant in the dark days of dictatorship.[6] Literature played a critical role in keeping collective memory alive in a society where the writing of history was a routine operation dedicated to the glorification of the regime. Not only history, but the names of towns, roads, and the like became mythologized. New toponyms, inspired by the Russian revolution, tended to abolish all diversity, whether regional or cultural. They homogenized the country, shaping it all in the image of the all-powerful centre. In a word, ideology replaced memory by imposing the imaginary notion of a uniform Soviet people. Literature taught otherwise.[7]

Under Fascism or other repressive regimes, the invasion of everyday private life by political agents contaminated memories of mundane events; how to write about family life under such circumstances was a profound challenge. Where 'normality' ended and the monstrous began is a question which may never be answered fully. A similar divide between recollections of the rhythms of daily life under the Nazis – private memories – and 'amnesia' about the disappearance of the Jews has spawned a huge interpretive literature. As Saul Friedlander has observed, 'the Nazi past is too massive to be forgotten, and too repellent to be integrated into the "normal" narrative of memory'.[8] This dilemma

---

[3] See the discussion in Alain Brossat, Sonia Combe, Jean-Yves Potel, and Jean-Charles Szurek (ed.), À l'Est la mémoire retrouvée (Paris: Armand Colin, 1990).

[4] Elizabeth F. Loftus, Mahzarin R. Banaji, and Rachel A. Foster, 'Who remembers what?: gender differences in memory' Michigan Quarterly Review, 1 (1987), pp. 26, 64–85.

[5] Nadezhda Mandelstam, Hope against hope, trans. by Max Hayward (New York: Athenaeum, 1974).

[6] Andrei Plesu, 'Intellectual life under dictatorship' Representations, 49 (1996), pp. 61–71.

[7] Luisa Passerini (ed.), Memory and totalitarianism, International yearbook of oral history and life stories, vol. I (Oxford: Oxford University Press, 1992), 'Introduction', p. 13.

[8] Saul Friedlander, Memory, history, and the extermination of the Jews of Europe (Bloomington: Indiana University Press, 1993), p. 2.

has been the subject of entire libraries; it has also informed painting, sculpture, architecture, and other facets of the visual arts.

It would be idle to assume that these problems are restricted to authoritarian regimes. Even the democratic West has had trouble in reconciling its official versions of the past with the memories of millions of ordinary people. This is especially true in the case of that other collective trauma of the twentieth century, that of the two world wars. Of course, the two histories – that of Fascism and communism on the one hand, and of warfare on the other – are inextricably mixed. The shape of 'the short twentieth century'[9] emerged from the catastrophe of the First World War. It is only now in the 1990s, after the collapse of communism, and at a time when the European state system created in 1919 is being reconfigured, that we are able to see clearly some of the fundamental features of this brutal century.

Historians have contributed to public conversations about the recent past. They have helped to organize exhibitions, create museums, and write both for their colleagues and students, as well as for a wider public. But it is important to separate any notion of 'collective memory' from historical knowledge. Collective memory is not what historians say about the past. These professionals try to provide a documentary record of events, but in doing so they almost always depart from private memories. Anyone who has conducted interviews with participants in public events can attest to that. Collective memory is not historical memory, though the two usually overlap at many points. Professional history matters, to be sure, but only to a small population. Collective remembrance is a set of acts which go beyond the limits of the professionals. These acts may draw from professional history, but they do not depend on it.

This is apparent in the uproar that greets some public exhibitions, presenting a narrative which varies from individual recollection, from the official version of events, or offends some particular sensibilities. Collective remembrance is apparently too important a subject to be left to the historians.

This is evident in the way wars have been remembered in public. In all combatant countries there has been a proliferation of monuments, understood as literary, visual, or physical reminders of twentieth-century warfare. Many are self-serving tributes; most go beyond state-sponsored triumphalism to the familial and existential levels where many of the effects of war on the lives of ordinary people reside.

Here too the dialectic between remembering and forgetting is visible,

---

[9] E. J. Hobsbawm, *The age of extremes* (London: Michael Joseph, 1994), p. 4.

and is especially salient in non-official forms of collective remembrance. This book is intended as a contribution to the history of collective remembrance in the twentieth century. Its focus is on wars, soldiers, and victims of wars in Europe, the Middle East, and North America. Its purpose is to examine collective remembrance as the outcome of agency, as the product of individuals and groups who come together, not at the behest of the state or any of its subsidiary organizations, but because they have to speak out.

Why? Here we are at the intersection of private memories, family memories, and collective memories. The men and women whose activity we explore in this book lived through war as trauma, understood as an overwhelming, sustained, and mass experience. Many were in mourning; most were torn by war from one set of daily rhythms and were in search of another. Their decisions to act in public – by creating associations, by writing memoirs, by producing films, by speaking out in a host of ways – were profoundly personal. But they were not only private matters, since they existed in a social framework, the framework of collective action.

This emphasis on agency, on activity, on creativity, highlights a different approach to the cultural history of this century. We too speak of 'collective memory', but depart from those who define it as the property of dominant forces in the state, or of all survivors of war in the privacy of their lives, or as some facet of the mental furniture of a population – what the French like to call their *mentalités*.

Instead, we privilege the term 'collective remembrance'. The primary advantage of this shift in terminology is the avoidance of generalizations which simply cannot be true. The 'collective memory' of war is not what everybody thinks about war; it is a phrase without purchase when we try to disentangle the behaviour of different groups within the collective. Some act; others – most others – do not. Through the constant interrogation of actors and actions, we separate 'collective memory' from a vague wave of associations which supposedly come over an entire population when a set of past events is mentioned. Given the centrality of the experience of war in this century, we can and must do better than that.

To speak of 'collective remembrance' is to begin that task. Wars, soldiers, and the victims of war have been remembered in ceremony, in ritual, in stone, in film, in verse, in art; in effect in a composite of narratives. All are charged with the weight of the event: twentieth-century warfare is infused with horror as well as honour; the proper balance in representing the two is never obvious.

Those who make the effort to remember collectively bring to the task their private memories. They also use language and gestures filled with social meaning. But the key mid-point, the linkage that binds their stories and their gestures, between *homo psychologicus* – the man of private memory – and *homo sociologicus* – the man of socially determined memory – is action. *Homo actans* is our subject. He or she acts, not all the time, and not usually through instruction from on high, but as a participant in a social group constructed for the purpose of commemoration. Their efforts are at the heart of this book.

Many different approaches obtain. But one unifying element persists. We stand at a mid-point between two extreme and unacceptable positions in this field: between those who argue that private memories are ineffable and individual, and those who see them as entirely socially determined, and therefore present whether or not anyone acts on them. With Blondel, we urge that such approaches are best located in 'the gallery of useless abstractions'.[10] In between is the palpable, messy activity which produces collective remembrance.

In this as in other areas, agency is arduous. Its opportunity costs – time, money, effort – are substantial. And it rarely lasts. Other tasks take precedence; other issues crowd out the ones leading to public work. And ageing takes its toll: people fade away, either personally or physically. The collective remembrance of past warfare, old soldiers, and the victims of wars is, therefore, a quixotic act. It is both an effort to think publicly about painful issues in the past and one which is bound to decompose over time.

This fading away is inevitable. But the effort to create artefacts or ceremonies in the aftermath of war has been so widespread that it is time to consider them not as reflections of current political authority or a general consensus – although some clearly are one or the other, but rather as a set of profound and evanescent expressions of the force of civil society itself. The history of collective remembrance of wars in this century is infused with both sadness and dignity; an understanding of its contours requires both.

Homo psychologicus

The difficult terrain between individual memories and collective remembrance may be traversed more safely in the light of the findings of two very different communities of scholars. The first studies cognitive psychology; the second, social psychology and patterns of action. Each has much to add to our understanding of remembrance as a social activity.

[10] As cited by Coser in his introduction to Halbwachs, *On collective memory*, p.13.

Many historians use the term 'memory' as if it were unproblematic. But here both scientific and historical disputes abound. Decades of empirical research in cognitive psychology have unearthed sets of terms and pathways which have a direct bearing on the nature of individual memory. And since collective remembrance is an activity of individuals coming together in public to recall the past, historians would do well to reflect on the findings of cognitive psychologists on how memory happens.

These findings are much too complex and varied to be discussed in detail. All we can do here is to provide a stylized and schematic summary of the major lines of interpretation in this vast and growing field.[11] When relevant, we highlight terms in the scientific literature which have a bearing on the historical problem we address below.

Social learning

Cognitive psychologists use the term *social learning*. It is a process to be distinguished from declarative learning, or learning facts about nature (which plant is poison ivy) or the human environment (how to tell the time). Declarative learning is storing away bits of information, such as how many centimetres are in an inch, or when the Battle of Hastings took place. Social learning, in contrast, is the assimilation by an individual of narratives or *scripts* about himself and his exchanges with other people. Given the slow pace of child development, and the care needed at an early age, it is a commonplace to say that we are never the first people to know who we are.

It should be evident why a student of 'social learning' cannot ignore the findings of cognitive psychologists. It is true that their experiments are unavoidably partial and 'unreal', in the sense of being unable to show the overlap and interaction of individuals and groups. But they force us to return to the individual, whose sense of the past is both the beginning and the end of all processes of 'social learning'.

---

[11] F. Bartlett, *Remembering* (Cambridge: Cambridge University Press, 1932); A. Baddeley, *Your memory: a user's manual* (London: Penguin, 1992; A. M. Hoffman and H. S. Hoffman, *Archives of memory* (Lexington, Ky.: University of Kentucky Press, 1990), esp. ch. 1; M. Howe, *Introduction to human memory* (New York: Harper & Row, 1970); L.R. Squire, *Memory and brain* (New York: Oxford University Press, 1987); Michael Schudson, 'Dynamics of distortion in collective memory', in *Memory distortion: how minds, brains and societies reconstruct the past*, edited by Michael Schudson (Cambridge, Mass.: Harvard University Press, 1995), pp. 353–73; D. J. Schachter, *Searching for memory* (New York: Basic Books, 1996); Y. Dudai, *The neurobiology of memory* (New York: Oxford University Press, 1989).

Memory traces

The process of recollection has a biochemical and a neurological dimension, both of which are still the subject of elementary research. Despite the sheer complexity of these processes, a number of rudimentary findings may be identified.

The first is the notion of a *memory trace*. Most experiences leave long-term *memory traces*, recorded in our *episodic memory* system – the system which encodes 'what happened', that is, events. It is to be distinguished from systems which record not 'what' but 'that' – mundane, matter-of-fact events or details about nature or human affairs, grouped under the rubric of *semantic memory*. Long-term memory is defined as the retention for more than one minute of either kind of information. All these traces differ, though, in their density.

They also differ in accessibility for *recognition* or for *recall*. The *density* (or weight of a memory) is shaped to a large extent by the dramatic nature of the experience, its uniqueness, its being reconsidered or reinterpreted after the fact as a turning point. Density is further enhanced by the emotional nature of the experience (quite often dramatic) and its autobiographical nature. *Autobiographical memory* appears to be the most enduring kind of memory. For example, combat experience is particularly dense because it is personal and dramatic. Harrowing moments are denser still.

Interference

There is no convincing evidence so far of the physical decay or disappearance of long-term memory traces. They seem to be deposited in the brain in an archeological manner; that is, they are there, even though other traces are on top of them.

Longitudinal studies have found these traces surviving over six decades. But some are not immediately available for retrieval. Why? Because other memory traces create 'layers' deposited on top of the original one, impeding its direct and immediate recall.

Psychologists refer to this obscuring or eclipsing of a memory trace by the terms *retroactive* or *proactive interference*. An instance of 'retroactive interference' is when newly encoded memory traces reshape, cover, or eclipse older memory traces. Proactive interference occurs when early memories shape our sense of the context or relative importance of later experiences.

Recognition and recall

The nature of interference is not the same with all memory traces. Here psychologists operate a distinction between 'recognition' and 'recall'. *Recognition* is an association, an identification of an issue; *recall* is its evaluation, requiring more active effort. Students may recognize the name 'John Milton', but only some recall the character and significance of *Paradise Lost*. For our purposes, the distinction is important, because recognition of memory traces may survive interference, even when recall doesn't. This is hardly surprising, since the amount of information stored up for purposes of recognition is much less than that needed for recall.

Distortion, reinterpretation, interpolation

Evidence produced so far supports the view that the *distortion* of memory traces does not usually happen after the initial *encoding/reconstruction* of the experience in the memory trace. Distortion precedes encoding.[12]

Another way of putting this point is to note that a memory trace is not an exact replica of an experience, even under the best of circumstances. Memory traces have a *telescoping/selective* nature. That is, a number of events or personalities are contracted into one, or some aspects of an experience are ordered and highlighted. In effect, some reinterpretation has already been made at this initial stage. It may be done through *schemata* or *scripts* which are either personal ('this is the story of my life'; or 'I'm always missing opportunities') or borrowed from the culture or sub-culture of which the individual is a member ('it's hard to be a Jew').

Here we come to an area very familiar to historians. Memory traces may be interfered with even after encoding, by a process of manipulation, or *interpolated learning*. Outside influences can persuade us of the truth of certain notions or the reality of certain events, by advertising, brain-washing, or propaganda.

The distortion and selection of visual memories is easier than in the case of verbal ones. But in both, interference operates either by manipulating major so-called 'facts' and/or by introducing key interpretive terms which have clear-cut resonances for the *semantic memory* of the individual and are, of course, culture-dependent. The result is a new script which integrates pieces of information brought to bear upon the

---

[12] E. F. Loftus, *Eyewitness testimony* (Cambridge: Cambridge University Press, 1979).

interpretation of the event. As we all know, such new scripts may vary dramatically from the original memory, let alone the event itself.

Rehearsal

Later access or recall of memories is greatly enhanced by the retelling of these narratives, either by individuals alone or in public. Conversation is a fundamental social act; hence the importance for the memory of war of the oral testimony of survivors. *Rehearsal* is done by the individual not by the society, through story-telling or meditation, though individuals reinforce their personal rehearsals in social events or rituals. Such rituals provide cues which are essential for triggering the process of recall/ retrieval. While individuals may have their own cues, ritual provides them with social cues – moments of silence, saluting the flag, and so on.

Some events are sufficiently powerful to be recalled initially without rehearsal. An earthquake is a good case in point. One hit San Francisco in 1994. Virtually everybody in the Bay Area had a recollection of the tremor, and held it passively for a time. This is indeed an exceptional case, in which a 'passive' collective memory exists, unfiltered through anyone's active attempt to make people remember it. What made it more than purely individual was that the media and word of mouth quickly made it just what each resident experienced at the moment of the jolt. Here the exception to the rule that collective memory is not passive memory is accounted for by the fact that the memory trace was so powerful that no rehearsal was needed initially to recall it. Sooner or later, though, these passive memories become formulaic – chants, such as 'where was I when John Kennedy was shot' – or fade away. Then recall requires rehearsal in public.[13]

In the retelling of memories, certain elements of the story are high-lighted. Psychologists refer to these facets as *primacy effects*, which enhance recollection. Salient events are more vividly remembered and recalled, especially when they are associated with a specific time and place. This is what is meant by the term 'context dependency'. *Context dependency* may be *extrinsic* or *intrinsic*. On the one hand, memory traces may be associated with certain external or 'extrinsic' features originating outside the individual: smell, colour, sounds. Such memories, on the other hand, may be linked powerfully with 'intrinsic' aspects of our mood or personal situation at the time the memory trace was encoded. A beautiful place may be recalled because of the elation or depression the visitor brought to it: that is an example of 'intrinsic' context

---

[13] We are grateful to Martin Jay for his comments on this point.

dependency. The evocation of a whole world triggered by a French pastry – Proust's *madeleine* – is an instance of 'extrinsic' context dependency.

Experiments have shown that 'extrinsic contexts' affect recall but not recognition. That is, if a student takes an examination requiring recall rather than simple recognition – interpreting *Paradise Lost* rather than knowing the name 'John Milton' – her grade is likely to be improved if the examination occurs in the room where the class initially studied the text. But when the test is a simple quiz, a test of recognition, no such positive enhancement of performance occurs through the location of the test. This finding may help to explain the importance of ritual in social learning, since rituals help to produce 'extrinsic contexts' which enhance the recall of memories at given moments and places.

Trauma

The encoding and revision of scripts are usually voluntary or deliberate acts; we learn through story-telling and its echoes in our own lives. But some events are harder to introduce into a script than others. There is a threshold of density of experience; when passed, that experience is usually referred to as a *trauma* or *traumatic*.

There are many different usages of this term, but for our purposes it is possibly best to consider the term simply as connoting a serious and enduring shock. Trauma, in this sense, is identified as latent or delayed memory, and is especially marked by its sudden recurrence whatever the individual's will to recall may be. A 'traumatic memory' may be triggered by extrinsic contexts, that is, similarities of ambience, noise, smell, mood. For instance, an individual walking through an American city during a particularly steamy summer may feel the anxiety of jungle combat, though it is only the heat and humidity which the two contexts share. What triggers the memory is the traumatic nature of the encoded experience. Under specific conditions, and occasionally long after the initial set of 'traumatic events', these extrinsic contexts can produce overwhelming recall. At this point the memory crowds out everything else; it is potentially paralytic.[14]

The work of cognitive psychologists here reinforces the findings of psychiatrists and neurologists, who have identified biochemical pathways of 'trauma'.[15] But, for our purposes, the key element of this

---

[14] Cathy Caruth, *Unclaimed experience: trauma, narrative and history* (Baltimore: Johns Hopkins University Press, 1996).

[15] Steve Southwick of West Haven Veterans Administration Hospital brought this research to our attention in 1995; see the chapter he co-authored in Daniel Schachter,

analysis is that 'traumatic' memories are not a separate category of remembrance, but simply an extreme phenomenon of processes of recollection we all share.

Implications for the historical study of memory

The study of how individuals remember is hard enough. Historians want to go one step further and study how groups of individuals remember together. It is evident that we need all the help we can get. For this reason, let us consider the implications of this body of cognitive psychological research for the history of 'collective memory'.

Social learning

Societies do not learn. Individuals in societies learn, but their learning has sufficient overlap for us to be able to speak metaphorically of social learning. It follows that for two or more individuals to hold the same memory, even if they have experienced the same event, means only that there is sufficient overlap between their memory traces. For this overlap to become a social phenomenon, it must be expressed and shared. In this sense, and in this sense alone, can one speak, again metaphorically, of 'collective memory'.

Shelf-life

Collective memory has no existence independent of the individual, and in consequence, 'collective memory' has a *shelf-life*, after which individuals cease to share and express it. Memory artefacts are produced by external rehearsal, but they are just that, memory aids. As long as there are individuals using these aids, whether internally or externally in order to rehearse their memories, then the process of remembrance is alive. It may die out or it may be given a new lease on life; at that point, the 'shelf-life' is renewed, but not forever. One example is the way an Israeli monument created by bereaved parents was adopted thirty years later by a municipality which wanted to create a locus for civic pride.[16] The 'shelf-life' of the monument was renewed thereby, but over time this usage will fade away too.

Ritual and rehearsal

Latent (and even implicit, fleeting, or overlapping) memories become active ('flash-bulbs lighting up') in specific times and places. Time is

(ed.), *Memory distortion: how minds, brains and societies reconstruct the past* (Cambridge, Mass.: Harvard University Press, 1995).
[16] I. Shamir, *Israeli war memorials*, PhD thesis, Tel Aviv University, 1995, p. 150.

especially connected with 'ritual', which is a series of stylized and repetitive actions. Spatial memory – which is to be distinguished from visual memory – is the transformation of latent into active memory when an individual occupies a site associated with an event or a ritual. After the passing of these encounters in a particular place and at these particular moments of social action, most individuals depart and store the experience as individual memory. Then collective memory ceases, though it can be revived through a return to the initial framework of action.

Agency, 'brain-washing', and manipulation

Much attention has been paid to manipulation/reinterpretation of memory by elites, particularly political/cultural ones, whether at the moment of the events, or much later. It is important, though, to note that much 'memory work' goes on spontaneously within civil society, especially after salient or dramatic events. This work goes on through exchanges among members of social networks, either those pre-existing the events or created as a result of them. Agency in the constitution of social learning about the past is crucial, but it operates from below, not only from above.

War and remembrance

So far we have considered the implications of this area of research for the study of historical remembrance in general. But the test of inter-disciplinary work is in the concrete results of research in one field, informed by the insights of another.

Our focus is on a particular problem in a particular time and place: twentieth-century warfare in Europe, North America, and the Middle East. Here it is evident that there is much of value to be derived from the work of colleagues working in allied disciplines. Let us consider a number of these implications, in the terminology described above.

Warfare is no doubt a time of dramatic, unique experiences, which leave dense memory traces, individual and social. This is particularly true in the twentieth century, with mass industrial warfare of conscript armies. Obviously, because this is contemporary history, many living witnesses are still around after each and every war and make a particular contribution to social learning about the past. Hypotheses about agency can thus be tested with greater accuracy and variety due to the presence of these living witnesses.

These witnesses may be defined as agents, whether surviving soldiers, members of families of those killed or wounded, surviving civil victims or their relatives, and even people peripherally affected by the war far from the front lines. Those people are involved in memory work, that is, public rehearsal of memories, quite often *not* in order to create social scripts or schemata for the interpretation of the war. They act in order to struggle with grief, to fill in the silence, to offer something symbolically to the dead, for political reasons. In most of their immediate concerns, they tend to fail. The dead are forgotten; peace does not last; memorials fade into the landscape. It is a moot question, at the very least, as to whether healing at the personal level follows.

This intense activity, in family, survivor, or other networks, rehearses the memory traces in the case of the agents involved and also transmits information and scripts about the war to other contemporaries, and beyond them, to generations born after the war. The scripts are based upon autobiographical memory, depict dramatic events, are ritualized in ceremonies, and thus impart many elements of social learning.

Other agents join in. Their activity has other objectives (profit or other gain, artistic expression), but their efforts overlap with the work of survivor networks. The difference, though, is that audiences (of a television series, a play, a book) cannot really be considered a network; it is extremely difficult to judge the variegated reactions of these consumers. The advantage of survivor networks is that their 'social learning' may be passed on to later generations. These younger people, uninitiated into the actual experience, carry emotion-laden stories very effectively. For some, carrying a survivor's narrative can approximate survivorship itself.

We must be reticent, though, before concluding that most wartime experience is remembered socially in this way. Much is forgotten, and necessarily so. The dialectic between the need to remember and the need to forget and to go on to a less harrowing phase of life has been and remains an ongoing one.

Different approaches to the question of agency and victimhood are evident in this book, for the question of who is a victim of war is a vigorously contested one. At one end is Samuel Hynes, writing about soldiers' narratives. 'Every narrator', he writes of soldier-writers, 'believes himself to have been to some degree an agent in his personal war, and agents aren't victims' (p. 219). In the middle are Aguilhar, telling the story of associations of disabled men, women, and children in post-Civil War Spain, for example, the Comisión de Madres de Soldados Muertos or Association of Mothers of Dead Soldiers; Winter, introducing the history of associations of disfigured men after the 1914–18 war; or Prost – like Hynes, an historian who has served in combat – who surveys Frenchmen who fought in the Second World War, and notes that 'The most legitimate victims, at the very end of the war, were the *résistants*, especially those who had been deported by the Nazis to the concentration camps' (p. 173). Here agency and victimhood cohabit. At the other end is Wieviorka, writing of the survivors of Auschwitz, men like Leon Weliczker-Wells, who opened the mass graves, extracting anything of value from the corpses. Wieviorka speaks of his testimony at the Eichmann trial (p. 136). His victimhood is self-evident. But was he an agent? Certainly at the trial; before then, perhaps, but by telling the story in 1962, he retained a recognizable human voice. Hynes himself takes a more nuanced view in an extended discussion of these issues elsewhere. Referring to the concentration camps, he notes that 'in this brutal world of powerless suffering it was possible, just possible, to be an agent – by small assertions of the will in opposting actions and, afterward, by telling. Because remembering is an action: to bear witness is to oppose.'[17] Victimhood and agency have always been and remain in problematic juxtaposition; they form a duality with different meanings in different historical settings.

Homo sociologicus

In these introductory remarks, we offer some suggestions as to how historians can learn from the neighbours. Our fundamental premise is that the subject of remembrance is so vast that no discipline can claim absolute authority in this field. For that reason, we turn to sociological and anthropological reflections on this subject, once again in search of allies.

Interdisciplinary work requires a clear notion of the limits of each discipline. For the historian, the insights of cognitive psychology are striking and suggestive. The problem remains, though, that *homo psychologicus* lives in isolation from his social setting. No man goes to war alone. However the conflict develops, it is always a social activity. It is necessary, therefore, to look beyond cognitive psychology to fully understand processes of remembrance in the aftermath of war.

One way forward is to explore sociological and anthropological thought on the subject of collective memory. Such work proliferated from the late nineteenth century. Many of these developments followed choices made about the carriers of memory, however defined. These carriers had different origins and functions. First came notions of racial

---

[17] Samuel Hynes, *The soldiers' tale. Bearing witness to modern war* (London: Allen Lane, 1997), p. 269.

memory, in which the 'race' is the carrier and memory is in the 'blood' or genetic equipment of a social group. Linked to this position, but distinct from it, were concepts of *Geistesgeschichte*, or the history of the spirit of an age, drawn out by elite interpreters of art, philosophy, or literature.

Against these two positions, a new point of view emerged associated with Emile Durkheim. His school located memory in the social structure, which provided individuals with the conceptual tools to remember the past. In the work of Maurice Halbwachs we can see the most elaborate development of this position.

More recently, historians of *mentalités*, or the mental furniture of a social group, have drawn from earlier notions of *Geistesgeschichte*. These scholars describe forms of thought and behaviour which are general within a population, usually a national population. But they abjure the study of elites, to concentrate on ordinary people. They are the carriers of a society's unspoken assumptions about time, modes of comportment, and emotion. The carriers of collective memory, thus defined, are the common people.

Anthropologists, following Roger Bastide, to whom we will return below, have accepted this position, with some qualifications. Their contribution is to specify the character of groups in which the people are organized and the pivotal positions of their leaders, the secondary and tertiary elites within those societies.

Racial memory

Before proximity to Nazi notions of racial identity contaminated and discredited concepts of racial memory, there were many scholars and public figures who developed notions of collective memory understood as racial inheritance. Some were anti-Semites or anti-immigrants, defending the supposed purity of the host population and its way of life against an alien wave. But others were simply carriers of nineteenth-century notions of collective heredity, in which talent or deviance were traits passed on from generation to generation.

Cultural memory

Some observers flirted with such hereditary notions as the source of cultural continuities. This kind of cultural genetics was evident in the writings of people of very different political outlooks. The German racialist Moeller van den Bruck took it that exotic elements in Botticelli's art came from the eruption of 'an Asiatic *karma*' which brought to the surface 'primeval Italian forms . . . Not only styles but also life, not only movement but also people come back.'[18]

The racial message was embedded in works of art, and those who could detect the charge therein, those (as it were) with Geiger counters to register the radioactivity of the object, were poets, philosophers, and historians. They were men who could take the pulse of their times. These scientific metaphors were common at the turn of the twentieth century, especially among the proponents of the school of collective memory known as *Geistesgeschichte*, through its outstanding cultural forms.

How the *Geist* moves over time was a subject for philosophical, not biological, inquiry. Conducting it were scholars or artists who could tease out the living presence of the past in artefacts or writings of a vanished age. Jacob Burckhardt's comments on classical elements in Donatello's 'David' are a case in point. Classical influences moved from ancient to Renaissance Italy, Burkhardt argued, 'by way of an invisible force, or through inheritance. Indeed one must never wholly forget . . . that the people of central Italy stem from the ancient population.'[19] The poet Rainer Maria Rilke returned time and again to the theme of blood inheritance in modes of thought and expression. 'And yet', he wrote in 1903, 'these long-forgotten [*sic*], dwell within us as disposition, as a burden on our fate, as blood that courses and as gesture that arises from the depths of time.'[20]

The German art historian Aby Warburg went beyond *Geistesgeschichte* in a theory of social memory directly concerned with the transmission of ancient forms and motifs to Renaissance art. The 'task of social memory', he noted, is 'through renewed contact with the monuments of the past', to enable 'the sap . . . to rise directly from the subsoil of the past'.[21] The charge is in the object; it is encountered and transmitted through the creative work of the artist or scholar. Thus the sensitivity of members of an elite liberates a message embedded in artefacts; then it becomes accessible to the world at large.

Note the scientistic metaphors: elsewhere Warburg spoke of his work as that of a ' "seismograph" responding to the tremors of distant earthquakes, or the antenna picking up the wave from distant cultures'.[22] He set up a library as a laboratory of memory. That collection, removed to London after the Nazi accession to power in 1933, still operates today.

---

[18] E. H. Gombrich, *Aby Warburg. An intellectual biography. With a memoir on the history of the library by F. Saxl* (Oxford: Phaidon, 1970), p. 240.

[19] As cited in Gombrich, *Warburg*, p. 239.

[20] Ibid. p. 240; see also his *Duino elegies*, written between 1912 and 1922. Rainer Maria Rilke, *Duineser Elegien* (London: Hogarth Press, 1963).

[21] As cited in Gombrich, *Warburg*, p. 250.   [22] Ibid. p. 254.

Its purpose, to Warburg, was to serve as 'a collection of documents relating to the psychology of human expression'. Its aim was to investigate how 'human and pictorial expressions originate; what are the feelings or points of view, conscious or unconscious, under which they are stored in the archives of memory? Are there laws to govern their formation or re-emergence?'[23] To this end, all disciplines must be tapped. This is the essence of *Kulturwissenschaft*, part positivist, part romantic meditation on the explosive power of works of art.

The memory of images is social memory to Warburg, in that a work of art 'derives from a collaboration among individuals and thus is a symbol that does not allow for the separation of form and content'.[24] To Warburg, art history is the study of style and meaning of creative works located in specific historical periods. Art described a world view, an expression of *Geistespolitik*, or the politics of the spirit of an age.[25]

Warburg's library covered many fields, but the specific focus of his own work was on the 'significance of the influence of heathen antiquity on the European mentality'. He believed that art was 'an inventory of the emotions of a given epoch'; artists in the Renaissance confronted Classical art and were stunned by 'the heritage of passionate [that is, sensual] experience stored in memory-form'. That encounter – frequently laden with fear – was controlled and transformed in the process of creation. The result is visible to us now as an efflorescence of images in various media.

This cultural historian of imagery explored 'the historical sum of all efforts made by man to overcome his fear'[26] of primitive emotion. The scholar registered both the charge released by antique art and the challenge accepted by later artists to master it. Cultural memory – or what he termed social memory – is the record of that confrontation between past and present, that profound dialectic between emotion and creativity.[27]

To be sure, Warburg was too sensitive a scholar to ignore the range of symbols to be found in popular art. He did not limit his gaze to the works of elite artists alone, but on occasion drew on the art of the Pueblo Indians, astrological pamphlets, and postage stamps. His interest extended as well to the iconography of First World War propaganda. The symbolic language of art was ubiquitous; sometimes lesser artists disclosed the codes of an age more transparently than did

---

[23] Ibid. p. 222.

[24] Leopold Ettlinger, 'Kunstgeschichte als Geschichte', *Jahrbuch der Hamburger Kunstsammlungen*, 16 (1971), pp. 7–19.

[25] As cited in Jan. Assmann, 'Collective memory and cultural identity', *New German Critique*, 65 (1995), p. 130.

[26] Ibid. p. 139.   [27] Assmann, 'Collective memory', p. 130.

the greater.[28] Teasing out the meaning of these codes and comparing cultural differences between groups were the primary tasks of the student of 'social memory'.

Collective memory

So far we have moved from racial memory to social memory. The first adopted biological images, which have had little residue in recent years. The second explored an idealist universe in which the history of ideas and creativity over centuries naturally privileged the elites which produced and sponsored art.

Warburg's collection was not limited to great works of art, but the initial direction of his project was towards the study of cultural history through masterpieces of what he understood as 'the spirit of the age' in which they were created. This inevitably elitist approach was challenged in the period in which Warburg was writing – he died in 1929 – by another, more populist school of cultural studies. Primarily (but not exclusively) in France, the focus shifted away from racial memory and the analysis of great works or art as the embodiment of historical memory to broader and more inclusive issues and evidence.

Here the work of Emile Durkheim and his school was fundamental. They located social memory not in race or in works of art but in the social structure itself. Contrary to the position developed contemporaneously by Henri Bergson, Durkheimians held tenaciously that individual memory was entirely socially determined.[29] Durkheim gathered a group of like-minded scholars around the journal *Année sociologique*, where from 1898 there appeared learned discussions of a decidedly interdisciplinary kind. Social psychology, demography, geography, history, and political economy were all invoked as elements of sociological analysis, which in Durkheim's system, superseded them all.

In this system, social facts are external to the individual's mind. The theory of their organization, institutionalization, and operation is what Durkheimian sociology was all about. Durkheim offered an analysis of collective memory diametrically opposed to notions of racial memory and remote from the elitism of much of the study of great art as the repository of cultural memory.

The implications of his work for collective memory were elaborated in

[28] Aby Warburg, 'Italian art and international astrology in the Palazzo Schifanoia in Ferrara', in Gert Schiff (ed.), *German essays on art history* (New York: Continuum, 1988), p. 33. Thanks are due to Mark Russell and Peter Burke for drawing this reference to our attention, and for critical comments on these points.

[29] Terry N. Clark, *Prophets and patrons: the French University and the emergence of the social sciences* (Cambridge, Mass.: Harvard University Press, 1973), pp. 168–70.

the inter-war years by a number of scholars, most notably Maurice Halbwachs (1877–1945).[30] Some of this work was done at Strasbourg, where he joined a remarkable group of intellectuals committed to inter-disciplinary research.[31] Among them were the historians Marc Bloch and Lucien Febvre, co-founders of the journal *Annales d'histoire économique et sociale*, on whose editorial board Halbwachs sat. We shall return below to the historical approach to collective memory which emerged from this collaboration, but first we need to survey Halbwachs's own contribution.

Halbwachs's work is a critique of individualism in approaches to memory. Contrary to Bergson, he argued that all individual memory is socially framed. Collective memory is the sound of voices once heard by groups of people, afterwards echoing in an individual who was or is part of that group. It is a form of individual memory, socially constructed and maintained.[32] The duration of collective memory is the duration of the group(s) producing it. In words echoing the concept of shelf-life discussed above, he wrote:

Forgetting is explained by the disappearance of these frameworks or a part of them, either because our attention is no longer able to focus on them or because it is focused somewhere else . . . But forgetting, or the deformation of certain recollections, is also explained by the fact that these frameworks change from one period to another.[33]

This is a critical element in Halbwachs's approach. Collective memory is not inscribed in the genes; it is not located in great works of art; it is imbedded in the social structure, and changes when social bonds weaken or dissolve, or when new bonds replace them.

Halbwachs held that 'a person remembers only by situating himself with the viewpoint of one or several groups and one or several currents of collective thought'. To recollect an event is to recall 'the viewpoint' of the social group through whose eyes we see the event.[34] Collective memory is thus the matrix of socially positioned individual memories. This is critical: memory does not exist outside of individuals, but it is never individual in character.

The collective memory, for its part, encompasses the individual memories while remaining distinct from them. It evolves according to its own laws, and any

---

[30] Ibid. p. 199.

[31] John E. Craig, 'Maurice Halbwachs à Strasbourg', *Revue française de sociologie*, 20 (1979), pp. 273–92.

[32] Maurice Halbwachs, *The collective memory*, translated by F. I. and V. Y. Ditter (New York: Harper & Row, 1980), p. 24. A new and completely revised edition of *La mémoire collective* has been published recently, in which Gerard Namer has restored some material left out of the earlier edition. See Maurice Halbwachs, *La mémoire collective* (Paris: Albin Michel, 1997). These changes do not affect our interpretation.

[33] Halbwachs, *On collective memory*, p. 172.

[34] Halbwachs, *The collective memory*, p. 33.

individual remembrances that may penetrate are transformed within a totality having no personal consciousness.[35]

La mémoire collective is not the reified memory of the collective – a notion filled with nationalist and racialist echoes. It is rather the individual's memory, fashioned by the social bonds of that individual's life. 'I need only carry in mind', Halbwachs asserted, 'whatever enables me to gain the group viewpoint, plunge into its milieu and time, and feel in its midst.'[36] Indeed, such 'social frameworks for memory' are essential prerequisites for individual remembering, since 'it is to the degree that our individual thought places itself in these frameworks and participates in this memory that it is capable of the act of recollection'.[37]

Annales *and the history of* mentalités

The influence of Halbwachs on subsequent studies in cultural history has been real, but muted by another facet of his work. In his rejection of Bergsonian subjectivity, he returned to the positivist side of Durkheimian sociology in positing an impossibly strict distinction between history (objective) and memory (subjective).[38] This bifurcation corresponded as well to a certain cavalier attitude of Durkheimian sociology to the study of history, relegated to a subordinate position rather than a true partnership in the development of the social sciences.[39]

That partnership was the foundation stone of a group of historians and social scientists who came together in the University of Strasbourg around the journal *Annales d'histoire économique et sociale*.[40] For our purposes, the major concept produced by this school is *histoire des mentalités*, which may be translated loosely as the history of implicit

---

[35] Ibid. p. 51.

[36] Ibid. p. 118; for an earlier formulation, see *On collective memory*, p. 53.

[37] Halbwachs, *On collective memory*, p. 38.

[38] Halbwachs, *The collective memory*, ch. 2. For a critique of Halbwachs's position, and the entire notion of 'collective memory', see Noa Gedi and Yigal Elam, 'Collective memory – what is it?', *History & Memory*, 8, 1 (1996), pp. 30–50.

[39] John E. Craig, 'Sociology and related disciplines between the wars: Maurice Halbwachs and the imperialism of the Durkheimians', in *The sociological domain: the Durkheimians, and the founding of French sociology*, edited by Philippe Besnard, pp. 263–89 (Cambridge: Cambridge University Press, 1983). Jacques Revel, 'Histoire et sciences sociales: les paradigmes des *Annales*', *Annales. Economies, sociétés, civilisations*, 34, 6 (1979), p. 1364.

[40] Carole Fink, *Marc Bloch: a life in history* (Cambridge: Cambridge University Press, 1989), ch. 5. See also André Burguière, 'Histoire d'une histoire: la naissance des *Annales*', *Annales. Economies, sociétés, civilisations*, 34, 6 (1979) pp. 1347–59.

collective assumptions, attitudes, and emotions.[41] A culture, Salman Rushdie tells us, is described by its untranslatable words.[42] This is one of them.

In 1941, one of the founders of the *Annales*, Lucien Febvre, offered this clarion call for the history of collective emotions:

The historian cannot understand or make others understand the functioning of the institutions in a given period or the ideas of that period or any other unless he has that basic standpoint, which I for my part call the psychological standpoint, which implies the concern to link up all the conditions of existence of the men of any given period with the meanings the same men gave to their own ideas.

Febvre complained that we have 'No history of love, just remember that. We have no history of death. We have no history of pity, or of cruelty. We have no history of joy.' The research agenda was clear: 'I am asking for a vast collective investigation to be opened on the fundamental sentiments of man and the forms they take'; in short, on the history of *mentalités*.[43]

The sweep, the daring, the profound desire to destroy the boundaries between the private and public realms are obvious here.[44] But the precise nature of the subject was (and is) still puzzling. The Frenchness of both the terms and the enterprise has been a mystery to many non-French scholars. Alphonse Dupront, one of the finest practitioners of the history of *mentalités*,[45] offered this discussion as a way into defining the subject:

I prefer to use the term 'the history of collective psychology'. It is not satisfactory, since it is equivocal: even in French it has the air of only one discipline, 'collective psychology' . . . and to foreign ears . . . it appears to be a Gallic secret . . . If we accept the Greek with its indefinite perfection, the term 'the history of the collective *psychè*' approaches what it entails. And in place of our strange but necessary expression about 'the analysis of the collective

---

[41] For a classic formulation, see Marc Bloch, 'Mémoire collective, traditions et coutumes', *Revue de synthèse historique*, 118–20 (1925), pp. 70–90.

[42] Salman Rushdie, *Shame* (London: Pan Books, 1992), p. 12.

[43] Peter Burke (ed.), *A new kind of history: from the writings of Lucien Febvre*, translated by K. Folka (London: Routledge & Kegan Paul, 1973), p. 24. For a recent and lucid discussion of the position, see Roger Chartier, *Cultural history: between practices and representations*, translated by Lydia G. Cochrane (Cambridge: Polity Press, 1988).

[44] For an *apéritif* of this heady approach, see Jacques Le Goff, 'Mentalities: a history of ambiguities', in *Constructing the past. Essays in historical methodology*, edited by Jacques Le Goff and Pierre Nora (Cambridge: Cambridge University Press, 1985). For an appreciation of the implications of Halbwachs's approach for one maverick historian of *mentalités*, see Patrick H. Hutton, 'Collective memory and collective mentalities: the Halbwachs-Ariès connection', *Historical reflections/Réflexions historiques*, 15, 2 (1988), pp. 311–22.

[45] Alphonse Dupront, *Du Sacré. Croisades et pèlerinages. Images et langages* (Paris: Gallimard, 1988).

mentality', perhaps a procession of terms will do: the history of values, of mentalities, of forms, of symbols, of myths, be it in general, or in a particular civilization.[46]

Anthropological approaches

For our purposes, the history of the *mentalités* concept has limitations. The emphasis on the common people homogenizes them, and also exaggerates their margin of manoeuvre, which may be shaped by elites whether primary or secondary. It also blurs the borderline between the individual and the collective, a problem we have encountered in Durkheim's and Halbwachs's work as well.

A response to this set of issues may be found in the anthropological work of Roger Bastide, derived from his comparative study of African populations in Haiti and Brazil from slavery to the present.[47] Bastide accepts that man remembers as part of a social group: individual memories are rehearsed and located in the past in reference to the individual memories of other people, that is, those persons who are significant at different levels for that individual. The intermeshing of individual memories creates collective remembrance, feeds it, and maintains its continuity. It is through this remembrance that human societies develop consciousness as to their identity, as located in time. A social group is composed of individuals who enter into an exchange relationship at the level of consciousness. This is what Bastide calls *networks of complimentarity*.

Bastide rejects the notion of collective memory as a reified, separate entity existing above individuals. Collective memory is the end product of that exchange relationship – exchange of information, memories, values – between the individuals who compose the group. Each individual contributes his own memories. The weight of various memories in this process is by no means equal. The contribution of elites carries greater weight. Priests in a historically based cult, elders who tell the history of the tribe are examples of these elite groups. Whoever expresses

---

[46] Alphonse Dupront, 'Problèmes et méthodes d'une histoire de la psychologie collective', *Annales. Économies, sociétés, civilisations*, 16, 1 (1961), p. 3, n. 2.

[47] Roger Bastide, *The African religions of Brazil. Towards a sociology of the interpenetration of civilizations*, translated by Helen Sebba (Baltimore: Johns Hopkins University Press, 1960); Roger Bastide, 'Mémoire collective et sociologie de bricolage', *Année sociologique* 21 (1970), pp. 65–108; Roger Bastide, *Applied anthropology*, translated by Alice L. Morton (London: Croom Helm, 1971). See also, Nathan Wachtel, 'Remember and never forget', *History and Anthropology*, 2 (1986), and L. Valensi, 'From sacred history to historical memory and back', *History and Anthropology*, 2 (1986).

his memories in the public space leaves a deeper impact than those who keep (or who are kept) silent.

It follows that the social group locates this exchange relationship between individual memories in two dimensions. The first is *organization*: that is, the relative weight of certain individual memories as compared to others within this network of complimentarity. Organization is shaped by the nature of the group, and particularly by its power structure. The second dimension is *structure*, a kind of interpretive code which endows individual memories with meaning according to the *living tradition* of remembrance of that specific group. This tradition may be passed on through rituals which give it an emotional, behavioural expression, but it may also be transmitted in a manner both emotional and rational through school textbooks, stories passed from father to son or mother to daughter, fiction, poetry, popular legends, and the like. This interpretive code fits in well with the notion of social scripts/ schemata suggested by cognitive psychologists.

Collective memory here is a matrix of interwoven individual memories. It has no existence without them, but the components of individual memory intersect and create a kind of pattern with an existence of its own. Strong colours or a salient location within the pattern represent the 'organizational dimension', while the overall layout represents 'structure', or the cultural interpretation. To change metaphors, it is possible to speak of collective memory, à la Bastide, as a sort of choir singing, or better still, a sing-along. This is a kind of event which is not very regimented, and in which each participant begins singing at a different time and using a somewhat different text or melody which he himself has composed or developed. But he does it according to norms – musical, linguistic, literary – accepted by other members of that informal choir. Moreover, when each sings, he hears himself in his inner ear, but he also hears the collective choir in his external ear. That is, he hears the product of the collective effort. Certainly, this collective product may modify or even slant his own singing, almost in spite of himself.

Bastide emphasizes that the end product is in a state of constant flux, due to the changing relationships between members of the group. Hence his use of the term *bricolage*, borrowed from his colleague, Claude Lévi-Strauss, who meant by it the eclectic and ever-changing composition of cultural forms.[48]

Bastide leads us inevitably to the study of civil society. This term describes the domain between family and the state. It is composed of

---

[48] Claude Lévi-Strauss, *Tristes tropiques* (Paris: Plon, 1955).

voluntary social groups, led by secondary elites. These elites help shape the process of remembrance, though their freedom of action is limited by the contribution of individual members of this group. Overall, they may be as important as the state in the overall processes of remembrance constantly ongoing in society as a whole.[49]

Homo agens

The literature we have surveyed is both necessary and incomplete as a guide to social processes of remembrance with respect to twentieth-century warfare. What is missing in cognitive psychology is the sense that experience is intrinsically social; what is missing in the sociological approach is the appreciation of remembrance as a process, dependent upon groups of people who act over time. It is this collective enterprise through which *homo agens* creates and maintains. If rehearsal is the key to remembrance, agents count. Among these agents, we have chosen to concentrate upon those coming from civil society because state agency and manipulation have been sufficiently well documented. Even in totalitarian situations, however, state agency does not control individual or group memory completely.

Civil society, as we have noted, links the family and the state apparatus. It includes the market place as well as private or corporate associations. Businessmen, entrepreneurs, filmmakers, producers, distributors, painters, sculptors, photographers all satisfy demands; they present versions of the past, and do so for a fee. Some times *homo actans* is in it for the money; sometimes not.

Artistic expression for the purposes of collective remembrance exists both within the market place and beyond it. The works of poets, novelists, painters, and sculptors about war, soldiers, and the victims of war are well documented. Their work constitutes points of reference for many social scripts, and have enduring intrinsic qualities. Still, as some of our essays will show, for example on Europe after the Great War and Israel during its half-century of warfare, their vision is not imposed on voluntary groups in society, but tends to be in tune with the sensibilities many groups develop on their own. It is the activity of these groups, important but neglected, as major agents of remembrance, which we study in this book.

We have selected remembrance of war not only because industrialized war is a central fact of the twentieth century. War is trauma, a situation

---

[49] For a fuller discussion of these and other issues arising from Bastide's work see Noelle Bourguet, Lucette Valensi, and Nathan Wachtel (eds.), *Between memory and history* (Chur: Harwood Academic Publishers, 1990).

of overwhelming, extreme, and violent pressure with enduring impacts. It disrupts equilibria and requires an effort to restore them. That effort (intentionally or not) contributes to processes of remembrance, a point to which we shall return below.

As the empirical evidence presented in the chapters which follow shows, that process has four central features.

Multi-faceted negotiation

The state is ever-present, but it is neither ubiquitous nor omnipotent. Civil society is where many groups try to work out their own strategies of remembrance alongside the state, sometimes against it. The fact that such groups do succeed in attracting individuals who after a war may feel a strong urge to resume their individual lives, is something which requires explanation.

Remembrance consists of negotiations between a multiplicity of groups, including the state. Obviously, the partners are not equal. Repression happens, but counter-voices may be heard. If some voices are weaker than others, at least in the context of a pluralistic society, this is not only because they lack resources – or to return to the metaphor of the choir – they are too far from the microphone. They may also be weak because of self-censorship due to lack of moral status in the eyes of others, or due to a low self-image.

Inconsequent intentions; unintended consequences

Groups do not necessarily raise their voice in the choir with the intent of shaping historical consciousness. They may do so for their own private reasons: in order to cope with grief, to create a powerful lobby so as to achieve material gain, for revenge or exoneration. They may or may not achieve these aims; in fact, some of these aims are beyond reach from the start: this may be called the 'law of non-consequent intentions', which is to say, the unlikelihood of the realization of a programme of action, such as keeping alive the memory of an individual son. The main unintended consequence of even a quixotic endeavour of this kind is its contribution to the overall process of remembrance.

The trajectory of shelf-life

Remembrance is by its very nature vulnerable to decay, and hence has shelf-life. Even under the delayed impact of the extreme conditions of war, memories do not necessarily endure, if only because there is interference from new memory traces. Constant rehearsal, group action, ingenuity in mobilizing resources are elements which keep memory traces alive: that is, they create a relatively more successful process of remembrance.

Groups of war victims deal with a particularly dense memory trace, that of autobiographical memory. But even their efforts are not always successful. Certainly the passage from the generation of victims contemporaneous with the event to the next generation is a very difficult one, given the inevitable change in social priorities.

Certain memories of war endure, while most others do not. Endurance and persistence require explanation. Forgetting and fade-out are usually the rule. To advance this argument is to go against the grain of the idealistic vision of representations as disconnected from social contexts, from interactions, and material conditions.

The notion of trauma suggests another dimension of 'shelf-life'. Some studies of war victims have adopted a notion of delayed impact to describe those so overwhelmed by war experiences as to be entirely unable to register them at the time.[50] This numbing is not a full protection from these injuries to the mind; later on, and involuntarily, these earlier events may be vividly recalled or re-enacted by sufferers of what is now known as 'post-traumatic stress disorder'.[51] The notion of shelf-life is perfectly compatible with this topology of recurrent memories. They may flare up at any time, even among those unafflicted with pathological conditions. A resurgence of memory work after the Eichmann trial in 1961 is a case in point among Jews all over the world (see chapter 6). The second generation of Japanese Americans gave the memory of their parents' internment (see chapter 7) not only a new lease of life but also a vigour lacking in the muted public expression of these members of the older generation.

It is not only rekindled interest among second or third generations of the victims which may help prolong shelf-life. As the case of the descendants of Holocaust survivors in Europe and North America proves, the availability of new techniques of information technology – the video-cassette recorder – enables testimony expressing 'authentic' autobiographical memory available to large audiences. These are reached in an audio-visual fashion, which can be revived decades after the original imprint of the testimony of war victims.

---

[50] See Cathy Caruth (ed.), *Trauma: explorations in memory* (Baltimore: Johns Hopkins University Press, 1995).
[51] For full references see: Daniel Schachter, (ed.), *Memory distortion: how minds, brains and societies reconstruct the past* (Cambridge, Mass.: Harvard University Press, 1995).

The ambiguity of the healing effects

Mourning is an essential part of the story of remembrance of war, but there is much evidence that it is problematic to consider remembrance in Freudian terms, as the work of mourning, leading to healing, reconciliation, and separation of the living from the lost loved-one. Our story is less optimistic and much less redemptive, as Walter Benjamin has argued (see chapter 11). Even when some healing occurs, it is at best healing for a while, and when old age sets in, healing may cease altogether and wounds reopen. Mourning may never end, and even when it seems to be completed, it may re-emerge. This form of mourning is usually termed 'melancholia'.[52] One case in point is the suicide forty years after the Second World War – and decades after the publication of his apparently healing memoirs – of the Italian writer Primo Levi. Another case is the suicide in old age of fathers of Israeli war dead, sometimes using their service revolver to end their lives at the grave of their sons.

The above generalizations represent what we can say in an introductory fashion about what our groups of researchers have found in their empirical work. Future research on *homo agens* may modify these findings, but these very palpable situations point out a number of mechanisms and processes involved. Given the limited number of cases we present, whatever we learn from them is indicative rather than conclusive.

In light of the chapters in this book, what are the mechanisms and processes of remembrance?

Scale

First, activity is above all *small scale*. Groups of individuals, usually victimized by war in some way, carrying autobiographic memory, meet face to face. Even if these individuals are part of a larger whole, they also have face-to-face points of encounter – as in veterans' organizations. They constitute 'networks of complimentarity'. Their vision is of necessity narrow even though their implicit concerns – for example, war as disaster – may be much wider. This brings us back to the two laws of 'unintended consequences' and of 'non-consequent intentions', referred to above. The groups may wish to do something which concerns their immediate circle – assistance for traumatized individuals, for example – but perforce they may wish to operate on a wider scale. This is evident

[52] Jay Winter, *Sites of memory, sites of mourning: the Great War in European cultural history* (Cambridge: Cambridge University Press, 1995), pp. 113–14.

in many of the cases discussed below, and in particular with regard to the Japanese American case, and the French–Jewish groups (see chapters 6 and 7).

In the aftermath of the First World War, a huge bureaucracy handled legitimate claims for compensation for war injury or loss. These bulky, rationalized, and hierarchical institutions exasperated survivors, by their inefficiency and their insensitivity to the personal dimensions of loss. To fill in that empty space, small-scale groups appeared. They provided the assistance in mourning and mutual help which no state apparatus offered. The scale of the local action of these groups was small, giving free range to the expression of sentiments of loss, and involving essentially egalitarian structures as a sort of counter-image of the state. The fact that this situation (see chapter 2) recurs in a much longer conflict, yet in a much smaller society – that of Israel (see chapter 9) indicates why such mechanisms proliferate in the twentieth century, with its centralized state and industrial warfare.

This is not to idealize civil society. Weak social groups may not have a voice at all; consider the case of the Muslim Harkis in France after the Algerian War, who lacked both articulation and a capacity for organization. As we have mentioned above, the low self-esteem of conscript soldiers made their voice somewhat faint. Interpolated social learning – also known as distortion – occurs vigorously in state-produced commemoration. But small groups do not have a more balanced view. In any civil society, there are contested views, diverging more or less radically about what happened in the past. Each group highlights elements close to its own traumatized members. German war veterans obscured the sacrifices of Jewish soldiers in the First World War; Israeli-born veterans highlighted the losses of their cohort in 1948, while disregarding the huge sacrifices made by new immigrants during the same war (see chapter 9). In both cases, it is the nature of the audience of the small group involved which determines the kind of telescoping or selection in the process of encoding memory traces. Here is a classic instance of the social framing of individual memory through reference to what the group shares.

But silences are not just a matter of who you highlight but also what you highlight and what you obscure or sanitize. Soldiers' memoirs recognize degradation but rarely dwell on it. The crimes committed by comrades are known by all; why elaborate if those for whom the account was written – namely, fellow soldiers – know this all along? Instead (see chapter 10), soldiers' stories reinforce the decencies that survive the indecencies of combat.

The nature of warfare

The nature of warfare is a critical determinant of the activity of remembrance. A succession of wars or other kinds of violent disruptions presents a different challenge to remembrance in the case of one single war, however large. The Russian and Israeli instances (chapters 3, 9) represent such limiting cases of decades of conflict, producing 'retro-active interference' which impinges upon memory traces of earlier decades of violence. The Russian case is particularly poignant because many of the upheavals were self-inflicted: civil war, famine, forced collectivization, purges. Israeli society coped better, perhaps because the range of options for remembrance was broader in a democratic setting. But even here the 'primacy effect' of the 1948 war – so powerful in the 1950s and 1960s – is on the wane under the retroactive interference of memory traces of more recent and more controversial conflicts.

Constraints within civil society

But *civil society* itself is a limiting factor in the work of remembrance. Civil society is defined by its position with respect to the state. A dictatorship or an authoritarian regime may set severe limits to civil freedom of expression and action, even in the realm of small-scale remembrance activity, let alone in full-scale action. In Russia (see chapter 3) even communication within families with regard to their experience of war and repression was greatly curbed; it could be done only in a haphazard manner, and in one-on-one situations. Still this case also shows the inventiveness of a heavily damaged civil society. For instance, despite the weakness of the Church, which had been the custodian of the traditions mediating existential issues, like death, civil society found ways of marshalling these resources. But let us not exaggerate what civil society can do under such conditions. To a great extent, the regime won; many memory traces vanished with the physical disappearance of the victims. Recall today of some aspects of that past may be well nigh impossible.

In Spain in the 1960s, before the demise of the dictatorship, another limiting feature of remembrance appeared. This multi-faceted negotia-tion between social groups arrived at a kind of implicit pact to avoid confronting the trauma of the Civil War and the repression which followed. The fear of a return to the polarization of Spanish society in the 1930s was the core around which the consensus emerged (see chapter 4). Here silence was a condition of the transition to democracy, and to its stabilization in the 1980s and 1990s under the Socialists.

Not everyone concurred. Those who wish to break the silence go against the tide. Some Spanish anarchists insist on doing so anyway.

Another instance not examined in this book reinforces the contested nature of such arrangements to limit open discussion even under conditions of democracy. In South Africa in the 1990s, a 'Truth and Reconciliation Commission' took evidence from people who had engaged in violent acts of repression during the apartheid era. An open admission of guilt is a ticket to amnesty. Families of victims, as well as political groups such as the Pan African Congress challenged this arrangement, but did not generate widespread public support.

We return here to the question raised by Walter Benjamin, of how healing occurs, if at all. Benjamin's complaint was against a kind of pseudo-healing that screens us off from confronting the deeper trauma beneath the apparent wound. Archbishop Desmond Tutu, a member of the Commission, argues that public repentance and forgiveness are essential for healing, both personal and social. Others suspend judgment, or reject this claim altogether. It is critical to note that these arrangements are not just imposed from on high. Both in Spain and in South Africa negotiation at all levels occurred, and is still ongoing.

Representations of war

Most of these groups tend to generate *representations of war* as primarily traumatic: overwhelming, nasty, and disruptive over a relatively long period. It is not the case that the evidence we present is selected to show this outcome. Mixed and dense memory traces appear in many war narratives and in the ways survivors speak of the event. Elements of elation, of pride, of camaraderie persist, but negative, disruptive memory traces exist too. The latter tend to motivate individuals to repeated rehearsal of memories in order to restore the equilibrium disrupted by war. In post-1918 Germany, the humiliation of defeat was the subject of reiteration as the centrepiece of a political movement dedicated to restoring Germany's national pride. The celebration of the 'war experience', the baptism of fire of a whole generation, took on sombre and defiant tones since its price was the humiliation of the Fatherland.

In the case of the more 'positive' memory traces, in victorious wars, such activity is not as urgently called for. This is why, over time, the voice of those who rehearse through lamentation is likely to dominate the chorus of small-scale remembrance more than the voice of those who celebrate moments of glory or valour. Lamentation, however, is not at all the same as a critique of war, because the blame can be put elsewhere: on fate, on the shoulders of the enemy, or of some alien domestic group, for instance, the 'stab in the back legend' of the 1920s in Germany.

Writers and poets codify images of war while the fighting is still on. Thereby they enlarge the interpretive codes available in the culture for the small groups engaged in their separate acts of remembrance. Later on, these words, verses, stories, may be appropriated by official organizations or by the state, but their origin is within civil society itself. One instance is the poem 'The silver platter', written in a premonitory mode by the Israeli writer Nathan Alterman during the mobilization of December 1947. Fighting had just begun, but Alterman was already visualizing the disappearance of a whole cohort of young men and women. Their ethereal bodies, in his vision, would constitute the 'silver platter' upon which the then unborn state of Israel would be presented to the Jewish people. Over the next year, while the war continued, the poem was used by families and comrades of those who were killed. Only later was it incorporated into the official liturgical code of the Israeli Memorial Day.[53]

Representations may be created for entirely commercial reasons. When Robert Graves wrote *Goodbye to all that*, a Great War novel/ memoir, he was trying (as he himself said) to cash in on the commercial success of another war novel/memoir, *All quiet on the Western Front*, by Erich Maria Remarque. So did many of the European post-1945 film-makers discussed in chapter 5.

The success of these filmic efforts is partly a function of their catching/exploiting the mood of the audiences who viewed them. Still, an unintended consequence of their work was to provide a set of codes about war and victimhood. These codes were not passed directly to individual members of the audience, but were mediated through families, yet another case of a small group. Film-going was still a family affair in the 1950s. Decades later, some of these films, for instance Rossellini's, may still appeal to new audiences on video because of their intrinsic artistic value, while renewing the initial message about survivors of the Second World War.

Soldiers' tales, as described in chapter 10, are expressions of codes shared by soldiers and reinforced in the telling. The positive, intriguing, or piquant stories repeated time and again are useful as a counter-weight against darker images. The result is neither the domination of one rhetoric nor another: at least in soldiers' stories, told by soldiers and for soldiers, and made available to others through publication, the outcome is never certain, but the conflict is not resolved.

Each of these groups presents war through a particular interpretive code – or 'structure', in Bastide's terms. But these are more often than

---

[53] Dan Meron, *Mul Ha'ach Ha'shotek* (Tel Aviv: Am Oved, 1992).

not selected from a range available in the culture. Complete departure from conventional forms is very rare, as in the case of the second-generation Japanese Americans who try to introduce concentration camp symbols into American history. As such they face heavy odds and their chances of integration into the American interpretive code remain in doubt. The case of French soldiers after the Algerian War shows how difficult it is to innovate. On the contrary, these men had two prior sets of representations of war – two social 'scripts' – standing in the way of their own story. The first was the moral crusade of French veterans of 1914 to 1918, whose representation of war was as a crime that must never be repeated; the second was the image of the *maquisard* of the Second World War, disturbingly similar to their enemies in Algeria (see chapter 8). Because their experience could not be located within either interpretive network, the range of social action available to them was severely limited. The Algerian War was not a 'good war'; neither was it (especially in the countryside) heroic; it was altogether desultory warfare.

Spatial memory

Artefacts matter: to state that process is crucial is not to deny this point. They are at one and the same time the product of such processes as well as 'memory aids' for its later trajectory. Artefacts are what the French designate as *les lieux de mémoire*.[54] In their absence, as not only in Russia but also in revolutionary China, memory work is much more arduous. Artefacts related to place enable the retrieval of dense memory traces, because they create 'extrinsic context dependency'. It should be noted that such 'extrinsic contexts', according to experimental psychology, help 'recall/access', but not 'recognition'. The case of the concentration camp exhibit in Los Angeles (see chapter 7) is apposite here. The organizers intended to re-trigger such memories among second generation Japanese Americans. Yet success is not guaranteed.

The history of family pilgrimage after the First World War to the battlefields is well known (see chapter 2). But other less obvious linkages are powerful. The French songwriter/performer, Marc Ogeret, offered a glimpse of this process in his *chanson*, entitled 'Verdun', written in the 1970s.

> I have seen Verdun
> I have seen Verdun
> I have seen Verdun in the rain . . .
> And I, who do not really like

54 Pierre Nora, 'Between memory and history: *Les lieux de mémoire*', *Representations*, 26 (1989), pp. 7–25.

That old veterans' line;
Now, I understand it,
I understand it.

Another instance in which spatial memory operates is the tangible character of war memorials. Those in mourning used them not only for ceremony, but also for a ritual of separation, wherein touching a name indicates not only what has been lost, but also what has not been lost. Visitors to such memorials frequently leave flowers, notes, objects, which serve as a focus of a ritual exchange. The dead have given everything; the living, symbolically or tangibly, offer something in return. The Museum of American History in Washington's Smithsonian Institution has a large store of such objects left at the Vietnam Veterans Memorial.[55]

This is hardly surprising, since the dead aren't present: hence the need to re-present them. The names are there, and so are the survivors, whose acts of exchange can only be symbolic at best. But the power of objects, as well as the power of place, cannot be denied.

The role of the state

The thrust of analysis in this book is towards highlighting the role of second- and third-order elites within civil society. The social organization of remembrance tends to be decentralized. This claim shifts the emphasis in this field away from the central organizations of the state, both from the top downward and sideways. That is to say, away from state central institutions, and towards civil society groupings, their leaders and activists.

Nevertheless, the state remains relevant both as the carrier of the brunt of warfare, whether conventional or counter-insurgency, and as a major producer and choreographer of commemoration. The key issue is the tension between these two foci of remembrance.[56]

Since the Second World War, and the end of decolonization, the character of military conflict has shifted away from interstate collisions towards violent contests, usually within the borders of one nation, for

---

[55] On the multiplicity of types of artefacts, see Maya Lin, Andrew Barshay, Stephen Greenblatt, Tom Laqueur, and Stanley Saitowitz, *Grounds for remembering. Monuments, memorials, texts*, Occasional papers of the Doreen B. Townsend Center for the Humanities, no. 3 (Berkeley, California: Doreen B. Townsend Center for the Humanities, 1995); and Marita Sturken, 'The Wall, the screen and the image: the Vietnam Veterans Memorial', *Representations*, 35 (1991), pp. 118–42.

[56] On state versus local affiliations, see Jay Winter, and Jean-Louis Robert, *Capital cities at war: Paris, London, Berlin, 1914–1919* (Cambridge: Cambridge University Press, 1997), ch. 1.

state power.[57] The process of remembrance following such conflicts is unlikely to vary in character from that associated with public recollection of earlier conflicts. This is already clear from the comparative study of conflict instigated by Fundamentalist movements in Shi'ite and Sunni Islam, in Hinduism and among Sikhs, in Judaism, as well as in Protestantism and Catholicism.[58]

We may suggest that the dialogue between agents working within civil society and state institutions, an ongoing process of contestation, is and is likely to remain one of the permanent features of remembrance. It is not the geographic location or level of economic development which is decisive here, but the nature of that complex and enduring social activity, remembrance.

[57] Martin van Creveld, *The transformation of war* (New York: Free Press, *c.* 1991).
[58] E. Sivan, 'The enclave culture', in M. M. Marty and R. S. Appleby (eds.), *Fundamentalism comprehended* (Chicago: University of Chicago Press, 1995), pp. 11–63; see also chapters 16–19 in the same volume, written jointly by G. Almond, E. Sivan, and R.S. Appleby.

2 Forms of kinship and remembrance in the aftermath of the Great War

Jay Winter

Agents of remembrance work in the borderlands linking families, civil society, and the state. There, during and after war, individuals and groups, mostly obscure, come together to do the work of remembrance. This entails their creating a space in which the story of their war, in its local, particular, parochial, familial forms, can be told and retold. The construction of the narrative – in stone, in ceremony, in other works and symbols – is itself the process of remembrance. Once completed in this initial phase, these 'sites of remembrance' are never stable, never fixed. In the process of composition, they begin to decompose, losing little by little the force and content of their original meaning and evocative power. The reason for this transformation is imbedded in the life cycle of agency itself. Those who join in this activity do so at the cost of other ventures; when their lives change, and other business calls, the bonds of such agency begin to fray, and unravel.

I would like to offer an interpretation of one facet of this process of public recollection of war in the twentieth century. I want to suggest that an antidote to the use of the term 'collective memory' in a general or ethereal sense, floating somewhere in the cultural atmosphere of a period, may be found in the insistence upon the significance of agency in the work of remembrance of particular groups of survivors, whose bond is social and experiential. Following anthropologists, these groups may be termed 'fictive kin', 'adoptive kin', or 'functional kin', as opposed to those linked by blood bonds or marriage.[1] I shall use the term 'fictive kinship' to denominate such associations.

[1] The anthropological literature on this subject is vast and highly contentious. See Meyer Fortes, *Kinship and the social order. The legacy of Lewis Henry Morgan* (Chicago: Aldine, 1969), pp. 241, 251, 110, 123, 239. For the distinction between blood kinship, fictive kinship, and figurative kinship, see Julian Pitt-Rivers, 'The kith and the kin', in J. Goody (ed.), *The character of kinship* (Cambridge: Cambridge University Press, 1973). For other approaches to the subject, see Ernest Gellner, 'Ideal language and kinship structure', *Philosophy of Science*, 24 (1957), pp. 235–41; Rodney Needham, 'Descent systems and ideal language', *Philosophy of Science*, 27 (1960), pp. 96–101; E. Gellner, 'The concept of kinship', *Philosophy of Science*, 27 (1960), pp. 187–204; Maurice Bloch, 'The moral and tactical meaning of kinship terms', *Man*, 6 (1971), pp. 79–87.

In them, the agents of remembrance have formed families of remembrance. They do more than merely describe the space of individual reflection, homage, and sorrow. That is why they act in concert. But such groups, such families of remembrance, do less than express what some scholars, following Halbwachs, call 'collective memory' as the repository of images and notions common to a social class or to a national society as a whole. Fictive kin are small-scale agents. That is why I prefer to use the term 'remembrance' to describe their activity. Their work is liminal. It occupies the space between individual memory and the national theatre of collective memory choreographed by social and political leaders. They flourish at a point between the isolated individual and the anonymous state; a juncture almost certainly closer to the individual than to the state.

Some of the people whose work I shall discuss may be described (following Bastide) as second-order elites. Others are more obscure than that. All take civil society as their point of departure, though they deal with the state time and again. In the vast literature on the effects of war, and on its deepening of the 'exuberance of the state',[2] perhaps it is time to give greater weight to the exuberance of civil society, and to highlight the tendency of ordinary people to come together and to reflect publicly on what happened to them, to their loved ones, to their particular world, when war descended on their lives.

The structure of this chapter is straightforward. I first examine some processes of remembrance within the structure of family life. I then turn to the creation and activity of a kind of kinship, 'fictive kinship', whose members engaged in many kinds of collective remembrance during and after the First World War.

Families and remembrance

In order to appreciate the work of families of fictive kin in the aftermath of that war, we must recognize the profound shock to family life that the upheaval of war brought about. First was the call to arms, leaving many women, old people, and children with the vital task of taking in the harvest alone. Then came long years of separation, ended for the lucky

---

In this chapter, I use the term 'fictive kin' simply as shorthand for a multiplicity of groups. The term 'fictive' implies 'constructed' and 'created', rather than 'imaginary' or 'untrue'. I prefer it to 'adoptive' since that word carries parental echoes, which do not decay over time; in addition much of the following discussion is about solidarity of a fraternal kind. The term 'functional kin' may have more precision, but it has a cold, perhaps manipulative, element in it too. By sticking to the term 'fictive kin', I want to convey the sense of social bonds as created and maintained through stories and acts.

[2] Françoise Boc, 'L'exubérance de l'état', *Vingtième siècle* (1989), pp. 1–12.

ones by a debilitating though non-lethal wound or by demobilization. For the unlucky, widowhood and orphanhood followed. Perhaps one-third of the men who were killed in the war were married; thus 3 million widows and between 7 and 10 million orphans were created by the war.[3]

That the war was a monumental disaster in family history goes without saying. But perhaps more surprisingly, despite its devastating repercussions, the upheaval did not undermine marriage patterns or fertility trends. The image of a generation of spinsters created by the war is a myth. Women adjusted their marriage patterns to escape the penury and marginality of widowhood or spinsterhood. Nuptiality rates were no lower in the 1920s than before the war. Indeed, there is overwhelming evidence that the First World War *increased* the strength of family life, reinforced the institution of marriage, and created powerful pressures towards the provision of family allowances along the lines of the separation allowances paid to soldiers' wives while they were on active service.[4] The 1920s were, therefore, a moment when family ties, so deeply threatened by the death toll of the war, were celebrated as never before.

It is not surprising, therefore, that the war was remembered initially and overwhelmingly as an event in *family* history. In a rush, with the war, family history and national history came together in unprecedented ways. To this day, through the study of genealogy, through retelling family stories, the war is kept alive as a vivid moment in popular history. This is the source of the huge wave of interest in the 1990s in fiction located in the First World War. Millions of young people today (1999) hear tales of their grandparents' early lives, as children during or after the war, and then read of this epoch in powerful works of narrative art. Pat Barker's trilogy *Regeneration*, *The eye in the door*, and *The ghost road*[5] and Sebastian Faulks's *Birdsong*,[6] best-selling and award-winning novels in Britain, have counterparts in France. Jean Rouaud's *Champs d'honneur*[7] and Sebastian Japrisot's *Un long dimanche de fiançailles*[8] create the same domestic setting for remembering war. What today's readers find in this literature is that their family stories are part of a wider code,

---

[3] J. M. Winter, *The Great War and the British people* (London: Macmillan, 1985), ch. 8.

[4] See J. M. Winter and R. Wall (eds.), *The upheaval of war: family, work and welfare in Europe, 1914–1918* (Cambridge: Cambridge University Press, 1988); and Susan Pedersen, *Family, dependence, and the origins of the welfare state: Britain and France 1914–1945* (Cambridge: Cambridge University Press, 1993).

[5] Pat Barker, *Regeneration* (London: Viking, 1991); *The eye in the door* (London, Viking, 1993); *Ghost road* (London: Viking, 1995).

[6] Sebastian Faulks, *Birdsong* (London: Hutchinson, 1993).

[7] Jean Rouaud, *Champs d'honneur* (Paris: Editions de Minuit, 1990).

[8] Sébastien Japrisot, *Un long dimanche de fiançailles* (Paris: Denoël, 1991).

perhaps even a 'master code' of stories about how we in the twentieth century got to be where we are.

I want to consider several such accounts of family history to illustrate this powerful framework of remembrance. The first is the recollection of rural life in Brittany, written by Pierre Jacquez-Hélias, *Le cheval d'orgeuil*, published in 1975. For him, the war presented a very mundane set of problems. He remembers being given the clothing his father had worn while on active service. For this, he (and others)

owed yet another debt to the war, but that one we could have done without. It was the lice which the soldiers were said to have brought back from the trenches. Day after day we had to fight a merciless battle against them. It wasn't all that bad for the boys, who as a rule had close-cropped heads. But the poor little girls wept every morning while their mothers combed their hair, energetically, over a white plate. When the black lice fell into it, the girls would crush them one by one under their thumbnails, 'the little lice-hammers'. We thus inherited our fathers' woes.

Jacquez-Hélias also observed another unexpected effect of the war, this time with a longer shelf-life. It was a shift in the comportment of the postwar generation. Before the war it was very rare for family members to kiss each other in public:

The First World War changed all that. The appalling losses during the first two years of it, which had decimated most families, the wretched life of the fighters; the newspapers, which everyone had begun to read and which had fed their anguish instead of making it easier for them to wait; the soldiers returning on leave and their departing yet again, with death in the offing – all that encouraged effusiveness. Once the heroes had returned, the people went on making shows of affection; it had become a habit.[9]

How general this change was is impossible to say; all it indicates is the range of adjustments family members had to make in the aftermath of war. Subtly, family bonds bore the imprint of war; the emotional language of everyday life had a hidden agenda after 1914, the indirect expression of anxiety through gestures of affection which only those who had gone through the experience of war could decode.

Here we encounter a critical element of story-telling about the Great War. The war was traumatic, in the sense of being a violent and over-whelming experience. The telling of stories within families, and their subsequent publication, was a means to convert trauma into misfortune, to prevent the events of the war from paralysing those who experienced them and to enable them to pick up again the threads of their lives.

Remembrance through story-telling was, therefore, a path to recovery.

[9] Pierre Jacquez-Hélias, *Le cheval d'orgueil. Mémoires d'un Breton du pays bigoudin* (Paris: Plon, 1975), p. 11.

Remembrance – within families and among families – provided a way to live with the war. Here family narratives, scripts highlighting the disruption of war, whether published or not, played a crucial role. When in print, they served as documents of collective remembrance.

Some soldiers created such books themselves. In 1919 the Provençal barrel-maker turned infantryman Louis Barthas put together a travelogue of his time at the front. His family published this book in 1978.[10] Other soldiers, turned novelists, adopted this format in deceptively straightforward ways. Robert Graves's war novel, *Goodbye to all that*, published in 1929, starts with the Victorian poet Swinburne staring at him in his pram in Wimbledon Common in London. Whether or not this event ever happened is beside the point; it merely serves to show the familial framework out of which the story of a junior infantry officer in the Great War unfolds.

Another set of family stories may illustrate this wider social phenomenon.[11] In 1991, the Canadian writer David Macfarlane published a book entitled *The danger tree. Memory, war and the search for a family's past*.[12] It is a family history, written by a great-nephew of the protagonists, and published a full lifetime after the Armistice. And that is precisely its point. It tells the life – and death – of an ordinary family, one that was shattered by war.

Here is the outline of the story. The Goodyear family were among the staunchest British patriots in Newfoundland, still in 1914 a British colony. They lived in the town of Grand Falls, founded in 1906 to service the timber industry, and in particular, the demand for pulp and newsprint of the London press. Louisa and Josiah Goodyear had seven children: six boys and a girl. Five joined up, and the youngest, Kate, became a nurse.

Three of the Goodyear boys were killed in the war. Raymond Goodyear was seventeen at the outbreak of war. Twice he ran away to enlist, twice he was retrieved by his father. Then he went to a recruiting meeting at which his father Josiah was the keynote speaker. 'Father, now can I go?', he publicly demanded, and finally got the answer he wanted. After three months' service in the Newfoundland Regiment, he was killed by shrapnel near Ypres in October 1916.[13]

A year later, his brother Stan was killed by a shell while transporting

---

[10] See the manuscripts published by his family of the memoirs of the French infantryman (and mutineer) Louis Barthas, *Les carnets de guerre de Louis Barthas, tonnelier 1914–1918* (Paris: Maspéro, 1978).

[11] See Sivan's essay in chapter 9 of this book.

[12] David Macfarlane, *The danger tree. Memory, war and the search for a family's past* (Toronto: Macfarlane Walter & Ross, 1991).

[13] Ibid. pp. 104, 107.

munitions to his unit near Langemark in Belgium. The third to die was their elder brother Hedley, who had enlisted while attending the University of Toronto. He joined the Canadian 102nd Battalion, and served on the Somme in August 1918. On 7 August, he wrote to his mother:

My eye is fixed on tomorrow with hope for mankind and with visions of a new world . . . A blow will be struck tomorrow which will definitely mark the turn of the tide . . . I shall strike a blow for freedom, along with thousands of others who count personal safety as nothing when freedom is at stake.[14]

The following day his unit did indeed take part in a major battle. In official accounts, Hedley was among the 110 men of his unit to die in the encounter. The truth is otherwise. He survived for another week, only to make one critical mistake. He shared a match with two Australians at night in the trenches near Chaulnes. The light was the last thing he saw: a sniper shot him through the head.[15]

Two other brothers survived. Joe Goodyear suffered a severe thigh wound, and was invalided back to Newfoundland. So was his brother Ken, also wounded. They both later re-enlisted and served in Scotland in the Newfoundland Forestry Corps. All five Goodyear boys in uniform were casualties of war.

Kate Goodyear also put on a uniform – that of a nurse attending to wounded men at St Luke's Hospital in Ottawa. Before she knew the fate of her brothers, she nursed a 19-year old private who had lost a leg. There was no room for him in the ward, so he was placed in the corridor. Being unable to sleep, he asked Kate for help. The only place of respite was a private ward, off limits to the soldier. Kate decided otherwise, and then had to face the wrath of the matron and superintendent. After the anticipated dressing-down, this is the explanation she offered:

I have brothers . . . I have brothers overseas. I don't know where or how they are, and I can't do much to help them. But I'll do what I can wherever I am, and I'd like to think that someone might do the same for them. So let me tell you. As long as I am in this hospital, and so long as there's an empty bed, no soldier will ever spend a night in a hallway. I. Will. Not. Have. It. I shall move them to the private rooms if I have to carry them up the stairs myself.[16]

For once, regulations gave way to compassion. This story, retrieved by a nephew fifty years after the war, was a classic family tale, repeated at frequent intervals to educate the young and restore – perhaps for a moment – the atmosphere of what once was.

For Kate Goodyear, and the surviving members of the family, the war didn't end in 1918. For seventy years, tears welled up in her eyes at unexpected moments. To her and millions like her, her family was

[14] Ibid. p. 203.   [15] Ibid. p. 196.   [16] Ibid. p. 188.

defined by those absent from it. As her great-nephew put it, on three birthdays a year, as well as on public days, what was remembered was

nothing . . . what was never to be, after the war was over. The best were gone by 1917 or doomed, and what the world would have been like had they not died is anybody's guess. The war left their things unfinished: enterprises conceived, projects initiated, routes surveyed, engagements announced. And that's where it ended.

The three Goodyears left behind their photographs, one or two letters, a few often-repeated stories, and an emptiness that steadily compounded itself over the years. It was a different family after the war. Something was gone from the heart of it . . . Somehow the wrong combination survived . . . A balance was never regained.[17]

That story – the transformation of a family through war – echoed through parlours and kitchens on both sides of the ocean. Through family gatherings, letters, photographs, and stories, the narrative was passed on. It is a script of sadness, but also of survival. Here story-telling was at the heart of the work of remembrance.

This narrative, drawn from a set of family stories, was unusual only in that it was published. Countless others existed only in oral form. Its author admitted that all he was doing was repeating family stories told time out of mind. Their recovery, preservation, and publication, were acts of remembrance.

The title of the memoir is significant. The 'danger tree' was a sniper's post in no man's land in one corner of Beaumont-Hamel, in the northern sector of the Somme battlefields. There on 1 July 1916, the Newfoundland Regiment was slaughtered in futile attacks on German lines. The land surrounding the 'danger tree' is now sacred ground for Newfoundlanders, who became Canadians only in 1949. The trench system has been preserved, and turned into a park of remembrance. The tree itself is an ossified piece of the landscape, perched dangerously in front of the Newfoundlanders' advanced position. It is frozen in time, and in space, just like the stories told and retold in the Goodyear family. It is a point of reference, enabling them to see what their family was, and what it lost because of the war. Here family stories and national monuments are fused; icons enter the common language of narrative, and remind those of us too young to have known those days how terrible they were. None of the Goodyear boys killed in the war died in Beaumont-Hamel. But in a symbolic sense they all did. Their loss is encapsulated, it is given meaning by the telling of stories.

Trauma is by definition unbounded by the ordinary. Its full force may not be felt initially, but returns unannounced and devastatingly at odd

---

[17] Ibid. p. 139.

moments. Perhaps one of the purposes of such family narratives as that of the Goodyears is to convert trauma into history, to locate it in time and in place, to unfreeze the 'danger tree', and let other shoots take its place.

Kin, 'fictive kin', and patterns of remembrance

The effort to rebuild the lives of the survivors quite naturally was lived within family units. But one of the striking features of the inter-war years was the extension of these families in a social rather than a biological sense. In every combatant country there emerged groups of people whose business it was to help each other recover from its traumatic consequences.

Partly this was simply a natural human response to a disaster. And as in the case of natural disasters, those able to help did so. After the war, support groups emerged in reaction to the unavoidable tendency for bureaucrats to see files rather than families, cases rather than people. The emergence of self-help associations trying to negotiate the passage to 'normality' for war victims, sometimes against and sometimes along-side the bureaucracy, demonstrates the strength of civil society in the aftermath of the war.

The disabled

'Fictive kinship' operated both on the sacred and the profane levels. After the Armistice, there arose a dense network of filiation, an array of people standing alongside victims of the war trying to help manage problems large and small. Here is the hidden pre-history of many, more visible, forms of collective remembrance.

Consider the millions of people living with the disabled veterans of the war. These were the men and women who saw the war literally inscribed on the bodies of their loved ones. They were everywhere after the war, on street corners, in public squares, in churches, and in family circles. The French textile worker Mémé Santerre described her village in the north of the country:

The agricultural laborers came back as amputees, blind, gassed, or as 'scar throats', as some were called because of their disfigured, crudely healed faces. We began to see more and more returning. What a crowd! What a rude shock at the railway station, where the wives went to meet their husbands, to find them like that – crippled, sick, despairing that they would be of no use anymore. At first, we had the impression that all those returning had been injured. It wasn't until later that those who had escaped without a scratch returned. But, like their comrades, they were serious, sad, unsmiling; they spoke little. They had lived in hell for four years and wouldn't forget it.[18]

Only a fraction of the men wounded in the war were permanently disabled, but their number was still sufficiently large to provide families with problems that they could not handle on their own. At that point families came together, joined by networks of aid and compassion working to support those struggling under the burdens the war had imposed on them.

The men with the broken faces

Again, one example of this kind of 'fictive kinship', this joining together to help families *in extremis*, may serve to disclose a wider phenomenon. The wounded came in many forms: psychologically damaged men, men who suffered from illness contracted during the war; men literally torn apart. Among those who came back from the war were thousands of ordinary men afflicted with extraordinary wounds. These were the *gueules cassées*, the men with broken faces. How many disfigured veterans were there? Estimates vary, but at least 12 per cent of all men wounded suffered from facial wounds. Perhaps one-third of these men (or 4 per cent of all wounded) were disfigured. Since in Britain, France, and Germany alone, roughly 7 million men were wounded, about 280,000 disfigured men in these three countries alone returned home after the First World War.[19] Of these men, perhaps one in ten joined associations devoted to their needs and their cause.[20]

Men without faces, without recognizable features, could not look in the mirror. They had literally lost their identities. Many other forms of identity were lost in the First World War, but for these men with the broken faces the road back to some semblance of ordinary life was tortuous indeed. It was only through the formation of groups of individuals surrounding the disabled men that these people could escape from a form of remembrance which was paralytic. These men needed to see that they were not reduced to their wounds or disabilities. They were men capable of acting with other men and women to resume their lives. Associative work helped people reduce trauma to handicap, so as not to let the war further truncate their lives.

A glimpse of how painful and fraught with danger this effort was may

[18] Serge Grafteaux, *Mémé Santerre*, trans. by L.Tilly (Boston: Schocken, 1982), p. 83.
[19] Sophie Delaporte, 'Les blessés de la face de la grande guerre', Mémoire de maîtrise, Université de Picardie Jules Verne, 1991–2, introduction; and S. Delaporte, 'Les défigurés de la grande guerre', *Guerres mondiales et conflits contemporains*, 175 (1994), pp. 103–21.
[20] I am grateful to Antoine Prost for his comments on this subject.

be found in the work of one woman who helped the *gueules cassées*. Henriette Rémi was a French nurse who learned of the fate of these men during the war. She visited a friend in the spring of 1918, an officer who had in his care a man with no face:

He has only one leg; his right arm is covered by bandages. His mouth is completely distorted by an ugly scar which descends below his chin. All that is left of his nose are two enormous nostrils, two black holes which trap our gaze, and make us wonder for what this man has suffered? . . . All that is left of his face are his eyes, covered by a veil; his eyes seem to see . . .

The wounded man talks of home, where his mother and sister live:

I cannot see them, it is true, but they will see me. Yes, they will see me! And they will care for me. They will help me pass the time. You know, time passes terribly slowly in hospital. My sister is a teacher, she will read to me. My mother's eyes are weak; she can hardly read; she sewed too much when we were kids; she had to provide for us; my father died when we were little.

The authorities at the hospital did not encourage family visits; they were potentially traumatic. But the time had come when this veteran would return to his family. He asks Rémi if they will recognize him. Certainly, was her hesitant answer, hoping that if their eyes did not find the man, their hearts would. Then the sister comes:

A young woman, fresh, pretty, approaches quickly; she searches in the crowd for her brother. All at once, her face pales, an expression of terror forms; her eyes grow in fright, she raises her arms as if pushing away a vision of horror, and murmurs, 'My God . . . it's he.' A little further away, a woman in black, a bit bent, advances timidly, searching with an expectant smile. And in an instant, those poor tired eyes grow terrified, those tired hands raised in fear, and from this mother's heart comes the cry: 'My God . . . it's he.'[21]

For this family, after the first shock of recognition, the long journey towards recovery began. But others were not so fortunate. One of the men Henriette Rémi tried to help was a Monsieur Lazé. He had been a teacher, and while recuperating, he looked forward to a visit in hospital from his wife and son. He was blind, but wanted to embrace his small son, Gérard, who had followed his father around on his last leave before being injured. On Gérard's first visit to the hospital, he asked the nurse if he could see his father, but was told not today; the next day his father would come to him on a home visit. Sister Henriette agreed to accompany him on the journey home. On the train, a child saw Lazé and asked his mother, 'what's wrong with that man?' Lazé replied: 'Have a good look, little one, and don't ever forget that this is war, this and nothing

---

[21] Henriette Rémi, *Hommes sans visage* (Lausanne: S.P.E.S., 1942), pp. 21–3. I am grateful to Sophie Delaporte for providing me with a copy of this remarkable memoir.

else.' At his village, he took his habitual route home. At the door, his wife welcomes him and calls their son.

Then the boy uttered a piercing cry: the boy shook. His father was shaken too, and stared at the floor. And Gérard turned and ran, much faster than he had come, crying in a loud voice: 'That's not Papa.' Lazé was desolate. His wife said: 'You've gone too fast; one must take precautions.'

At the other end of the garden, Gérard continued to say 'That's not Papa.' Henriette tried to help.

I approached him slowly, but Gérard didn't want to see me. He was shaking; better to leave him to his mother. He hid in her skirts.

Lazé was rooted to the spot. He took his head in his hands and said: 'Imbecile, imbecile! But how could I have known how horrible I am. Someone should have told me!'

Henriette agreed: 'Despair, shame, impotence shook me. Yes, he was right. At the hospital we had but one desire: to make them believe that they were not terrifying, and now look at the result.'

Henriette took Lazé back to the hospital. Everyone told him the child would forget. He refused to believe it. He told Henriette:

Having once been a man, having once understood the meaning of this word and wanting nothing more than just to be a man, I am now an object of terror to my own son, a daily burden to my wife, a shameful thing to all humanity.

Another attempt to return home; another failure: again his son cries,

'That's not Papa.' Lazé recoiled. 'It's finished. It's too late. I terrify him.' That night, back in hospital, Lazé committed suicide. He opened the veins in his wrist with his penknife.[22]

This terrible story brings us to a critical feature of what I have called 'fictive kinship' in the aftermath of the Great War. The war provided challenges too heavy for most individuals or families to bear on their own. There were two alternatives open to them: to rely on the state for help; or to create associations which would demand recognition, assistance, and respect for those disabled in the service of the nation. Given the financial constraints under which states operated after the war, and the inevitable headaches of bureaucratic procedure, associative action was the only way out of despair and penury for millions of families after the Armistice.

Lacking an identity easily reconstructed in civilian life, many disabled men and their companions succeeded in forming a new identity, a corporate one through their own associations. Let us again consider the *gueules cassées*. The Union of Disfigured Men (later the National Federation of Trepanned and Disfigured Men) was but one of a host of

---

[22] Rémi, *Hommes*, pp. 89–109.

veterans' associations in postwar France. But it remained separate from the larger organizations of veterans or of wounded men. The disfigured had special problems of sociability, which only their own association could address.[23]

The idea to form such an association was hatched by two disfigured men, who had met at the Val-de-Grâce military hospital in Paris, and invited all those they knew there to join together. Their first meeting was on 21 June 1921, four years after other, inclusive groups of veterans began to create their own associations.[24] Like all other such associations, they had their own newspaper. Their leader was a disfigured officer, Colonel Picot, aged fifty-nine in 1921, the father of the organization, and a towering figure in the veterans' movement as a whole. He always affirmed the special character of the association, drawing upon men who had formed strong bonds during their long stays in hospital. They met at a banquet twice a year, and drew on each other's strength to meet the terrible problems they had to face. In 1927 their association opened a country house for its members at Moussy-le-Vieux in the Department of the Seine-et-Marne, where disfigured men could rest without fear of encounters with a still uncomfortable public.[25] This chateau with 100 acres of land, 40 kilometres from Paris, would not be a place of suffering, but of rest and celebration. As Colonel Picot put it, it would be 'a place worthy of them, a chateau like those acquired by the men who got rich when we lost our faces'. Some men came for short stays; others for good. Their families were welcome too. All were invited to join in farming; even those who thought they were unemployable were put to work. In 1934, a second home opened in the south of France, at Le Coudon, near the port of Toulon. There Colonel Picot died in 1938.[26]

This one case was not an isolated one. The proliferation of this form of fictive kinship, lived out in the life of associations built on remembrance is one of the key features of the social history of the inter-war years. These groups had a 'collective memory', but it was not shared by the larger collective, the state. The 'collective memory' of these men and women was theirs and theirs alone. They had to wrest from the state what we might think they deserved by right: decent pensions and assistance in rebuilding their lives.

---

[23] Antoine Prost, *Les anciens combattants et la société française 1914–1939* (Paris: Presses de la Fondation Nationale des Sciences Politiques, 1977), II, p. 52.

[24] J. M. Winter, *Sites of memory, sites of mourning. The Great War in European cultural history* (Cambridge: Cambridge University Press, 1995), p. 36.

[25] Delaporte, 'Les blessés', ch. 2.   [26] Ibid. pp. 200–13.

Helping the orphans

It would be a mistake, though, to characterize fictive kinship as entirely a struggle of state versus civil society. There were many who worked through state institutions to help the victims of war. Among the most prominent were teachers. Their job was to stand in for the millions of missing fathers, to present their orphan sons with a sense of their own worth, of hope for the future, a future which – to a degree – their absent fathers had earned for them by their sacrifice. In this effort, such teachers were not hostile to the state. They brought to these young victims of war a sense that they were not abandoned.

One example of how this happened is that of the Algerian-born writer Albert Camus. Camus's father Lucien was wounded in 1914 during the Battle of the Marne, when his son Albert was eleven months old. Lucien Camus was evacuated to a hospital at Saint-Brieuc in Brittany, from which he wrote to his wife reassuringly that he was recovering. Four weeks later, he was dead. Catherine Camus received the official notification, followed by shell fragments removed from her husband's body. For the family, these relics were all that remained of Lucien Camus.

She took her two small children and moved in with her mother in the Belcourt district of Algiers. Already deaf and illiterate, though able to lip-read, Catherine's speech became twisted and more limited. She worked in a cartridge factory during the war, and thereafter, lived a passive life of laundry work and obedience to her mother. A full four years after her husband's death, she began to receive a widow's pension. No one at home could write to fill out the form, so the claim was made only when a neighbour helped.[27]

Catherine Camus's young son Albert grew up in this household, with the shadow of the absent father a constant companion. His mother was a benign cipher to the boy, but his father was simply unknown. There were no household documents, since no one could read; there were very few family stories, and only one or two pictures. A postcard or two, and the bits of metal that had killed him.

Throughout his life, Albert Camus searched to find who his father had been. In 1953, at the age of forty, he made a pilgrimage to the cemetery in Brittany where his father lay. He found the grave, in the first row of the military section of the Saint Michel cemetery. There he read the date:

'1885–1914', and automatically did the arithmetic: twenty-nine years. Suddenly he was struck by an idea that shook his very being. He was forty years old. The

[27] Herbert R. Lottman, *Albert Camus. A biography* (London: Weidenfeld and Nicolson, 1979), chs. 1–2.

man buried under that slab, who had been his father, was younger than he.

And the wave of tenderness and pity that at once filled his heart was not the stirring of the soul that leads the son to the memory of the vanished father, but the overwhelming compassion that a grown man feels for an unjustly murdered child – something here was not in the natural order, and, in truth, there was no order but only madness and chaos when the son was older than the father.

Wandering around the cemetery, he saw other graves and 'realized from the dates that this soil was strewn with children who had been the fathers of greying men who thought they were living in this present time'. He puzzled over who this missing father was, this 'younger father'.

In a family where they spoke little, where no one read or wrote, with an unhappy and listless mother, who would have informed him about this young and pitiable father? No one had known him but his mother and she had forgotten him. Of that he was sure. And he died unknown on this earth where he had fleetingly passed, like a stranger.[28]

Could the son still discover the secret of this 'stranger's' life? All the son saw was the shadow of his father, like the 'light ash of a butterfly wing incinerated in a forest fire'.[29] But even at the age of forty, this orphan of the war 'needed someone to show him the way'.[30] Without a father, he lacked a sense of heritage, of a past. He had 'never known those moments when a father would call his son, after waiting for him to reach the age of listening, to tell him the family's secret, or a sorrow of long ago, or the experience of his life'. Consequently, he – the son – had had to become 'the first man', and 'without memories and without faith' enter 'the world of the men of his time and its dreadful and exalted history'.[31]

The 'dead stranger of Saint-Brieuc',[32] the fallen soldier and father 'consumed in a cosmic fire' was like millions of others. The war had created hundreds of 'new orphans each day, Arab and French' who 'awakened in every corner of Algeria, sons and daughters without fathers who would now have to learn to live without guidance and without heritage'.[33]

What rescued this orphan from despair? Almost certainly the bond he formed with one of his teachers, a veteran lucky enough to come back unscathed. Louis Germain, who taught Camus from the age of nine, was the most formative influence in his life. This former soldier was able to give Camus and his peers the sense that what they thought and felt mattered and that the world was there to be discovered. Germain also

---

[28] Albert Camus, *The first man*, trans. David Hapgood (New York: Alfred A. Knopf, 1995), pp. 25–8.
[29] Ibid. p. 314.   [30] Ibid. p. 297.   [31] Ibid. pp. 195, 197.   [32] Ibid. p. 82.
[33] Ibid. pp. 73, 70.

felt a special responsibility for war orphans like Camus. At the end of each term the teacher took up his copy of a war memoir, *The cross of wood* by Dorgelès. There he read of the war and 'of a special kind of men, dressed in heavy cloth stiff with mud, who spoke a strange language and lived in holes under a ceiling of shells and flares and bullets'. Camus 'just listened with all his heart to a story that his teacher read with all *his* heart', a story of the war 'that cast its shadow over everything in the children's world'.[34]

Germain helped to persuade Camus's mother and grandmother to forego his wages so that he could study for a scholarship enabling him to go to the *lycée* (or secondary school). They remained life-long friends. Years later, Germain gave his gnarled copy of Dorgelès's novel to Camus, who (the teacher said) had earned it by the tears he had shed while the book was read aloud in a class in Algiers in 1922.[35]

Camus was fortunate. He had had a surrogate father, a man who had suffered in the trenches, and who had retained the view that the 'generation of fire', the men of 1914, had a duty to raise the sons of their fallen comrades. He gave his pupil Camus the belief that he could be more than a stranger, that he could find his way in a world disfigured by violence.

Commemoration and fictive kinship

The story of the Goodyear family, of surrogate fathers like Louis Germain, of nurses like Henriette Rémi, tell us much about forms of kinship and forms of remembrance of the Great War. Above all, these stories fill in the space between the war and the efflorescence of commemorative statues and ceremonies that have embodied the 'collective memory' of the Great War. No doubt, war memorials carry powerful collective messages, but they must be seen not only as projects with a life-history of their own, but also as outcomes of earlier projects, of earlier and ongoing efforts to tell the story of the war and its victims.

When the Cenotaph in London was unveiled on 19 July 1919, it elicited an overwhelming public response. The British Cabinet commissioned the architect Edwin Lutyens to build a temporary Cenotaph for a victory parade down Whitehall in London. They were astonished at the outpouring of public feeling surrounding the monument. Perhaps one million people made a pilgrimage to the spot in 1919 alone.[36] The

[34] Ibid. pp. 147, 148.   [35] Ibid. p. 149.
[36] David Lloyd, 'Pilgrimage in the aftermath of the Great War in Britain and the Dominions,' PhD dissertation, University of Cambridge, 1994.

temporary catafalque was turned into a permanent – the permanent – monument of mourning.

This one instance encapsulated events which occurred in many obscure corners of Britain and other combatant countries in the following years. War memorials were constructed by local committees composed in various ways of notables, ex-servicemen, and the families of the dead. They offered the town, village, or *quartier* a very simple and very powerful narrative of the war, inscribed in the list of names of the dead. These men took up arms, they say; they left the town, never to return. That is all. Inscriptions vary, but the style is overwhelmingly sombre and un-celebratory. In small towns, the faces of the mourners were very familiar. On Armistice Day, when townspeople gathered to pay tribute to the dead, they were also joining together, at least for a few moments, with the survivors.

Thanks to the work of a wide array of historians, the iconography and social geography of the war memorials of the 1914–18 conflict are relatively well established.[37] What I want to emphasize in this chapter is how these forms of official commemoration rested on a rich under-growth of unofficial activity, which antedated these statues and carried on long after they were unveiled. If we want to appreciate what those who survived the war brought to these monuments when they passed them, either on Armistice Day or on any ordinary day, we would do well to look beyond them to the small groups of people, whether linked by blood or experience, who dealt with the more obscure, but no less important legacies of the war.

The gathering together of such groups took place in many forms. For

---

[37] For Britain and the Dominions, see the work of Ken Inglis: 'A sacred place: the making of the Australian War Memorial', *War & Society*, 3, 2 (1985), pp. 99–127; 'War memorials: ten questions for historians, *Guerres mondiales et conflits contemporains*, 167 (1992), pp. 5–22; 'World War One memorials in Australia', *Guerres mondiales et conflits contemporains*, 167 (1992), pp. 51–8; 'The homecoming: the war memorial movement in Cambridge, England', *Journal of Contemporary History*, 27, 4 (1992), pp. 583–606; 'The right stuff', *Eureka Street*, 4 (1994), pp. 23–7; 'Entombing unknown soldiers: from London and Paris to Baghdad', *History & Memory*, 5 (1993), pp. 7–31. For France, see Antoine Prost, 'Les monuments aux morts', in P. Nora (ed.), *Les lieux de mémoire. I. La République* (Paris: Gallimard, 1984), pp. 195–225; and Annette Becker, *Les Monuments aux morts* (Paris: Errance, 1989, and *La guerre et la foi. De la mort à la mémoire* (Paris: Armand Colin, 1994). For Germany, George Mosse, *Fallen Soldiers. Reshaping the memory of the world wars* (New York: Oxford University Press, 1990), and (in advance of his definitive study of German war memorials) Reinhart Koselleck, 'Kriegerdenkmale als Identitätsstiftungen der Überlebenden', in Odo Marquard and Karlheinz Stierle (eds.), *Identität* (Munich: Wilhelm Fink Verlag, 1979), pp. 237–76; 'Der Einfluss der beiden Weltkriege auf das soziale Bewusstsein', in Wolfram Wette (ed.), *Der Krieg des kleinen Mannes. Eine Militärgeschichte von unten* (Munich: Piper, 1992), pp. 324–43; and 'Bilderverbot. Welches Totengedenken?', *Frankfurter Allgemeine Zeitung*, 8 April 1993.

those adhering to conventional forms of religious belief, the churches offered consolation. Others tried to bring the dead back to their homes through séances, frowned on by the churches, but popular nonetheless. Groups of spiritualists, either family members or fictive kin, met in a domestic setting where a medium 'reunited' families with the spirits of the dead. Here the deceased hinted at the story of their lives after death, and offered the living consolation. In a nutshell, their message was very simple: It's all right, the dead reassured the living; I'm safe and well. You can go on living.[38] And that is what they did, not in national units, or large collectives, but through local affiliations and in the rhythms of their daily lives.

The extended family of Käthe Kollwitz

One final story may help to uncover some of the essential features of this, the hidden face of remembrance after the Great War. Peter Kollwitz, the 18-year-old elder son of the Berlin lithographer and sculptress Käthe Kollwitz, volunteered for military service on 4 August 1914. He was one of approximately 140,000 German men out of 4 million men mobilized who joined up voluntarily early in the war. These idealistic youths – overwhelmingly students or in middle-class occupations – have been taken to be representative of 'war enthusiasm' in the nation as a whole. In fact, that 'enthusiasm' was strictly limited to a few days and a narrow part of the population.[39] But among Peter's circle, it was real enough.

The sight of troops marching off to the war convinced Peter that he had to join up before the reserves were mobilized. 'My fatherland does not need my year yet', he told his sceptical father, a Berlin physician working in a poor working-class neighbourhood, 'but it needs *me*.' Peter enlisted his mother's aid in getting his father to agree. He did, and Peter joined up, alongside his closest friends and classmates.

This acceptance of the principle of sacrifice by the youth of Berlin initially made some sense to Käthe Kollwitz. Throughout her life, her Protestant belief in a 'calling' infused both her notion of what she must do as an artist and how to serve the people of her country. Peter's decision to volunteer for the army fitted in to that framework. But as soon as the first news of battle and casualties reached Berlin, she began to see that it was 'vile', 'idiotic', and 'harebrained' that these young men, at the beginning of their lives, were going off to war.

---

[38] For details see Winter, *Sites of memory, sites of mourning*, ch. 3.
[39] Jeffrey Verhey, 'The myth of the "Spirit of 1914" in Germany, 1914–1945', unpublished manuscript, ch. 3.

Peter Kollwitz left home on 5 October 1914. He said farewell to his mother on 12 October. Ten days later he was dead. He was killed in Belgium in a field about 20 kilometres northeast of Ypres. One of the friends with whom Peter had enlisted brought the news of his death to the family.

For the next thirty years, Käthe Kollwitz grieved for her son. That story has been told.[40] For our purposes, I want to concentrate on one related theme. Emmanuel Sivan has shown in chapter 9 of this book how Israeli families created kinship bonds among the the friends of their fallen sons, friends with whom they had served and who were lucky enough to come back alive. In a very different context, Käthe Kollwitz and her family did the same.

Ritual attended this kind of bonding. The Kollwitzes left Peter's room intact. They put flowers on the chair next to his bed, and tried to conjure up his spirit in the room. Friends came by and read letters and texts there with the bereaved parents. They put a Christmas tree behind the bed, with eighteen candles, for each of Peter's years. On subsequent Christmases and New Years, additional candles were added, to mark the age he would have reached had he been alive. Birthdays were marked there. This was a sacred space both for the family and for those who had joined in these acts of remembrance.[41]

Such gestures were not just extensions of traditional forms of family gatherings. They were there because the process of healing was so difficult, so slow. Käthe Kollwitz used to sit in her son's room and try to commune with him. At times she drew strength from this effort; at times she believed that 'I walk in twilight, only rarely stars, the sun *has long since set completely.*'[42] The black sun, the aura of depression, was a constant companion.[43]

Some comfort came from Peter's friends; among them she found some solace. She corresponded with them, welcomed their visits. To them she was 'Mother Käthe' or 'Mother Kollwitz'. 'I must retain my feeling of connection to the boys', is the way she put it on 9 October 1916;[44] they were part of her household, part of her life.

This informal 'adoption' of those familiar young men who had shared Peter's fate, both the living and the dead, marked Kollwitz's life. It also became the centrepiece of her commemorative art. Before the First

[40] Winter, *Sites of memory, sites of mourning*, ch. 4.

[41] See the important article by Regina Schulte, 'Käthe Kollwitz's sacrifice', *History Workshop Journal*, 41 (1996), pp. 193–221.

[42] Käthe Kollwitz, *Die Tagebücher*, ed. Jutta Bohnke-Kollwitz (Berlin, 1989), pp. 368–9.

[43] Julia Kristeva, *Black sun. Depression and melancholy*, trans. L. S. Roudiez (New York: Columbia University Press, 1989).

[44] Kollwitz, *Die Tagebücher*, p. 278.

World War, her art encompassed many subjects. Prominent among them were historical and epic themes – peasant uprisings, great sweeps of protest and its suppression. After 1914, images of historical tragedy receded; images of family tragedy loomed large. Her art became more maternal, more familial. In effect, the collective of suffering portrayed in her drawings, etchings, and sculptures had collapsed inward.

From early on in the war Käthe Kollwitz was determined to create a war memorial for her son and for his generation of friends. Initially her idea was to form a single family circle in stone. Her early sketches show two parents holding their dead son; over time, the son became detached from the parents and ultimately he disappeared. Part of the meaning of this shift in iconography from a nuclear family to an extended family, is located in the process of mourning, in the slow and terrible effort to let her son go. But part of the meaning is to be found in Kollwitz's commitment to gather to her family those young men who had had to endure the war at its worst.

On 25 June 1919 she wrote hopefully: 'If I live to see Peter's work [the memorial sculpture] completed and good, commemorating him and his friends on a beautiful site, then perhaps Germany is past the worst.'[45] On 13 October 1925, she described the project as one in which 'The mother should kneel and gaze out over the many graves. She spreads out her arms over all her sons.'[46] Seven years later the memorial was inaugurated in the German military cemetery at Roggevelde. The sculpture is of Käthe and Hans Kollwitz, on their knees, in front of a field of graves, including that of their son. The mother's arms are not extended, but wrapped around her own body, as are her husband's around his. It is a profound statement about individual grief for a collective catastrophe. The parents mourn for this 'flock of children', this ill-starred generation, whose elders could not prevent the disaster which had enveloped them.

It is only with difficulty that the visitor can find the plaque on which the name of Peter Kollwitz is written. He has become one among many, a child mourned by the parents of a family which once was very large, but is now reduced to two old people unable even to support each other in their separate grief. All they can do is beg on their knees for forgiveness, and offer their love and their grief, fixed in stone forever.

At this point we are on the border between metaphor and lived experience. To say that at Roggevelde these were Käthe Kollwitz's lost sons is, on one level, poetic licence. But on another level, her gathering of her son's generation into her family was an essential element in her

---

[45] Ibid. p. 428.   [46] Ibid. p. 603.

effort to express the 'meaning' of the war for her whole generation. One family's loss was terrible; how much more terrible the loss of so many young men, so much promise, so much hope. Like the Goodyears, hers was a family which was defined by those who weren't there. There were millions of them in the aftermath of The First World War.

Conclusion

This chapter has tried to illustrate the need to approach the history of war and remembrance of war from the angle of small-scale, locally rooted social action. Many of these phenomena were family-based, but others were among people whose ties were based on experience rather than marriage or filiation.

I have used the term 'fictive kinship' to characterize these associations. They arose during the war itself. From 1914 on, I argue, kinship bonds widened, through a process of informal or figurative 'adoption'. The *locus classicus* of such work was that of the Red Cross, which operated in every combatant country not only to ensure fair treatment of prisoners, but also to find out what happened to the millions of men who simply went missing in battle. Parallel to the Red Cross, many confessional groups worked to help those stricken by the war. The Protestant voluntary tradition came into its own in this effort, but Jewish and Catholic groups also worked to ease the plight of widows, orphans, and aged parents who had lost their sons in the war. Men who suffered mutilation or illness during the war needed long-term help, and joined in the wider population of victims of war who created and were served by such organizations. Many of these groups were supported by the state; others tried to compensate for the shortcomings of central authorities, frequently too mean or preoccupied to provide adequately for those whose circumstances were reduced by the war.

All these groups were agents of remembrance. Their activity antedated public commemoration and continued long after the ceremonies were over. Yes, on 11 November these groups joined the nation, the wider collective. But that was not their origin, nor their centre of gravity.

I have insisted that remembrance is an activity of agents who freely congregate on the borderline between the private and the public, between families, civil society, and the state. Their work is the subject of this chapter. As we have noted in the introduction, it may be helpful to adopt Bastide's approach to the 'organization of memory' at this point. Remembrance, he posits, is an activity, built up arduously through exchange relationships of a concrete kind. The 'collective' thus formed is never independent of the individuals who create it by their own efforts.[47]

This form of small-scale collective memory – the thought-process of kinship, both fictive and filial – was both powerful and brittle. At the time, it gave men and women a way to live on after the horrors of war. But as those agents of remembrance grew tired or old, developed other lives, moved away, or died, then the activity – the glue – which held together these cells of remembrance atrophied and lost its hold on them.

What has remained to this day are the traces of their work and the envelope in which they operated: the national framework which was but a thin cover over a host of associative forms arduously constructed over years by thousands of people, mostly obscure. Today we see the 'collective memory' in national ceremonies; but in the decades after the Armistice of 1918, there were other, locally based collectives engaged in remembrance. They have vanished, but it would be foolish to merge these activities in some state-bounded space of hegemony or domination. What these people did was much smaller and much greater than that.

[47] See chapter 1 in this book.

3   War, death, and remembrance
       in Soviet Russia

Catherine Merridale

Modern warfare is a potent generator of memories. The involvement of
every citizen, the unaccustomed collectivities, the emergencies and
shock, the loss, the private totems and shared superstitions leave
indelible prints on the imagination. Total war, whether experienced as a
combatant or as a civilian, is an almost uniquely vivid story in the life of
any individual. But personal memory is only a part of the social process
of remembering. Indeed, it can come to appear irrelevant or even
subversive to national projects of commemoration. Even in democracies,
the corporate, usually national, use of images of war is only loosely
linked to the reality which people remember. Conversely, too, the
individuals who file past the eternal flame may well rehearse in their
silence memories and stories which have little to do with the ceremonial
which has provided the occasion for their presence. The state and the
individual interact, their exchange mediated, in democracies, by voluntary groups such as veterans' societies, local charities, widows' and
orphans' groups. The process, a contest between competing images and
claims, is complex, its outcomes – the image and historical memory of
the war – provisional. The war generation will die, individual memories
– painful, exciting, unresolved – will be lost, but the story of the war will
remain collective property, open to periodic reassessment with each
change of government.

How do these observations apply in an authoritarian single-party state
like the former Soviet Union? What happens when the public expression
of individual memory is censored? How does commemoration work
where there can be no voluntary associations of veterans independent of

Some of the material presented in this paper appeared in *History Workshop Journal* in
October 1996 (issue 42, pp. 1–18). I am grateful to the editors of the journal for
permission to use it here. An earlier version of the same paper was presented to Bristol
University's Critical Theory Seminar in March 1996, and I would like to thank the
organizers and all the participants for their comments. I would also like to thank Jay
Winter and Emmanuel Sivan for their invitation to think about this material, the Harry
Frank Guggenheim Foundation for its support in the organization and funding of two
workshops on the subject, and Dori Laub for his support and advice.

state control and funding? What occurs when the regime collapses and memories are released? This chapter explores some of these themes. Its starting point is the Second World War, the Great Patriotic War of 1941–5, an event, or series of events, commemorated with elaborate official ceremony. The style of this commemoration recalled other nations' acts of remembrance; the same images were used, the same exclusions made, the same goal of patriotic affirmation served. What was unique about the Soviet case was not, arguably, the commemoration of the war in question but the silences which lay behind it, the unspoken grief for the millions – victims of other wars, and of repression, famine, and industrial disaster – whose loss was scarcely acknowledged until the final years of Communist rule.

It is sometimes suggested that the iteration of one kind of memory involves the forgetting of others.[1] Memorials may commemorate a version of events, but it is an exclusive one. Much that is left out, runs the argument, is ceremonially or architecturally forgotten. But is it? In the Soviet case, the exclusions were clear enough. Great Patriotic War memorials and histories recalled the young, handsome, innocent soldier, the victim who fell in battle repelling the Nazi invader. In so doing, they excluded the older men and boys, the women, the victims of disease, accident, and of mass executions carried out by their own side. They excluded, too, the people who fell behind the lines, including innumerable victims of continued police repression. Those who fell in the winter war against Finland were virtually ignored. For years, too, the true cost of the Great Patriotic War, in human and other terms, was concealed. Stalin admitted to 7 million Soviet war dead, Khrushchev to 20 million. One of the tasks of recent historical research has been to unearth more accurate statistics. It now appears likely that 26 million Soviet deaths can be attributed to the war, and some Russian historians have inflated the figure to 37 and even to 40 million.[2]

The story of exclusion can be extended beyond the Great Patriotic War in either direction. Most First World War graves are hardly marked

[1] See, for example, Michael Ignatieff, 'Soviet war memorials' *History Workshop Journal*, 17 (Spring 1984), pp. 157–63; George L. Mosse, *Fallen soldiers* (Oxford: Oxford University Press, 1990).

[2] The highest serious figure has been given by V. I. Kozlov (*Istoriya SSSR*, 2 (1989), p. 133), who calculated that the population deficit in 1945 was between 45 and 48 million, suggesting that approximately 38 million excess deaths occurred between 1939 and 1945. Other Russian calculations are rather lower, and correspond more closely to the estimates of Western demographers such as Alain Blum. E. Andreev, L. Darskii, and T. Khar'kova, for example, suggest a total of 26 million. 'Otsenka lyudskikh poter' v period velikoi otechestvennoi voiny', *Vestnik statistiki*, 10 (1990).

today.[3] The 'fraternal grave' of 300 Russian troops who fell defending Moscow at the battle of Borodino in 1812 was surreptitiously moved in 1953 to make way for the development of apartment blocks along Kutuzovskii Prospekt.[4] More recently, the boys who fell in the early months of the Afghan War from 1979 also received scant commemoration. Many were buried separately, the cause of death left vague in the epitaph, a civilian photograph attached to the headstone, in order to conceal the scale of Soviet military losses.[5] Such concealment in these and other cases contrasts with the patriotic importance deliberately assigned to the war of 1941–5. Depending upon circumstances and its own perception of *raison d'état*, the Soviet state was as skilled at destroying the material basis of collective memory as it was eager to commemorate the selected fallen of Mother Russia in concrete and stone.

Historians have understandably focused on this attempted destruction of social memory, linking it with starker instances of censorship and denial. The issue even became front-page news, briefly, when the Communist Party Central Committee's last rehabilitation campaign was at its height in 1988. This focus on official denial, however, has diverted attention away from the fact that private and personal stories were often obstinately preserved. Proscribed memories – tales of arrest, disappearances, lost parents, orphans – survived, despite the odds, through the Stalin years and the later period of stagnation under Brezhnev. They were kept alive as family secrets, private narratives rehearsed in kitchens, out at the dacha on long summer evenings, in whispers at the funerals of each survivor as they died. How and why did memories survive? How, more troublingly, did people acquiesce in official distortions while simultaneously repeating their own stories to friends and children?

In searching for answers to these questions, the literature on trauma and collective memory has much to offer.[6] But the bulk of the evidence on which it is based has been drawn from work with survivors of the Holocaust. Here, simultaneous knowing and not knowing is well documented. But recollection took place against a background of the wide public acknowledgement, to say nothing of physical commemoration, of

[3] I. A. Kremleva, *Pokhoronno-pominal'nye obychai i obryady* (Moscow: Institut etnologii i antropologii RAN, 1993), p. 35.
[4] Timothy J. Colton, *Moscow. Governing the Socialist metropolis* (Cambridge, Mass.: Belknap Press of Harvard University Press, 1995), p. 338.
[5] Svetlana Aleksiyevich, *Zinky boys: Soviet voices from a forgotten war* (London: Chatto & Windus, 1992), p. 15.
[6] I discussed these issues in more depth in the article 'Death and memory in modern Russia', *History Workshop Journal*, 42 (October 1996), pp. 1–18.

some of the key events. In this sense, refusal to discuss personal memories of the Holocaust has been accurately described as 'silence', a marked contrast to the 'secrets' which Russians rehearsed in the long years of repression.[7] Virtually every Soviet family had 'secrets' of some kind. The first fifty years of the twentieth century in the Soviet Union were marked by a succession of disasters, each accompanied by large-scale population losses. The state publicly denied much of the mortality, but official records were nonetheless preserved, and these tell a tale of repeated demographic catastrophe.[8] Assessments of the scale of losses at each stage vary according to the individual demographer's assumptions about such issues as migration, fertility, and infant mortality, but a reasonable estimate would place the total number of excess deaths for the whole period somewhere around 60 million. Between 23 and 26 million people died prematurely in what would become the USSR between 1914 and 1922. Collectivization, the famine, and the purges – the Stalinist revolution from above – resulted in about 10 million further excess deaths, of which political executions probably accounted for roughly $1\frac{1}{2}$ million. Finally, the war years 1939 to 1945 saw in excess of 26 million premature deaths, some in combat, some related directly to war, but many also products of a continuing campaign of state repression. Even families which saw little in the way of combat or terror were likely to have suffered in the succession of famines and outbreaks of epidemic disease which characterized the period of Soviet state-building.

Losses on this scale defy attempts to picture the reality which they catalogue. Even disasters familiar to West Europeans assumed incalculably greater proportions in the East. For example, the First World War was more costly, in terms of human lives, for the Russians than for the Western European powers because of the large number of men they fielded. It was followed, moreover, by a vicious civil war in which further millions perished. Both wars were accompanied by massive movements of population. As Lorimer put it in 1946, 'during the years 1915–23, the Russian people underwent the most cataclysmic changes since the Mongol invasion in the early thirteenth century'.[9]

The civil war was followed almost immediately by a severe famine.

---

[7] I am grateful to Dori Laub for pointing out this distinction, and for directing my attention to the work of Daniel Bar-On.

[8] The most complete of the current surveys of the demographic literature is Alain Blum, *Naître, vivre et mourir en URSS, 1917–1991*, Paris, 1994. For a survey of the current state of the debate about numbers, see R. W. Davies, Mark Harrison, and S. G. Wheatcroft, *The economic transformation of the Soviet Union, 1913–1945* (Cambridge: Cambridge University Press, 1994).

[9] Cited in Davies, Harrison, and Wheatcroft, *Economic transformation*, p. 60.

This was most destructive in southern Russia, and especially the Volga region and Ukraine. Total mortality in these regions is estimated at between $1\frac{1}{2}$ and 4 million. The picture is complicated by infanticide, which was not new, and also by cannibalism, which had not been reported on such a scale before. The authors of a contemporary study of the famine admitted, for example, that cannibalism in any form was virtually unknown in 1891, when hunger had been almost as severe.[10] But in 1921, possibly, according to the same source, because of the brutalizing effects of the First World War, cases where dead bodies were consumed by survivors, even if graveyards had to be robbed, ran to several thousand. The murder and eating of neighbours, and especially of children, although less common, was also widely reported. With careful Bolshevik rationality, the authors explained that such behaviour was a desperate last resort, and that the guilty seldom survived to acquire a taste for human flesh.[11] Rather than making a sensation out of these cases, readers were told, they should look for parallels with this behaviour among animals, many species of which, 'and especially rabbits', consume their young at times of food shortage.[12] What the survivors were to make of their unspeakable memories was not discussed. Still less attention, moreover, would be given to the succession of disasters which followed. The famine of 1932–3, indeed, was officially denied at the time. The open commemoration of the eight or more million who died would be left to exiles for fifty years.

By 1939, then, the Soviet Union had already sustained proportionately more excess deaths than any other industrializing European society. Most were far from heroic, material neither for patriotic monuments nor state-building mythologies. As we have noted, such was the official concern about the scale of loss that statistics about it were concealed and the reality of mass death publicly denied. The first census conducted under Stalinist rule, that of 1937, was suppressed before a line of its conclusions had been published.[13] Denial was not merely the work of the state, however. Every individual with a personal memory of loss, every witness, in some measure colluded in the process. It has been suggested that mass death brutalizes its witnesses, that they become hardened to violence.[14] The Soviet case is more confusing, however. For the victims collaborated with an apparently brutal suppression of

---

[10] L. A. and L. M. Vasilevskii, *Kniga o golode* (Petrograd, 1922).
[11] Ibid. pp. 175–8.   [12] Ibid. p. 182.
[13] See Catherine Merridale, 'The 1937 census and the limits of Stalinist rule', *The Historical Journal*, 39, no. 1 (1996), pp. 225–40.
[14] Mosse, *Fallen soldiers*, pp. 159–60.

mourning while simultaneously preserving their private memories for years afterwards.

How did people cope with loss on this scale? What was its impact? In other societies a natural response would have been to turn to the traditional comforts of religion and ritual, public or private. But here again, the Soviet case was exceptional. The violence of the Stalin era was compounded by a parallel and simultaneous assault upon religious practices of all kinds, including those surrounding death. The impact of this attack on Russian mentalities can be understood only by considering the importance of tradition in the years before Stalinism. Even for a pre-industrial society, Russia was richly endowed with superstition, custom, and ritual when it came to the treatment of death and bereavement.[15] Beliefs about the relationship between the body and the soul, and even about the condition of the corpse itself, incorporated pre-Christian influences, accretions from traditional folklore and adapted orthodox ideas and language. Superstitions which had persisted for centuries were widely held, affecting practices across European Russia. The rapid violation of these would have been shocking on its own. But their more or less enforced abandonment at a time of widespread violence compounded a major social catastrophe.

In the light of what was about to happen, two principal sets of issues stand out as particularly important. First, the body itself was treated with careful reverence – washed, dressed in special garments, laid in its coffin with an assortment of possessions and tokens to ease its passage to the 'other side'. Second, the place of burial acquired a lasting importance. The holding of ritual meals at the graveside, regular visits to the plot, the tending and decoration of graves – these are traditions which still survive. Family members might converse with the deceased by the grave; sometimes messages were sent in the keeping of the recently dead for those who had gone long before. A sense of continuity was preserved at the burial site. Cremation, which the Bolsheviks attempted to introduce in the 1920s, was entirely alien to Russian funerary culture. The practice disappeared, indeed, more or less at the same time as Christianity arrived in Kiev.

Fear of and respect for death were manifested through ghost stories and the belief that potentially vengeful spirits must be appeased. The purpose of many of the more elaborate aspects of funerary ritual was to circumvent the possibility of haunting or other revenge. At the moment of death, for example, doors were locked and a window opened to allow the spirit to leave by an unfamiliar route, thus making its return to the

---

[15] See G. A. Nosova, 'Traditsionnyi obryady russkikh: krestiny, pokhoronny, pominki', *Rossiiskii etnograf*, 6 (1993), p. 5.

house more difficult.[16] The soap with which the corpse had been washed was buried in an uncultivated corner of the yard, and the water disposed of outside the house. Body and spirit were hardly separate – violations of a corpse could result in an angry haunting.[17] Whether individuals fully believed in these superstitions is at one level unimportant; their persistence indicates that they were at least effective as strategies for allaying the collective anxiety about death in a high-mortality world.

How did the Bolsheviks deal with death? Their ideology was officially atheist. Unease about death, however, is universal. Before the Revolution, 'red' funerals, with their processions of workers, red banners, and hortatory speeches in place of religious imagery, had been arranged for individual Marxist heroes.[18] These were exceptions, however. The creation of a state ritual was a matter for the post-revolutionary leadership, but one which they confronted within hours of the seizure of power. An early task for the new government was to bury the 238 heroes who had died in the struggle for Moscow. Here, perhaps, lies the origin of official amnesia about the First World War. For Bolshevik ceremonial appropriated martial imagery, stripped it of its imperial and religious trappings, and pressed it into service for the fallen of the people's revolution. Red Square, which only four years before had seen celebrations for 300 years of the Romanov dynasty, now hosted its first mass rally for the new regime.[19] Every factory, office, and theatre in the city was closed for the occasion. Open coffins were carried through the city to their burial place in the Kremlin wall. The choice of ceremony, even the choice of music and the presence of keening women, combined the old and familiar with elements of Communist state theatre. The addition of military guards and political slogans, neatly replacing the trappings of traditional religion, was intended at this stage to honour the fact that the 'heroes' had died fighting. This war, the revolutionary struggle, had symbolically to supersede the sacrifices made on behalf of Tsarism since 1914. Selection and censorship had begun at once.

The hero's funeral, repeated several times in the next three years,[20]

---

[16] Details from D. K. Zelenin, *Vostochnoslavyanskaya etnografiya* (Moscow, 1926; reprinted 1991).

[17] Elaborate ghost-rituals survived in rural Siberia into the twentieth century. See M. M. Gromyko, *Dokhristyanskie verovaniya v bytu sibirskikh krest'yan XVIII–XIX vv.* (Moscow, 1967).

[18] On this, see N. S. Polishchuk, 'Obryad kak sotsial'noe yavlenie', *Sovetskaya etnografiya*, 6 (1991), pp. 25–39.

[19] My description of the funeral is based on accounts reproduced in A. Abramov, *U kremlevskoi steny* (Moscow, 1984).

[20] Notably at the funerals of the assassinated Bolshevik, Zagorskii, and of Ya. M. Sverdlov, the first general secretary of the Party.

would reach its high point in the public obsequies for Lenin in 1924. In its seventh year, the new regime had yet to perfect the atheist funeral; Lenin deserved the deepest solemnities, but Communism, with its simple slogans and direct messages of equality and consumption, could provide little that did not smack of bathos. The choice of music, for example, was problematic. The heroes of 1917 were buried to the strains of the *Internationale* – less than two weeks after the Revolution little else seemed appropriate. But the commission which met to organize the ceremony for Lenin's interment included men whose tastes had been formed in Western Europe. They reached instinctively for the requiem masses of Verdi and Mozart, to say nothing of the heroic romanticism of Wagner's *Götterdämmerung*. Memoranda flew from the commission to the office of Lunacharskii, Commissar for Education. It was the latter who discarded all the religious music, rejected Wagner on aesthetic grounds, and opted for Chopin and Beethoven interleaved with frequent repeats of the *Internationale*.[21]

Lenin's funeral and the embalming of his corpse raise questions which reach beyond the scope of this chapter. Here it is enough to note that it provided the occasion for the most spectacular public ritual of the Revolution's first decade, and indeed possibly also of the entire pre-war period. Its cost, at a time of economic stringency, was considerable.[22] Red Square itself was refurbished, numerous small buildings, and even a tram line, were removed, and a temporary mausoleum constructed. The military demonstration which accompanied the ceremony was rigorous to the point of barbarism – 162 soldiers suffered frostbite standing to attention along the route of the cortège.[23] But the official object was achieved. Lenin's funeral was treated as a moment to renew one's allegiance to the new regime; from the premature death of the hero would flow new life in the form of a new world order. The leader's body, like that of a pre-revolutionary saint, would not corrupt. Preserved in his perspex coffin, moreover, the dead hero watched – albeit impotently – over the regime he had created. His death, like those of other heroes, glorified the collective enterprise of building socialism. Such a sense of purpose assuaged the grief which, bereft of any sense of a compensatory afterlife, could otherwise only mourn, and even seek to avenge, the senseless obliteration of life.

If Bolshevism appropriated some of the symbolism and ritual of pre-

---

[21] The papers relating to Lenin's funerals are in the Lenin *fond* at RTsKhIDNI, *fond* 16, *opis* 1, *delo* 105.

[22] For a lavish account of the building of the Lenin mausoleum, see N. N. Stoyanov, *Arkhitektura mavzoleya Lenina* (Moscow: Gosizdat, 1950).

[23] RTsKhIDNI, *fond* 16, *opis* 1, *delo* 91.

revolutionary Russia for its leaders, however, in practice the deaths of common people were treated with less reverence. A regime which originally attempted to maintain the Provisional Government's ban on the death penalty for both civilian and military offences soon found itself presiding over summary executions running at scores or even hundreds a day.[24] Eye-witnesses recalled piles of bodies littering the streets of provincial cities, the nightly echo of rifle fire. As Lenin put it, 'no revolutionary government can do without the death penalty, and the essence of the question is only against what class will the weapon of the death penalty be directed'.[25] Some of the killings were intended to have a deterrent effect. In 1922, for example, Lenin called for the religious protesters of the city of Shua to be punished 'so brutally that they will remember it for decades to come'.[26] The first official victim of the death penalty administered by Soviet justice was Aleksei Shchastny, Admiral of the Baltic fleet, executed for treason in June 1918.[27]

The bulk of the political killings of the early Soviet period received little publicity, however, especially those which did not involve prominent figures or elaborate trials. Public, theatrical, execution was not a staple of a regime which preferred to despatch its many enemies with a swift bullet rather than risk the spectacle – and possible focus for revolt – of an overcrowded public gallows.[28] By the 1930s, indeed, by which time techniques for removing opponents had become routine, individuals who were purged simply disappeared. Although recent testimonies, for example from Belarus, speak of people kept awake at night by the sound of rifle or revolver fire, most of the Great Purge killings of 1937–8 took place in secret. Even prominent figures from the revolutionary era – Bukharin, Kamenev, Zinoviev, and others – were killed in cellars or remote wooded compounds away from public view. Purge victims were often shot in the back of the neck, a method of execution which spared the executioner from eye contact with his target and, apparently, minimized the post-mortem spilling of blood. Their human bodies, several

---

[24] The death penalty was abolished after the February Revolution. It was formally reinstated in September 1918, but had in practice been revived from as early as March. See Ger P. van den Berg, 'The Soviet Union and the death penalty', *Soviet Studies*, 35, 2 (April 1983), p. 155.

[25] *Polnoe sobranie sochinenii*, fifth edn, vol. 39, pp. 183–4.

[26] On this remark, and the literature about it, see van den Berg, 'The Soviet Union and the death penalty', pp. 156 and 168.

[27] Ibid. p. 155.

[28] A comparison might be made here between the use of the guillotine in the case of Louis XVI's execution – the deliberate distancing of the crowd from the moment of death – and the more elaborate secrecy, or at least, the absence of publicity or ceremony, in the bulk of Soviet executions. For Louis's execution, see Richard Sennett, *Flesh and stone: the body and the city in Western civilization* (London: Faber & Faber, 1994).

million of them over the whole Soviet period, simply disappeared.[29] Of the remaining victims of Stalinism, many died in complete isolation from society, starving or perishing from cold in the labour camps of the far north and east. The scale of the political killings was nearly always downplayed. The dictatorship of the proletariat could be baptized lightly with the blood of martyrs, but there was nothing to be gained from advertising its total immersion in that of its real and imagined opponents.

The Civil War provided many seminal images for the new state, and references to its heroes echoed a decade later in the martial language of Stalinist industrialization. While military metaphors and the language of emergency and heroism were retained, however, the enemy featured in extreme, almost dreamlike, burlesque. A desire to deny even the basic humanity of alleged criminals was reflected in their depiction in the press as spiders, rats, pigs, vultures, dogs, hyenas. The official images were carefully censored. Ex-combatants of the Civil War were known to be racked by nightmares of slaughter and mutilation, their nerves shattered, their bodies incapable of work.[30] But while the medical and Party journals discussed the problem from a clinical point of view, scant public acknowledgement was made of the scenes which had driven them to such a pass.

The Civil War was an extreme crisis; the reverent disposal of corpses could hardly have been a high priority. But even behind the lines, long-held burial customs were under pressure from the moment Soviet power was declared. The Bolshevik Party correctly recognized that institutions such as the Orthodox Church would resist its officials and subvert attempts to divert resources away from religious establishments. But the attack on organized religion which followed the Revolution was not solely aimed at the institutional power of the priesthood. Popular religion, custom, and folklore all posed an ideological challenge. Funerals provided ideal opportunities for the parade of superstition, the collective indulgence of religious belief and for group speculation about the benefits or costs of the new political order. The traditional funeral, and the customary rites of memorial during Lent and after Easter, were objects of particular concern to militant atheists in the Bolshevik Party; but they were also the least susceptible of religious rituals to violent suppression. As late as the 1960s, by which time the majority of other rites of passage (such as marriage and the naming of children) had

---

[29] The public reopening of mass graves, for example those at Butovo near Moscow and Levashovo near St Petersburg, began in the late 1980s. Up to then, their existence was a matter of general but secret knowledge, unconfirmed and largely undiscussed.

[30] A survey cataloguing some of this damage was published in the Party journal, *Bol'shevik*, 21–2 (1925), pp. 61–74.

acquired an almost universally accepted secular ritual, burial remained a predominantly religious affair.[31] Even the Bolsheviks, so heavy-handed in their treatment of many survivals of traditional Russia, were aware that death and burial were more than usually sensitive.[32] But this awareness did not prevent them, in the Revolution's early years, from attempting to eradicate what they saw as offensive elements of the 'cult'.

A number of arguments were used in the attack on traditional practices. The most persuasive, arguably, was based on considerations of public health. It was no coincidence that the first Soviet decree on cemeteries was passed at the height of the typhus epidemic of 1918–19.[33] Cemeteries near the centres of increasingly overcrowded cities posed a threat to ground water; excessively shallow graves – often the result of the successive interment of several bodies in the same plot – could even result in the exposure of bones and rotting human remains. Meanwhile, the Bolshevik policy of closing churches left traditional cemeteries untended and raised questions about the future use of the space. The proposed solution to these problems, neatly including an anti-religious element, was to introduce the practice of secular, scientific cremation.[34]

One problem with this innovation, which it shared with other 'invented' ceremonies, was that the atheist ritual lacked dignity. 'The needs of individuals for emotional expression were not only ignored', observed an otherwise sympathetic commentator, 'but individual sensibilities were often violated.'[35] The official instructions for cremations called for 'order' in the cremation, 'complete silence, no smoking, shouting, or spitting on the floor'. A list of documents was required before cremation could take place; ashes, similarly, could not be collected without the appropriate form. 'Ashes cannot be kept in the house', concluded the directive, 'but every other way of dispersing them – scattering them in the mountains, dropping them from aeroplanes, keeping them in institutes and museums – is permitted. They may only be taken abroad with the appropriate documentation.'[36] This brutalism was not the main problem with crematoria, however. Far more impor-

---

[31] A. I. Kvardakov, 'Religioznye perezhitki soznanii i bytu sel'skogo naseleniya i puti ikh preodoleniya', *Aftoreferat dissertatsii* (Novosibirsk, 1969), p. 12.

[32] Christel Lane, *The rites of rulers* (Cambridge: Cambridge University Press, 1981), p. 82.

[33] The first decree on cemeteries was passed on 7 December 1918, and it attempted to control 'private enterprise' and 'small family concerns' in the burial business. GARF, *fond* 482, *opis* 4, *delo* 31, p. 40.

[34] For the hygienic arguments, see V. Lazarev's account of the 1923 exhibition of crematoria and cremation in *Sotsialisticheskaya gigieniya*, 3–4 (1923), p. 175.

[35] Lane, *Rites of rulers*, p. 62.   [36] GARF, *fond* 5263, *opis* 1, *delo* 12, pp. 7–8.

tant was the fact that the physical destruction of the corpse violated a deep taboo. The Orthodox Church required that bodies decompose naturally, a process which was deemed to parallel the soul's gradual detachment from the world of the flesh.[37] Traditionally, too, the spirit of the dead person did not leave his or her relatives at once; the commemorative services which were held forty days and a year after death were survivals from an older tradition of appeasing the courts of Heaven and even exorcizing the earth-bound spirits of the dead. Cremation required the premature annihilation of human remains, and also deprived the survivors of the possibility of revisiting the grave with the traditional gifts of food deemed necessary to forestall misfortune.

The introduction of cremation had, therefore, to be backed up by the suppression of cemeteries. Here again, careful regulations set out the procedure by which grave ornaments and lead could be removed and turned over to government use. A watch on such cemeteries was needed to prevent hasty (and thus unhygienic) burials from taking place even after official closure. The task fell to the secret police, who also monitored the activities of wandering priests and sectarian groups.[38] Procedures and regulations were prescribed to prevent unnecessary violence and the abuse of local believers, but in fact over-zealous officials could expect little in the way of reproof if they exceeded their tasks. Cases of so-called *proizvol*, arbitrariness, which could include the banning of prayers for the dying and religious funerals, were seldom investigated.[39] The priority at this stage was to break the universal grip of religion. Crematoria, which never superseded graveyards in the popular mind, were publicized as the socialist alternative to burial. The contrast between the meagre ritual there provided, the rapid disposal of physical remains, and the traditional pomp surrounding Lenin's corpse could hardly have been greater.

Even for those who died peacefully, then, Soviet power brought changes, many of which made mourning more difficult for those who survived. For the families of those who died violently, and for the victims of famine, the processes of loss and mourning were disrupted beyond recognition. Written records from the famine regions, for example, stressed the appalling casualness and haste of disposal. Bodies

---

[37] Monakha Mitrofana, *Zagrobnaya Zhizn', kak zhivut nashi umershie, kak budem zhit' i my posle smerti* (St Petersburg, 1897).

[38] Ibid. pp. 1–5.

[39] A petition sent to Kalinin in 1930 complaining about such practices, and noting instances of suicide in the face of repression and uncertainty, met with the reply that 'Comrade Kalinin is not in the least interested in the question of religion in this instance. He merely wants to know what violations of the law took place.' GARF, *fond* 5263, *opis* 1, *delo* 7, 12, 72–8.

were piled up on carts and in morgues and buried by the score – if there was anyone available to bury them – in communal pits. Sometimes the dying were loaded on to the mortuary carts with the dead to save a second tour of the village. Memoirs describe the looting of bodies, thefts of clothing. From the early 1920s onwards, moreover, reports of cannibalism, and especially the hasty butchering of corpses, accompanied every food crisis. During the siege of Leningrad, for example, stories were told of putrefying corpses being used as food, and even of the butchering of bodies lying in a hospital yard. 'It was an hour or so sometimes and body parts would be taken', a survivor recalled in 1986.[40]

Beyond death, there was also little or no formal remembrance for the millions who died in the unacknowledged catastrophes of the Stalin era. As many have observed, the social recognition of violent death is a crucial stage in the process by which the bereaved come to terms with loss individually and as members of society as a whole.[41] Remembrance involves the conferring of a certain status on the bereaved, the construction of dignified narratives to explain the necessity and value of the losses.[42] The Soviet Union was not the only state to obstruct this process. The fallen of 1920s civil-war Ireland have become almost invisible in social terms, as, for a time, did slaves who perished without record in the days before civil rights. Where Soviet Russia differed from most other cases, however, was that many memories did not merely rot but were actively suppressed. Millions of manilla files were preserved in the miles of underground corridors beneath ministry buildings, but the public had no access to them, and scant awareness of their existence, let alone their true extent.[43]

As far as the public was concerned, historical, and even personal records, were distorted throughout the Soviet period. Even war deaths, as we have noted, were recorded selectively. Other losses, as we also saw, were denied and evidence of them locked away so securely that people came to think that it had been destroyed. The state was clearly the instigator of this process of deceit. But it was not the only actor in the

---

[40] William C. Moskoff, *The bread of affliction: the food supply crisis in the USSR during World War II* (Cambridge: Cambridge University Press, 1990), p. 197.

[41] For a recent exposition of this, see Jay Winter's introduction to his *Sites of memory, sites of mourning* (Cambridge: Cambridge University Press, 1995).

[42] Mosse's idea of the 'myth of the war experience' stresses the nationalistic purpose behind this process (p. 7); Winter places more emphasis on the collective 'transcendence' of grief.

[43] For a discussion of the files, see Stephen Kotkin's 'Terror, rehabilitation, and historical memory. An interview with Dmitrii Iurasov', *Russian Review*, 51 (April 1992), p. 238. According to Iurasov, who worked in a number of archives, there were $2\frac{1}{2}$ million files in store at the Supreme Court alone.

process of memory destruction. In many cases the circumstances were such as to encourage individuals to collaborate actively in the suppression of documents and other items. The example of the 1933 famine illustrates this process at work. Reports from the area suggested that although food was critically scarce everywhere and prices high, starvation itself was uneven. Some villages were virtually wiped out while others, though suffering, survived. At the same time, refugees from famine areas were to be found at rail heads across Southern Russia and the Ukraine. Under these circumstances, the denial of mass death – the very word starvation was banned in 1932 – cannot have convinced many people. But there was no public outcry against this blatant official concealment. Part of the reason for the silence was the habit of collusion which fifteen years of Soviet power had begun to instil. Organized political opposition was no trivial crime by 1933. Speaking out, moreover, would bring few rewards in a political system where the possibility of alternative forms of government, or even of finding different personnel, had dwindled to nothing. It was on this basis that official lies about the famine paid off. The suppression of mortality data four years later, in the 1937 census, was effected without protest.[44]

Repression, however, or the threat of it, was not the only reason for the people's silence. For those who had suffered most directly, silence may have been preferable to repeating a story which could not publicly be acknowledged. Because there was no chance of healing recognition, the rehearsal of the experience would have brought only further suffering, material as well as psychological. Many had fled the countryside, moreover, to avoid further harm. Their guilt, as survivors, would have been reinforced by their desire to forget in order to begin a new life. Survivors have recalled in interview how they lied about their origins to escape the discrimination reserved for 'former' people and their children.[45] Finally, untold numbers benefited directly from the famine.[46] Some appropriated land or chattels; some, more grimly, were known to have looted the dead. Those who resettled abandoned villages, however innocently, would also have had good reason to be silent about the

[44] On the denial of the famine and suppression of the 1937 census, see Merridale, 'The 1937 Census'.
[45] This material is based on the author's current interview project, which involves recorded discussions and interviews with survivors of the purges, famines, and wars of the first half of the twentieth century in Russia. The research has been funded by the ESRC, and a book developing its findings will be published by Granta in 2000.
[46] On the appropriation of goods, and more generally on the exploitation of collectivization by some peasants, see Sheila Fitzpatrick, *Stalin's peasants: resistance and survival in the Russian village after collectivization* (Oxford: Oxford University Press, 1994), especially chapter 9.

recent past.[47] For all these reasons, the suppression of public discussion was not simply an act of violence perpetrated by the state. Private memories were preserved, though partially. But a sense of collective understanding, a social memory, developed only episodically and lacked immediate political impact.[48]

The same kinds of observation could be made about the purges. For most relatives of the arrested, it was actively dangerous to preserve material evidence of the existence of repressed enemies of the people. The work of destruction began with the individual. Photographs would be destroyed, or the faces of the deceased mutilated and erased. Manuscripts were burned, as were letters, keepsakes, and diaries. These acts, which took some time and would have forced a certain amount of reflection on the part of the mourner, might be portrayed as a kind of anti-commemoration, a process which aided mourning in its early stages. But they were also, crucially, violations of memory. Private narratives were sometimes, as we have seen, preserved within families. But the scale of the losses, the breadth of the disaster, could not have been apparent to the majority of people. Many were not even certain that their relative was dead. Such information was seldom officially given. At the time of the Great Purge of 1937–8, relatives who inquired would be told that a victim had been sentenced to 'ten years' imprisonment without right of correspondence', the inscrutable official euphemism employed when a person had been shot. As late as the 1980s, most survivors might only have received 'incomprehensible pieces of paper testifying to rehabilitation, and another piece of paper with false information about dates and places of death. Some people had no information of any kind.'[49] It was only after 1991 that individuals were able to ask for, and receive, the bare statement that their relative had been shot, together with the date. Many have yet to discover where the bodies lie.

Personal grief had no wider framework, no mirror in which to observe itself gradually diminishing. In this sense, the official denial of loss compounded initial acts of state brutality. To make matters worse, the widows or children of purge victims might well be obliged to denounce their disgraced relative, and this not once, but repeatedly in everything they did for the rest of their lives. A complex pattern of survivor-guilt emerged from interviews I conducted with such people in 1997. Many

---

[47] Some of these observations are based on interviews with famine survivors conducted by the author in Moscow in 1995.

[48] Exiles were more readily able to establish a connected story, the classic case in point being the Ukrainian community in Canada.

[49] Kotkin, 'Terror, rehabilitation, and historical memory', p. 259.

argued vigorously for their own innocence, citing precise clauses of the criminal law and constitution, while allowing for the possibility that many other victims of Stalinism were guilty at some level and even guilty as charged. Many continued to buy into the Stalinist dream, and even to be active Communists (if they were permitted to be Party members), thereby closing off the possibility of seeing their victimhood as part of a larger state crime. For these people, the revelations of the Khrushchev thaw in the 1960s offered little comfort. They continued to hide their own pasts and to deny their membership in a community of victims. None could have predicted, as they embarked on this lifetime of denial, that its end would be the springtime of glasnost and the fall of Communism itself.

Ostensibly, the war was a different story. Public commemoration of the Great Patriotic War was ubiquitous in the Soviet Union. But it was also selective. The overwhelming repetition of some memories, the pointed exclusion of others, was conceived as a form of censorship as powerful as any blanket official denial. Certain kinds of pain, including, for example, a child's sense of the strangeness of step-parents or the specific grief of Jewish Holocaust survivors, were censored out of public discussion.[50] But was this selectivity effective? Memories do not disappear within a generation. War mourning was specific, it required a channelling or sublimation of other griefs. And if wartime losses could be concentrated into the public commemoration of the unknown soldier – male, white, a fallen combatant – so, indirectly, could those which had preceded the war itself. The war was a catastrophe without parallel. As well as serving as a totem in its own right, it was used, by the state and by individuals who had enjoyed no opportunity to reconcile themselves to the pain of the 1930s, as a healing fire. The 1930s was a decade of unspeakable private pain on a mass scale. The war, terrible though it was, and damaging even to survivors, was a collective triumph, and the recollection of it still brings a smile of remembered comradeship to the people who speak of it. For those who survived, it was probably the most vivid set of episodes they would ever know, and sharing the memory with others was – and remains – a psychological imperative.[51] Arguably, too, commemoration and the re-enactment of national soli-

---

[50] Step-mothers in particular were identified as a group which should no longer be seen in a negative light, and folk tales were amended accordingly at the end of the 1940s. The identification of Jews as the special victims of Nazi violence was played down in favour of a more generalized story of atrocities aimed at the whole Soviet people.

[51] For accounts of shared commemoration, see Svetlana Aleksiyevich, *War's unwomanly face*, translated by Keith Hammond and Lyudmila Lezhneva (Moscow: Progress Publishers, 1988), which is composed of interviews with woman survivors and veterans living in Belarus.

darity enabled individuals to transcend earlier griefs which had few other outlets. The woman whose husband had disappeared in 1937 (and who had nonetheless given all her energies to the war effort for five years) could bring her grief, if not a story about it, to the solemn meetings in May every year as easily as her neighbour, the war widow.[52]

To assert that alternative, unofficial memories survived and were brought to remembrance ceremonies and memorials it is not necessary to deny the validity of the argument that state-sponsored commemoration aimed to rewrite the national story. Invented tradition to some extent fed upon the past at the same time as it sought to overshadow it.[53] State-sponsored ceremonial sank hungry roots into the deep well of historic pain and loss. Obviously, Soviet military parades were designed to overwhelm, to drown individual memory in the clamour of patriotic ceremonial. Observers became participants despite themselves as the martial music played and the tanks rolled by. But at the same time, the very crudeness of the ceremony, so effective as a shaper of crowds, guaranteed that alternative memories would survive. The groups which were excluded or overlooked were so numerous that they could not fail to muster some kind of counter-memory in the very shadow of the official story. Most obviously, men suffered disproportionately in each of the Soviet Union's wars. Twenty million more women were alive than men after 1945.[54] Soviet remembrance, like most of its genre, was oppressively masculine, from the parades of weaponry to the goose-stepping youths and the veterans on the stands. But the majority of the population, and, above all, of those who grieved and remembered, was female.

These women were not all isolated widows. After a war in which many had found themselves in sole charge of their families, where the men had vanished, they did not need formal associations to unite them at the local level. Despite the considerable disruption of the family involved in collectivization,[55] networks older than Communism still linked village women and their daughters, while new kinships of grief bound women who had previously been scattered within towns and cities.[56] Many women, even girls in their teens, were united further by their direct

[52] Comparable examples from other socialist societies are described in Rubie S. Watson (ed.), *Memory, history and opposition under state socialism* (Santa Fe: School of American Research Advanced Press, 1994).

[53] I would see the process as far more contested and ambiguous than Ignatieff suggested in 1984 ('Soviet war memorials'). However, he was writing before glasnost and also at a time when the war veterans were younger and the war twelve years more recent.

[54] On the long-term demographic impact of the war, see Blum, *Naître, vivre et mourir en URSS*.

[55] See Fitzpatrick, *Stalin's peasants*, especially pp. 220–4.

[56] For accounts of similar networks after the Afghan war, see Aleksiyevich, *Zinky boys*.

experience of military service, including combat. And those who survived were not consigned to the domestic (and therefore isolating) spheres of child-rearing and household management after the war ended. Most had to take over the work of their lost men, hard physical labour which perpetuated the associations and networks of wartime. 'In every other hut or so', recalled one village woman, 'there was a widow or a soldier's wife. We were left without men. Without horses – they were taken for the army, too. And after the war . . . the village women took the place of men and horses.'[57]

What can this larger section of the Soviet people have thought as it watched parades in honour of the very militarism which had killed their men? At one level, commemoration of the war was a near-sacramental act, militarism was not identified with loss, but with triumph, and the women who witnessed parades were proud to be associated with victory in any shape. But this adoring commemoration was also shot with paradox: angry memories conflicted with loyalty to the cause for which the men had died, bitterness mixed more or less equally with the limitless patriotism and respect for the uniformed men who claimed still to be protecting the motherland. 'My neighbour Vasil came in with his medals and other decorations', recalled a widow of a Victory Day parade. 'People were greeting him and the chairman of the collective farm seated him beside himself on the podium. But my Ivan and my son – one of them lying in Romania, the other in Voronezh. So wasn't it my day as well?'[58] Despite the pain, however, many individuals were proud to associate with the heroic and patriotic images of war. Most women veterans, for instance, appeared content to disregard their femininity and the specific stories which it implied, proud to be seen as the equals and even the near-equivalents of male soldiers.[59]

As far as personal loss and memory were concerned, individual experiences varied widely. Some mourners brought specific, completed personal stories to the remembrance ceremonies, details of the date and place of their husband's death, possibly even memories of a grave once visited. 'I've forgotten what happened yesterday', recalled one widow, 'but I remember the war. How I brought him home, how I buried him . . . How I wanted to kiss him for the last time, but the coffin was made of zinc, so I kissed the place where his face would have been.'[60] But these women, in some respects, were the lucky ones. Many others never knew what had happened to relatives or partners. In these circumstances, commemoration was a poignant event. One old woman, 'long past seventy', was to be seen wandering the Victory Day parade in the

---

[57] Aleksiyevich, *War's unwomanly face*, p. 206.   [58] Ibid. p. 207.
[59] Ibid. pp. 50 and 120, for example.   [60] Ibid. p. 179.

1980s with a worn-out placard round her neck which read, 'Looking for Thomas Vladimirovich Kulnev, reported missing in besieged Lenin-grad in 1942.'[61] For her, as for many others, remembrance was more complicated than official ceremony allowed. Whatever the individual memory, moreover, when the parade was over, and the tea was poured, the stories, individual and family-based, would also flow. Here again, remembrance took many forms. Men, typically, recounted their stories in the yard, on benches in city parks, or around the stove in winter hazes of tobacco smoke. Women talked separately, usually in the kitchen, and their stories had a different, often more personal, tone and content.[62]

Any list of excluded categories is likely in itself to be partial and thus misleading. There were many types of loss which official commemora-tion overlooked. But if gender was one of the more important sources of alternative perception, nationality was surely another. The absurdity of Mother Russia's monumental presence as a memorial outside the Ukrainian city of Kiev has been pointed out elsewhere.[63] Great Russian patriotism tended to conflate national and ethnic differences, although gestures of recognition for certain nationalities were made at the expense of others. Some members of ethnic minorities acquiesced in this incorporation. Identities were not fixed in the early Soviet period.[64] And to some extent the very excesses of Nazi brutality indeed united the Soviet people in a common cause. But the Russian focus of remem-brance, and the unknown soldier's assumed Slavic ethnicity, were not consistently acceptable to those who grieved.

The paradoxical, contested nature of remembrance in Russia con-tinues to be apparent. The war is not mere history yet. Throughout the Soviet period, it remained a matter of the deepest reverence and a focus for genuine grief.[65] Survivors still invest remembrance with near-religious significance. But with the fall of Communism came a discre-diting of the Stalinist political style, a rejection of the language of sacrifice and deference. Youth culture had little time for the past. Evasions of national service became more open, and young men trained in Moscow's suburbs not to fight for their country but to defend their gang. The fiftieth-anniversary commemoration ceremonies in Moscow in May 1995 were surprisingly low key. The veterans themselves com-

---

[61] Ibid. p. 81.
[62] These observations are largely based on my own interviews, conducted in 1994 and 1995. However, the specific patterns of female recollection are confirmed by Aleksiyevich in both the works of oral history already cited.
[63] Ignatieff, 'Soviet war memorials', p. 158.
[64] See Merridale, 'The 1937 census', pp. 232–3.
[65] Ignatieff, 'Soviet war memorials', pp. 160–1.

plained about the plastic medals with which they were issued, the poor-quality chocolate, the lack of sausage.[66] Meanwhile, the Chechen crisis continued its challenge to Russian military claims. It was in 1996, as the election approached, that militarism resumed its accustomed place. The war commemorations in May of that year were more elaborate, if more troubled by fears of terrorism, than those of the previous spring.[67] Stalin's war, with its victorious military imagery and underlying story of continued national danger, was used in an attempt to redeem Boris Yeltsin, just as twenty years before it had been used to rejuvenate Leonid Brezhnev.

For those whose prime concern is the immediate rebuilding of the Russian state, this abuse of history can appear to be a diversion. Young people, and not only the young, have argued that too much interest in the past is unhealthy. They stress this line with even greater vigour when the focus shifts from the war to the excesses of Stalin's terror. Their argument runs that the last survivors will soon be dead, and that the old hatreds are best left to die with them. The case was made frequently in the late 1980s, at the height of the rehabilitation campaigns. On the other hand, for those with memories of loss, the commemoration of Stalin's victims is no less important than the remembrance of war. When the Memorial society mounted a commemorative exhibition about the victims of repression, a million visitors attended it in a week. Thousands wrote to Iurasov, one of the organizers, soon after. 'All wanted to talk about their tragedies', he recalled.[68] Memorial's volunteers worked to recover as much information as possible about every person who had disappeared during the Soviet period. The society also undertook the construction of physical monuments to the repressed, the most famous of which now occupies a central position in Lyubyanka Square. But despite the support for its activities, a vocal section of the population has consistently maintained that the opening of old wounds can only cause pain and divert attention away from present tasks.

Who is right? The question has no final answer. One can look to the experience of postwar Germany and Eastern Europe since 1989 to draw comparisons, but each case has a number of special features which make generalization difficult. What is clear from Eastern Europe, including the Czech republic and former East Germany, is that witch hunts, the

---

[66] Observations collected by the author in Moscow in 1995. I personally tested the chocolate.

[67] The residential area around the victory monument at the end of Kutuzov Prospekt was at one point scheduled for evacuation, for example.

[68] Kotkin, 'Terror, rehabilitation, and historical memory', pp. 258–9.

search for collaborators, are dangerous and partially counter-productive affairs.[69] In the case of post-Soviet Russia, furthermore, virtually every living citizen over the age of forty, and many who are younger, bears some responsibility for collusion, however passive and unwilling. The boundary between victims and perpetrators is too fluid to be certain about the criteria for innocence.

But witch hunts and mourning are separate processes. Where mourning is concerned, Russia may have something to learn from postwar Germany. The problem there, as in Russia, was the question of collusion. Even for Holocaust survivors, guilt and uncomfortable memories of missed opportunities made commemoration problematic. But for the mass of the German population, even those who were not active Nazis, overwhelming guilt, together with unvoiced fears about collaboration and responsibility, made the Holocaust and the excesses of Nazi domestic policy into almost taboo subjects outside the prescribed curriculum of the schoolroom until well into the 1960s.[70] Psychologists working with German civilians and with former Nazis have noted the unwillingness of individuals to discuss their personal role in past events, an unwillingness often only breached with the approach of their own deaths.[71] Here, as in Stalin's Russia, censorship about sensitive matters was not merely imposed from above.

As we have noted, a crucial difference between the two catastrophes has been that on some issues at least the Russian silence was preserved only in public. Holocaust survivors protected themselves and their children in a relatively stable postwar world by avoiding the subject of their trauma. In a society where repression continued and the political danger was omnipresent, Soviet parents attempted to warn and protect their children by initiating them into family secrets. How much they told them, however, what words they found for personal trauma, remains unclear. More research is needed here to find points of comparison and contrast.

In Russia as in Germany, later generations have tried to escape the legacy of the past by attempting to ignore it. But evasion is not so easily secured. Psychologists have noted that the pathways through which secrets or deliberate silence can emerge include depression and other psychological disabilities such as anxiety. In Russia, enhanced rates of suicide, notable especially among males, may be linked at least in part to

[69] For some thoughts on the recent round of trials, see Timothy Garton Ash, ' "Neopagan" Poland', *New York Review of Books*, 43, no. 1 (January 1996), pp. 10–14.

[70] Alexander and Margarete Mitscherlich, *The inability to mourn: principles of collective behavior* (New York: Grove Press, 1975).

[71] For examples, see Barbara Heimannsberg and Christoph J. Schmidt, *The collective silence: German identity and the legacy of shame* (San Francisco: Jossey-Bass, 1993).

the undiscussed stresses of a prolonged and large-scale series of traumas.[72] The people affected come from generations who knew little or nothing of large-scale suffering at first hand, but whose lives were marked by the silences and undiscussed distinctiveness of their parents. In this, as in other ways, the comparison with Germany is not a question, Nolte-style, of reducing the magnitude of either disaster by relativizing both.[73] We should beware of applying the findings of one group to another, observing all the time that the conditions each experienced were unique, the historical, social, and cultural settings very different. But if the argument about trauma has validity for one cata-strophe, it is at least possible that it applies to others. For contemporary Russia, the consequences, if it does, are profound.[74]

Some of these consequences have policy implications. In the first place, Russian attitudes to death and to the value of life have probably been affected, in the medium term, by repeated exposure to un-mourned, unvalued death. What others have described as the brutal-ization of society[75] may have some applicability to Russia, though distinctions need to be made between those directly exposed to violence and those who experienced it at second hand or as children. More directly, faith in the state as the provider of care and advice on matters relating to health, hygiene, life, and death is likely to have taken a long-term beating. At every turn this century, ordinary people have looked to each other, to their friends, for the support and even the basic informa-tion which the state denied them. The consequences for any government interested in combating smoking, alcohol abuse, and even poor driving are obvious. But finally, and more controversially, it may be that there is, in the end, no avoiding the painful task of witnessing, of reliving, in diminished form, the traumas of Stalinism. If the psychoanalytic argu-ment about the long-term legacy of trauma is correct, they are present no matter how deliberately one attempts to ignore them.

If mourning cannot be avoided, then commemoration may yet have a crucial and even healing role to play. The political and civic uses of

---

[72] The full explanation for the increase in Russian death rates, including, but not exclusively, death from suicide, remains unclear. See Judith Shapiro, 'The Russian mortality crisis and its causes' in Anders Aslund (ed.), *Russian economic reform at risk* (London: Pinter, 1995).

[73] On the Nolte controversy, see Norbert Kampe, 'Normalising the Holocaust? The recent historians' debate in the Federal Republic of Germany', *Holocaust and Genocide Studies*, 2 (1987).

[74] Since writing this, I have modified my views as a result of extensive research and interviews with survivors and their children. A longer discussion of these issues appears in my book, *Night of Stone*, forthcoming, Granta, 2000, where the idea of 'second generation syndrome' in the Russian case is explored more fully.

[75] Mosse, *Fallen soldiers*, pp. 159–68.

memory remain controversial. But the public's need to remember may transcend political expediency. Clearly, the Soviet state was adept at devising patriotic ceremonial commemorations of the Great Patriotic War. But while they served some of the interests of the Soviet regime, these acts of remembrance were not fakes. As a commentator observes, 'it is impossible, in the long run, to impose ritual on unwilling people without destroying the ritual in the process'.[76] The commemoration of Soviet Russia's other fallen, however, will be harder to establish. The ceremonies and words, even the physical monuments, will have to be invented, if they are to be created at all. Nonetheless, as we have seen, a vocal group insists that memorials be built and invested with reverence. 'While humankind survives', concluded one of the Memorial society's founders, 'it must preserve the memory of its forebearers [sic], to remain human and to avoid becoming ... people without memory, whom it is easier to make slaves.'[77]

[76] Lane, *Rites of rulers*, p. 57.
[77] Kotkin, 'Terror, rehabilitation, and historical memory', p. 262.

4   Agents of memory: Spanish Civil War veterans and disabled soldiers

Paloma Aguilar

But in the black corners
in the blackest ones, they lie down
to weep for the fallen,
mothers who gave them milk,
sisters who bathed them,
brides once of snow
but now in the black of mourning,
and now with fever;
dazed widows,
shattered women,
letters and photographs
which portray them as they were,
there, eyes bursting
from seeing them so much and so little,
from so many silent tears,
from so much absent beauty.[1]

The traumatic collective memory that most Spaniards have, even today, of the Civil War is explained not only by the events of the war of 1936 to 1939, but also by the experience of millions of Spaniards in the aftermath of the conflict itself.[2] During the last weeks of the war as many as half a million Spaniards on the losing side fled to escape the justifiably feared repression of the victors. Most of the exiles who crossed the French border were confined in appalling conditions in refugee camps in the south of the country. Some managed to escape the German invasion of France and went on to Latin America, and above all Mexico. Yet many Republican veterans remained in France and joined the Resistance, so suffering a second experience of war even before they had

---

[1] From the poem 'Llamo a la Juventud' (1937) by Miguel Hernández, poet and combatant on the Republican side in the Civil War, who died in a Francoist prison shortly after the end of the war. Miguel Hernández, *Poemas sociales de guerra y de muerte* (Madrid: Alianza Editorial, 1977).

[2] I would like to thank Justin Byrne for the revision of the English version of this essay.

had time to recover from the first. Two decades after the end of the Civil War, some 300,000 Republicans remained in exile.[3]

The fate of those who stayed in Spain after the end of the war was no less dramatic. Thousands were executed for their real or alleged activities during the Second Republic or the war itself, victims of the immense wave of repression unleashed by the victors. Hundreds of thousands were imprisoned for political motives, sacked from their jobs, or had their property confiscated, measures sanctioned by legislation introduced during or after the war by the Francoist dictatorship.

Over and above all these individual and collective tragedies, the fratricidal dimension inherent in a civil war only heightened the traumatic nature of this particular conflict. When the echoes of the battle had faded, and the wartime propaganda ebbed, the time came for the Spaniards to confront the most traumatic elements of the war. It was then that most people, and especially those who had lost family members, inevitably began to reflect on the sense and purpose of the deaths, injuries, and sickness, the destruction, famine, and fear brought about by the war. Before the Nationalist side had had time to begin to question the sense and purpose of such a destructive conflict, the regime initiated an extensive and intensive programme of monument-building,[4] street-naming, and commemorations,[5] in honour of their own fallen, that is, the soldiers and civilians killed on the Nationalist side alone.[6]

---

[3] On these peoples' lives, the most complete archive on the Spanish exiles in general, and the disabled veterans in particular, is held by the Fundación Universitaria Española (FUE) in Madrid. I was grateful for the opportunity to consult these records.

[4] The most famous of these monuments, is the Valle de los Caídos (the Valley of the Fallen), an immense church and mausoleum built to commemorate the Nationalist victims of the Civil War (for a history and study of the symbolism of this monument see Paloma Aguilar, 'Collective memory of the Spanish Civil War: the case of political amnesty in the Spanish transition to democracy', Working Paper CEACS, no. 185 (Madrid: Instituto Juan March, 1996). Monuments and inscriptions were erected in every Spanish village in this period. Most Catholic churches, for example, built war memorials listing the local men and women who had died fighting on the Nationalist side, many of which still stand today. Since the return to democracy, some of these memorials have been taken down or replaced by others which also pay tribute to the Republican dead. In some places this gesture of reconciliation proved very divisive, provoking bitter confrontations within the local community.

[5] The most important of these was the 'Victory Parade' (*Desfile de la Victoria*) held each year between April and May (the official 'Victory Day' was 1 April) from 1939 to 1976. As its name suggests, this did not celebrate the end of the Civil War, but the victory of one half of Spanish society over the other. The last time this parade took place, less than six months after Franco's death, the salute was taken by King Juan Carlos I.

[6] One sector of society continued to suffer the physical consequences of the war even after this was over. These were the peasants, above all children, who were maimed or killed by the unexploded mines and bombs left all over Spain. The victims were totally neglected by the regime, receiving none of the honours and benefits accorded to the nationalist war veterans.

Although mourning is never a simple or easy process, in this case it was much easier for the victors than for the vanquished in the conflict. Not only did the former enjoy considerable support from the regime, but they were also given the opportunity to express their grief through a variety of different channels. A number of agencies were created after the war to provide material and psychological assistance to the Nationalist veterans, their families (mainly widows and orphans), and the disabled. In short, most of those on the Nationalist side who had suffered in one way or another the terrible consequences of the Civil War received material benefits from the regime. Moreover, they were able to create private agencies, or benefit from the official ones, and so participate in the joint elaboration of the memory of the war and thus achieve some form of moral and psychological relief.

The Franco regime was too vindictive ever to forgive the vanquished, or even show them any mercy. Not only were they the object of fierce institutionalized repression during the early years of the dictatorship, but for almost forty years, until Franco's death in 1975, they were also denied the material and moral assistance accorded to the victors. Even after the return to democracy, some years passed before the Republican veterans were granted full equality with their Nationalist counterparts. This came too late for as many as 50 per cent of those who had fought on the losing side, who were by then either dead or living in exile from which they would never return.

One of the groups which suffered the consequences of the war most directly was the war wounded. At a rough estimate, some 80,000 veterans on the two sides were left permanently disabled. At least half of these had fought in the government forces. The majority of these Republican veterans remained in Spain at the end of the war, where many were imprisoned in concentration or work camps or purged from the jobs they had held before the war. Many, in any event, were no longer capable of work. An unknown number of the Republican disabled went into exile, above all in France.[7] Although, the situation of the Republican disabled in exile was far from easy, it was certainly very different to that of their counterparts in Spain. A third group of disabled veterans consisted of those who had fought on the victorious Nationalist side. They enjoyed the protection and some privileges from the new regime, and showed no sympathy for those Republicans who had shared their fate. When Franco died in 1975, there were three different main associations of disabled veterans: the Nationalist one, the organization

[7] The Republican Disabled League in France, at its peak had a membership of some 3,000; Antonio Trabal, *Breve historia de la Liga de Mutilados e Inválidos de Guerra de España (1936–1939) en France* (Barcelona: Creaciones Gráficas Fernando, 1986), p. 22.

of the Republican disabled inside Spain (which was still illegal), and that of the Republicans in exile. Each of these groups had very different memories of the Civil War. Whilst this is only to be expected in the case of the Nationalists and the Republicans, it is perhaps more surprising with respect to the two Republican groups. Here it will be argued that their different perceptions of the past reflected their distinct experiences in the postwar period.

Disabled veterans' associations during the Civil War

Less than a year into the war, disabled Republican veterans began to mobilize independently from the state and the official institutions. Even though neither their personal situation nor the political climate favoured collective action of this type, after a considerable struggle they managed to create the Liga de Mutilados e Inválidos de la Guerra de España (LMIGE) or League of the Wounded and Disabled of the War in Spain.

The first preparatory meeting of the LMIGE took place in Madrid in May 1937. Over a year later, in August 1938, it held its first Congress in Valencia, where the Republican government had moved to escape the Francoist offensive against Madrid. This congress brought together representatives of the local branches of the LMIGE that had been set up in different parts of Republican Spain. At the same time, a separate organization, the Asociación de Inválidos de Cataluña or Association of the Disabled of Catalonia, had been created in that region in the north-east of the country, by then virtually isolated from the rest of Republican Spain.

During the first few months of the conflict, the only provision for the disabled was the legislation that had existed before the outbreak of war. In theory at least, this guaranteed them a disability allowance. Whilst it is impossible to judge the extent to which this weak and fragmented government was in fact able to meet its obligations, given the scant resources available and the lack of global coordination within the administration, it is highly unlikely that the disabled veterans received any significant economic assistance from the state. In any event, the leaders of the LMIGE considered that it was necessary to organize their members for a number of explicit purposes, at the same time stressing that they did not want to be a burden on the state. This point was repeatedly emphasized in the pages of the LMIGE's official newspaper, *Mutilado* (*The War-wounded*), fourteen issues of which were published between July 1938 and February 1939.

On the one hand, the LMIGE emphasized its commitment to the Republican war effort, and its desire to contribute to this, above all through activities carried out behind the front. In the first issue of *Mutilado* one of the LMIGE's members described the organization's aims in the following terms: 'It is the disabled veteran who creates his League not only to dispose of an organization which concerns itself with obtaining medical material, educating him, or making him a useful man in the production and the reconstruction of Spain, but also to participate actively in the mobilization of the entire people against the invader.'[8] Whilst this type of discourse evidently responded to the requirements of wartime propaganda, it also reflected the real need the disabled experienced to feel that they were 'useful' human beings, that they had some role to play in what was a critical situation. The LMIGE's members were not only well aware of the terrible consequence that a Republican defeat would have for them, but also felt an urgent and heartfelt need to justify to themselves the terrible wounds they had received. Thus, they were seeking a means of coping with their new and traumatic personal circumstances, and did so by identifying a practical and important task in which they could immerse themselves.

During the war itself, the tragic dimension of the LMIGE's discourse, which would become dominant after the end of the conflict, was matched by the emphasis given to these veterans' heroism. Thus, one of the LMIGE members wrote that the disabled veterans were

a symbol of the piercing shrapnel which stabs without compassion in the flesh of men who suffer with the proud arrogance of those who know their duty, the blows of the beast which tears off part of their body, which destroys their virility, which destroys their lean and manly figure, turning it into a useless piece of meat, a horrendous marionette in a grotesque puppet show. The disabled veteran is undeniably the true martyr of the war.[9]

These lines reveal the tragedy which, despite the rhetoric of wartime propaganda, these victims were experiencing. The only possible psychological consolation for their wounds was the social recognition of their bravery and sacrifice. Thus they also asked for support: 'Republican Spain has the moral obligation to give the disabled the succour of a mother . . . The disabled of this war of independence should occupy the place of honour in the hearts of the Spanish people. Whilst the dead deserve all our respect, the disabled deserve all our affection.'[10]

On the other hand, the LMIGE also had a number of more immediate and practical objectives. It campaigned for the state to provide special schools for disabled veterans, as well as the artificial limbs they needed if they were to be able to lead some kind of normal life. It is very difficult to know how much was achieved in this respect, or the source of the money spent on providing these services. In 1939 the Republican

[8] *Mutilado*, 1, 31 July 1938, p. 8.   [9] Ibid. p. 3.   [10] Ibid. p. 3.

government approved laws instituting positive discrimination in favour of disabled veterans for some low-ranking civil service posts. Equally, some public institutions made special provision for the war wounded; the Ministry of Education, for example, gave occasional grants to the LMIGE for training courses for its members.

The LMIGE did not rely exclusively on official support, but also developed its own sources of income. All members, for example, had to pay dues, and it seems likely that some money was obtained from the sale of *Mutilado*. The organization also set out to raise money from the general public. In 1938, for example, it launched a national subscription for disabled veterans. 'All Spanish anti-fascists' were called upon to contribute to the fund, which was to be spent on 'reeducation in order to continue the struggle in the war today and in peace tomorrow, and for this we need training schools and orthopaedic devices to substitute the amputated limbs'.[11] Emotive advertisements appealing for donations were placed in the Republican press: 'Anti-fascist. Your duty is to collaborate with the subscription in favour of the disabled veterans'; 'The disabled veterans need your financial support. Can you refuse it? Collaborate in the national subscription in favour of the disabled veterans'; 'The disabled veterans defended you from the invader. Now you must show consideration for them by contributing to the national subscription in favour of the disabled veterans.'[12]

The LMIGE, therefore, combined the pursuit of practical objectives, such as raising money to provide special schools or artificial limbs, with wider psychological aims, such as campaigning for public recognition of these veterans' 'generous sacrifice' in defence of the 'nation'. Over and above all this, the members of the LMIGE felt an urgent need to give some meaning to the mutilation they had suffered, as well as to begin to face up to this and to create a shared interpretation of the past, a memory that might console them in the future. However, the vindictive attitude adopted by victors at the end of the war effectively destroyed these early achievements of the Republican disabled veterans.

The disabled veterans and civilians on the Nationalist side faced the same physical and psychological problems as their Republican counterparts. However, they benefited from the support of a more efficient government, as well as that of a very prominent general who had himself been disabled in a previous armed conflict. This was the founder of the Spanish Foreign Legion, General Millán-Astray, who had been seriously injured at least three times during the Spanish colonial wars in Morocco. According to the apocryphal biography that a fellow Francoist

[11] The Republican *ABC*, 20 April 1938, p. 7.
[12] The Republican *ABC*, 20 April 1938, p. 3; 22 April 1938, pp. 3 and 4.

general wrote of Millán-Astray, at the end of 1937 Franco himself charged him with the task of organizing an association for disabled veterans. He set to work immediately, founding in the early 1938 the Benemérito Cuerpo de Mutilados de Guerra por la Patria or Honourable Corps of Disabled in the War for the Homeland. Whether or not the alleged conversation between Franco and Millán-Astray ever took place, it seems clear that the creation of an agency for the disabled Nationalist veterans responded to an official, rather than private, initiative.

Millán-Astray was well aware that if *his* veterans were to obtain the assistance they required, it was crucial that a solid organization should be created whilst the war was still on. He realized that when the needs of wartime propaganda had passed, it was all too likely that 'the enthusiasm for those who fell injured would begin to dwindle, and the sympathy inspired by their sufferings and lost limbs would begin to fade'. He feared the possibility that 'society might come to hate them, or even refuse them assistance and treat them as an onerous burden, considering them to be no longer of any use, as a source of sorrow'.[13] The Honourable Corps was officially created through a law passed in April 1938, but some years passed before the organization could claim to include the majority of the disabled Francoist veterans. In the 1950s, official sources claimed that some 20,000 disabled veterans were working for a living. The pre-war Corps for Disabled Persons was disbanded and its former members (who numbered over a thousand) were incorporated into the ranks of the Honourable Corps. As a result of this merger, the organization came to have a membership of some 54,000 members.

The Republican veterans in the postwar period

Throughout the Franco dictatorship, the vanquished who remained in Spain, their families, the widows and orphans, as well as the disabled (whether from wounds received on the battlefield or from bombing behind the lines), were not only subject to legal persecution but were also denied the opportunity to express their grief in public; nor were they able to commemorate their victims, or organize to elaborate a collective memory that might alleviate their anguish. Besides being forced to live under a hated dictatorship that never considered them to be equal citizens, the disabled Republican veterans were prevented from mourning their dead relatives and friends.

[13] Carlos de Silva, *General Millán Astray (El Legionario)* (Barcelona: Ediciones AHR, 1956), p. 207.

As a result of this explicit discrimination and repression, the disabled Republican veterans were unable to establish any private agency in Spain, and their achievements during the war itself were totally destroyed. They vanished as an organized group, only emerging from this enforced obscurity and dispersal in the late 1960s, when a few of their number embarked on the arduous task of reconstructing a formal association.

Thus, this heterogeneous group endured something even more complex than the 'post-traumatic stress syndrome' so commonly suffered by war veterans. The Republican veterans experienced what might be labelled 'delayed mourning', meaning that, in most cases, their memory of the war remained untouched, frozen, and was not relieved by the process of exposure helping to overcome the nightmare. Coming on top of their experience of the war itself, their defeat in this, the postwar repression, the state of fear in which they lived, and their inability to mourn their dead properly, the burden of the past must have been almost unbearable for the vanquished in general, and for those who had lost family members in particular. The disabled veterans, in turn, faced the additional tribulation of being handicapped and without pension rights, at the same time as their disabilities and their Republican past combined to make it especially difficult for them to find work.[14]

Research carried out by psychologists suggests that it is very difficult for war veterans to recover from 'post-traumatic stress syndrome' without adequate medical diagnosis and treatment. That is, that their condition 'does not improve spontaneously (at least this is true in many cases) with the passage of time', but that it must be treated 'as soon as possible, even in the same geographic area as the battle'.[15] None of the Republican veterans enjoyed any such treatment. In fact, most of them had no access to any form of psychological therapy. Even those who did, namely the exiles, could not be treated 'in the same geographic area'; hence they could not benefit from the kind of help that has proved crucial for treating this mental disorder. 'Social and psychological support received during and after the trauma' has also been shown to play an important role in the successful treatment of people affected by traumatic war experiences. For obvious reasons, no support of this kind was available to those Republican veterans who remained in Spain.

---

[14] It was paradoxical that whilst the veterans of the División Azul, the force of Spanish volunteers who fought alongside the Nazis in the Soviet Union during the Second World War, received pensions from Social Democratic German governments, the veterans of the Republican army received no pension in Spain.

[15] Pas Corral, Enrique Echeburúa, Belén Sarasua, and Irena Zubizarreta, 'Estrés postraumático en excombatientes y en víctimas de agresiones sexuales: nuevas perspectivas terapéuticas,' *Boletín de Psicología*, 135 (1992), pp. 7–24.

'Post-traumatic stress syndrome', finally, is also particularly prevalent amongst those who are seriously wounded in battle, as well as amongst those who have simply experienced combat, witnessed extreme violence, or suffered the death of family or friends.

Other factors which contribute to the intensity of the syndrome is the age at which the trauma is experienced. A study of 250 survivors of war, including a number of Republicans exiled in France, carried out in the late 1960s showed that many were still suffering the consequences of war traumas. Some 37 per cent of women and 28 per cent of men were found to suffer from chronic depression, as were 46 per cent of all those aged twenty or under at the time of their war experience. Psychologists also found extreme levels of irritability in 83 per cent of the cases studied, and that 45 per cent of survivors suffered from serious sexual disorders. Finally, psychosomatic conditions were identified in 85 per cent of survivors, and suicide was not unknown. This is the hidden face of war, the uncomfortable legacy of psychological instability and physical ill health from which so many 'survivors' never recover.[16]

The absence of proper mourning, and the negative consequences this would later have, are also explained by the fact that the fundamental priority for most Republicans and their families was survival.[17] Given the terrible conditions existing in postwar Spain in general (widespread famine, illness, destruction), and facing the vanquished in particular (repression, unemployment, fear), they could do little more than attempt to assure their most basic needs. The Mitscherlichs have described a very similar process in postwar Germany. They show how the Germans invested all their physical and mental energy in the reconstruction of their country. Absorbed in this task, they were largely

---

[16] In the light of these figures, the author of the study, himself a Republican and survivor of the Civil War, declared that 'tolerance and love of one's country must prevent another tragedy of the type now being commemorated, and concord and dialogue must be the only weapons brought to bear to settle our differences' (Francisco Fernández Urraca, 'En torno al exilio de España en 1939', *Cuadernos Republicanos*, 1, 1 (1989), p. 40). This was the main lesson most Spaniards drew from the Civil War. As will be seen below, this lesson was studiously applied during the transition to democracy, both by the Spanish people in general and the political elites in particular (Paloma Aguilar, *Memoria y olvido de la Guerra Civil Española* (Madrid: Alianza Universidad, 1996)).

[17] The journalist Carlos Elordi has recently published a book based on ordinary people's accounts of their very different experiences of the Francoist dictatorship. One of the testimonies is that of a man born into a 'vanquished' family, some of whom suffered severely from the repression of the postwar years. Nevertheless, he describes the silence and the need to forget the past that predominated within the family, affirming that 'we spoke very little about this at home. There all that mattered was to get on' (Carlos Elordi, *Antes que el tiempo muera en nuestros brazos. Recuerdos y reflexiones de quienes vivieron con Franco* (Barcelona: Grijalbo, 1996), p. 157).

able to overlook their very uncomfortable memories of the past and to elude the mourning process.

Finally, many of the vanquished who stayed in Spain remained silent in order to protect their families, and above all their children. Parents did not want their children to be marginalized or repressed by the regime in consequence of their own political affinities. They also feared that their children might repeat outside the relative safety of the home what they heard of their parents' experiences in the war, or their criticism of the dictatorship.[18] A large number of autobiographical accounts of growing up in Republican families in this period testify to the almost unbroken silence which surrounded the past. This climate of fear and discretion, which deterred many of the vanquished from speaking about the past, made it even more difficult to recover from post-traumatic stress syndrome. It meant that the vanquished could not benefit from the 'exposure therapy' which research has shown to be one of the most effective ways of treating this syndrome. Essentially this therapy encourages the patient to talk about what happened, to verbalize his or her traumatic experiences and work through these memories with relatives and friends. Evidently, very few of the vanquished were in a position to do this in postwar Spain, and then only within the family and amongst their closest and most trustworthy friends.

The plight of *los topos* or 'moles' who came to light (sometimes literally) during the transition was the most dramatic example of the silence and invisibility of the vanquished. These were men who went into hiding at the end of the Civil War from which they only emerged after Franco's death in 1975. They usually hid in caves or small rooms in the family home, which only their wives, and in some cases their children, knew about, whilst their wider family and neighbours believed that they had died or gone into exile. In some cases, their wives had spent years in mourning to complete the subterfuge.[19]

The vanquished Republican exiles faced a very different situation. Certainly many of them suffered the further trauma of the Second

---

[18] Some Republican families, of course, did socialize their children in liberal and anti-Francoist values, although this does not necessarily mean that they also passed on their family history. These non-, even anti-official values were largely transmitted through a small number of liberal schools, books, and pamphlets, and in private conversations. Nevertheless, many important leaders of the democratic opposition came from Francoist rather than Republican families; in these cases, their democratic socialization usually took place whilst at university, where they came into contact with certain influential texts and academics. For an exhaustive study of this process, see José M. Maravall, *Dictadura y disentimiento politico* (Madrid: Alfagura, 1978). For the slow but nonetheless solid reconstruction of civil society in Spain, see Víctor Pérez-Díaz, *La primacia de la sociedad civil* (Madrid: Alianza Universidad,1993).

[19] Jesús Torbado *Los topos* (Barcelona: Planeta, 1977).

World War, in which large numbers lost their lives serving with the Allied forces or in the Nazi concentration camps to which they were deported from France. However, in direct contrast to the Republicans who remained in Spain, the exiles who survived the world war now found themselves on the winning side. This put them in a comparatively privileged position. On the one hand, they received material assistance from agencies such as the Spanish Refugee Aid, the International Relief Rescue Committee, or the Service Sociale d'Aide aux Emigrants, as well as from a number of national governments; the French government, for example, awarded pensions to Republicans with a 'political refugee card'. On the other hand, these veterans were able to create their own organizations, to participate in the re-elaboration of their shared memory of the past, to openly commemorate and grieve their dead, as well as to express the hostility and anger they felt towards the Spanish dictatorship.

This is not to suggest, however, that life was easy for the Republicans who fled Spain at the end of the Civil War. Indeed, there can be little doubt as to the hardship they experienced, above all when they first went into exile. Numerous contemporary accounts testify to the miserable conditions in the refugee camps set up in southern France at the end of the Civil War. Here they had to endure appalling accommodation, food that was nearly always scarce and all too often inedible, the despotism of the French authorities, and a generally very unhealthy psychological climate.

A few years ago, Eulalio Ferrer published his diary covering the time he spent as an adolescent, and in the company of his father, in a number of these refugee camps. One of the most interesting aspects of this first-hand account of life in the camps is his description of a common mental condition which the inmates christened *arenitis*.[20] These were the delusions of the men living in the sand on the beaches on which most camps had been set up. According to Ferrer, who described the symptoms seen in a number of cases, most of the people suffering from *arenitis* were convinced that their families were about to come and take them to Latin America. They talked about this all the time, generally to themselves. In some cases, they even drowned themselves when, fully dressed and carrying their suitcase in one hand, they walked into the sea to take the boat which they imagined was moored there to take them to America. Ferrer also described the terrible state of the disabled veterans, reporting that some asked the camp doctors to put them out of their

[20] Eulalio Ferrer, *Entre alambradas* (Barcelona: Grijalbo, 1988), pp. 49, 94, 121, 129–30, 147, 151, 153, 165, and 182.

misery, whilst another, who had lost a hand and a leg in the fighting, committed suicide in the camp hospital.[21]

Ferrer is one of the survivors who puts most emphasis on the brutality and senselessness of war. He appears to have an almost obsessive interest in the legacy of the conflict, the madness, fear, violence, anxiety, nightmares.[22] At one point he writes that 'ours was a loathsome and brutal war. Not only because of the people who died in it, but also for the legacy of terror that it left in so many. In some this comes out in their dreams, but for so many this can be seen in their day-to-day behaviour. They were delirious men, who said and did the strangest things. Many people found this delirium amusing, but the overall impression is painful and distressing.'[23] Later in his diary, Ferrer writes that it was through the war that 'I discovered for the first time what a pistol was and the extreme violence and barbarism, which I will never forget, of a civil war'.[24] This survivor has much stronger memories of the traumatic rather than the epic nature of the conflict, and draws from this the lesson that 'never again' shall Spain suffer a civil war.[25]

It was precisely in these camps that the refugees began their mourning for the Republican war victims. Ferrer recounts the way in which the Republican refugees took advantage of a number of symbolic dates to pay homage to their dead. A month after the end of the war, banners proclaiming: 'We honour through our remembrance the martyrs for Spain' were hung on many barracks on International Labour Day (1 May). The Republicans marked Bastille Day by writing the message 'We honour our fallen' in stones on the sand.[26] Just a few days later, on the third anniversary of the beginning of the Civil War, a number of sculptures were created in sand on the beach bearing the words 'a tribute to the fallen', whilst the refugees kept a minute's silence in honour of their dead.[27]

Associations of Nationalist and Republican veterans and disabled soldiers

Some years after its foundation in April 1938, the association of disabled Nationalist veterans was renamed the Honourable Corps of Disabled Gentlemen (Benemérito Cuerpo de Caballeros Mutilados). By then, the Francoist regime had already passed a large number of laws and regula-

[21] Ibid. p. 94.
[22] See, among many examples, Ferrer, *Entre alambradas*, pp. 49, 94, 121, 129–30, 147, 151, 153, 165, and 182.
[23] Ibid. p. 43.   [24] Ibid. p. 115.   [25] Ibid. p. 115.   [26] Ibid. p. 106.
[27] Ibid. p. 112–13.

tions granting these Nationalist veterans social protection, economic benefits, and a number of other privileges and rewards.[28] Thirty per cent of low- and middle-ranking civil service posts were reserved for disabled veterans, and suitable jobs found for those capable of working. Pensions were also provided for people caring for those disabled veterans totally incapable of work. Both groups enjoyed other benefits such as almost entirely free medical treatment, artificial limbs, and major reductions on public transport.[29]

Further legislation was later passed widening the scope of these early measures. The 1938 law, for example, only applied to those blind or mentally ill veterans who had also been physically wounded by the enemy. As a result, none of the Nationalist veterans who had gone mad as a consequence of their experience of the tragedies and horrors of war enjoyed the benefits accorded to their physically disabled colleagues. The Francoist authorities were evidently reluctant to admit to the existence of these men, since they did not fit the heroic vision of the conflict propagated by the regime. Only in 1945 were these two groups of war victims incorporated into the 'Honourable Corps', and hence granted the same benefits and privileges as the physically disabled.[30]

On the other hand, many of the unwounded Nationalist veterans, especially those who joined the army during the conflict to serve as junior officers, created their own organizations in the postwar period. The most important of these was, and remains today, the Hermandad de Alféreces Provisionales or Brotherhood of Provisional Subalterns. This was created in 1958 by men who, although not originally professional soldiers, decided to remain in the army after the war and pursue a military career. The existence of large numbers of these men, whose social origins were quite different to those of most traditional officers, led to important changes within the army.[31] In contrast to the professional soldiers from the pre-war period, their formative military experience had been the war itself, something which had an enduring influence on their understanding of both politics and the role of the armed forces. They had a much more orthodox ideology than the armed forces as a whole, and created the Brotherhood in part to serve as a

---

[28] Similar benefits were provided for other groups of Nationalist war victims, including the widows and orphans of Nationalist servicemen, as well as people imprisoned by the Republicans during the war.

[29] Almost fifty years after the end of the Civil War, underground train walls still had the signs *Asiento Reservado para Caballeros Mutilados* or 'Seat Reserved for Disabled Men'.

[30] This delay had far more serious consequences for the mentally ill than for the blind veterans, since a unique and highly successful organization was created for the latter during the war itself.

[31] Julio Busquets, 'Las alféreces provisionales hasta la creación de la hermandad (1937–1958)', *Historia* 16, 19 (1986), pp. 44–55.

pressure group to oppose any moves towards liberalizing the Francoist regime. Their particular way of commemorating their fallen brothers in arms largely consisted of defending the 'essence' of the 'spirit of 18 July' (*espíritu del 18 de julio*), that is, the ideals supposedly represented by the *coup d'état* that sparked off the Civil War. Their distinctive identity was also reflected in their construction of special memorials to their own fallen in the war.

Other veterans' associations were founded with similar goals. The veterans of the Fourth Division of Navarre in Catalonia, for example, raised money to erect war memorials on the sites of a number of battles. The mere existence of all these private veterans' organizations, which created their own places of mourning, shows that even the many official initiatives to commemorate the Nationalist fallen were insufficient to meet the emotional needs of the survivors: despite the construction of the pharaonic 'Valley of the Fallen' and an incalculable number of war memorials and inscriptions in churches and cemeteries all over Spain, many people felt the need to participate in more modest and personal forms of remembrance in an attempt to relieve their pain.

As for the Republican disabled veterans who remained in Spain, on 29 March 1939, three days before the war officially ended, the LMIGE's headquarters was closed down and its bank account confiscated by the new political authorities. The National Committee that had been elected in the Valencia Congress in 1938 met Millán-Astray, the president of the 'Honourable Corps', in an attempt to secure for the Republican disabled veterans the same pension rights and privileges as those enjoyed by their Nationalist counterparts. In this they were completely unsuccessful, Millán-Astray reportedly declaring that the only disabled veterans worthy of help were those who had fought on the Nationalist side.[32]

Three decades went by before a few disabled Republican veterans attempted to reorganize the LMIGE inside Spain. Inevitably they had to work in hiding. Their first task, and one which would prove extremely difficult, was to try to locate their comrades scattered all over Spain. At the same time, secret meetings were held in various small churches in Madrid at which they defined their strategy. Despite their failure to obtain official authorization for their association, they continued organizing and entered into contact with some of the *procuradores familiares*

---

[32] According to the official history of the LMIGE, Millán-Astray rejected its demands declaring that: 'You are no more than depraved beings who, in pursuit of absurd ideals, have lost some arms and legs. But in Franco's Spain the only help that you can expect is that obtained by appealing door-to-door for holy charity ' (Pedro Vega, *Historia de la Liga de Mutilados* (LMIGE) (Madrid: M. C. Martínez, 1981), p. 30.

or 'family representatives' in the Cortes who had shown themselves most inclined to consider opening up the regime and ending the discrimination against the vanquished in the Civil War.[33] These *procuradores* were the principal source of all the reconciliatory measures proposed in the Cortes, including a number of initiatives to have the Republican servicemen and civilians who had been purged at the end of the war readmitted to their pre-war jobs. Significantly, all moves in this direction failed. And so too did their numerous attempts to win government approval for proposals to provide economic assistance to the disabled Republican veterans.

Thus, while the Nationalist disabled were treated as heroes and enjoyed the title of 'gentlemen', even in the 1960s the Republican disabled veterans were often treated with contempt and, in many cases, forced to beg for a living. Despite this, however, they displayed little bitterness or desire for revenge. Rather they strove for reconciliation and mutual respect and tolerance; after Franco's death, members of the LMIGE even claimed that on a number of occasions they had attempted to form a single organization of disabled veterans, by merging not only with the exiled veterans, but also with the Nationalist disabled. This was one of the many differences between the reconstituted League in France and the LMIGE: the exiles were totally opposed to any talk of unification with the Nationalist association, or what they described as 'false' and 'negative' unity.[34] They argued that the Disabled Gentlemen had never called on the Francoist regime to show any mercy towards their Republican counterparts, or shown any interest in the idea of a joint association.

Even before the end of the Second World War, the disabled Republican veterans in France had begun to work on rebuilding the organization that had existed in Spain during the Civil War. The German occupation forced the exiles to discontinue their activities, but on the overthrow of the Vichy regime they rapidly set to work again. A first meeting was held in Toulouse in July 1945; four months later they met to approve new statutes; and the formally reconstituted League-in-exile held its first Congress in early 1947. Here the organization's leaders declared that, besides campaigning and providing assistance to its members, one of their principal objectives was to denounce the Francoist regime and its responsibility for the Spanish tragedy. A common

---

[33] The *procuradores familiares* were the only elected members of the Francoist Cortes (though elected on a family franchise rather than through universal suffrage), and, along with the local councils the most representative body in the entire institutional apparatus of the dictatorship.

[34] Trabal, *Breve historia*, p. 150.

feature of mourning processes is the attribution of responsibility for the tragedy to a well-defined enemy; this helps to externalize the victims' anger and establish a target for present and future action. In this case, the exiles' target was the Francoist regime, and the organization's first priority the destruction of this regime; only then would their wounds be healed.

The exiles' obsession with this goal prevented them from favouring any action which, in their view at least, might have helped to postpone the overthrow of the dictatorship. This explains why the exiles opposed the attempts made by the Republican disabled inside Spain to secure from the regime some of the benefits enjoyed by their Nationalist counterparts. The exiles considered that all their efforts should be devoted to overthrowing the dictatorship, and that any contact with it constituted an intolerable act of submission. The disabled Republicans in Spain had a very different perception of the situation. They never received any of the material benefits available to the exiles; many were purged from their jobs and/or imprisoned, often with long sentences; and few knew anything but hardship. In these circumstances, their priorities were understandably different to their comrades in exile. They were more concerned with their own economic situation than with the nature of the political regime. Whilst this did not mean that they accepted the dictatorship, they could not afford to adopt a maximalist position, as did the exiles. Given their own personal difficulties, and faced by a repressive and relatively stable regime, all they could do was to try and advance some practical and unthreatening demands.

The two groups' different experiences in the postwar period help to explain their very different attitude towards politics, as well as their distinct memories and interpretations of the Civil War. This confirms that 'subsequent information may profoundly alter or affect memory'.[35] Equally, further traumatic experiences may also contribute to the reinterpretation of earlier memories. Thus, it can be suggested that these two groups assigned different meanings to and drew different lessons from their Civil War experience as a consequence of later events.

One of the arguments that the LMIGE in Spain used in its attempts to obtain material assistance from the Francoist regime was that many of the Republican veterans were victims of a 'geographical accident'; that is, that many of them had not fought in the Republican army by choice, or for ideological reasons, but because they had been caught in government-held territory at the outbreak of war. The exiles, however, totally rejected this line of argument. They maintained that all the members of

---

[35] Alice M. Hoffman and Howard S. Hoffman, *Archives of memory* (Lexington, Ky.: University of Kentucky Press, 1990), p. 130.

their association had fought in the Civil War out of deep political commitment, and considered the use the disabled Republicans inside Spain made of this argument as a betrayal of the Second Republic and a capitulation to the Francoist regime. In fact, it is certainly true that many of those who fought on both sides had been forced to enlist. Moreover, the LMIGE's use of the 'geographical accident' argument during the dictatorship was not merely opportunistic, since the organization continued to adhere to it even after Franco's death. Thus, the LMIGE's official history, published some years after the return to democracy, emphasized the ideological pluralism of its membership, composed of Republicans and Monarchists, Communists and Falangists, Catholics and anarchists.[36] Finally, in direct contrast to the exiles, the LMIGE emphasized its political neutrality; it had been formed exclusively 'to secure from the state our rights of association and a dignified pension which will allow us to keep our families, but never for political purposes'.[37]

It is possible that the disabled veterans in exile passed through a similar process to that experienced by many Jewish survivors of Nazi concentration camps. Many autobiographical accounts and a vast body of literature testify to the enormous burden of guilt they carried with them for having survived the horror whilst so many died, and the great distress this caused them. The exiles may have felt something similar, since they had been able to flee Spain, and so escape the evils of the Francoist regime in the postwar period: death penalties, imprisonment, repression, the lack of liberty, famine. They knew that despite all their unsatisfied dreams and aspirations, their situation was in many ways more comfortable than that of their counterparts inside Spain. In fact, in the book they later published they felt the need to try and justify their failure to give all but very limited help to the disabled in Spain, claiming that the LMIGE did not wish to cooperate with them.

The Republican veterans after Franco

During the two first decades of the Francoist dictatorship, the regime's principal if nonetheless very precarious source of legitimacy was its victory in the Civil War. It was for this reason that official rhetoric was full of references to the conflict. Later, however, major economic development in the 1960s brought the regime further, more substantial, sources of legitimacy in the form of prosperity and social mobility. These structural changes, together with the passage of time, made it

[36] Vega, *Historia*, 82.   [37] Ibid. p.88.

possible for younger generations in the political elite to modify the by then out-dated rhetoric of the war years. At the same time, the most active groups within Spanish civil society, above all workers and students, were beginning to thwart the regime's efforts to control them and emerged from apparent passivity to engage in clandestine political activity and public protest. One of the most important demands shared by the numerous, though often weak and fragmented, social movements which opposed the dictatorship was a full amnesty for all political prisoners. This demand was conceived as a step towards reconciliation, in that it would place the victors and vanquished in the Civil War on an equal footing. Broadly speaking, most political prisoners in Spain could be considered the ideological heirs of the vanquished, who, almost forty years after the end of the war, were finally transformed into victors with the return of democracy.

In October 1977 a full amnesty was approved as the result of the consensus reached by the main political parties represented in the first democratic parliament. Two groups, however, were excluded from this otherwise generous and wide-ranging bill. One was the Republican veterans of the Civil War, who were still prohibited from membership of the armed forces. This meant that they were denied the economic benefits (and above all pension rights) enjoyed by the Nationalist veterans, as well as their symbolic rehabilitation so many years after the end of the war. The democratic political forces were forced to accept this exception from the amnesty because those who had the greatest potential to put an end to democracy, and who for this reason could not be offended – the armed forces – strongly opposed this gesture of reconciliation. The military rejected any step which challenged their own heroic memory of the Civil War, as the incorporation of the Republican veterans into their ranks would certainly have done.

Other groups of Republican war victims, the disabled veterans and the war widows, also had to wait a number of years before obtaining rights equal to those of their Nationalist counterparts. It was only in 1981, after a number of pension reforms had left their status unaltered, that they were put on an equal footing with the victors in the war. Nevertheless, even after this step towards reconciliation, the different organizations of disabled veterans did not merge. Even now, there are three different associations of war veterans: the two Republican organizations and the successor of the Nationalist one. After the return to democracy, the Nationalist Honourable Corps of Disabled Gentlemen was rechristened the Asociación Cultural de Inválidos Militares de España (ACIME), the Cultural Association of Spanish Disabled Soldiers. All disabled servicemen now automatically belong to it; hence it will survive. In contrast, both the LMIGE and the League in France are destined to disappear as their members die.

The different collective memories of these two associations of Republican disabled veterans are evident from a reading of their official histories. Both books serve as a means of mourning their dead and expressing their grief for all they have suffered. Significantly, however, the way in which they recall the war and the dictatorship are very different. The League-in-exile declares that the Nationalist role in the Civil War constitutes an 'unforgettable' and 'unforgivable' crime. It repeatedly emphasizes that 'nothing can make up for the forty years of misery and suffering', and that the Francoists alone must bear all responsibility for the war. The exiles appear to be obsessed by the fear of being forgotten, and the demand that the authorities should pay public homage to their fallen. They themselves acknowledge that whilst they have not called for a purge of the administration inherited from the dictatorship, they are very reluctant to forgive and forget.

In striking contrast, the LMIGE speaks in terms of reconciliation and forgiveness, the need to recognize that both sides must accept their share of the blame for the atrocities committed during the war. This spirit inspired the joint meeting of the LMIGE and the Nationalist Honourable Corps in July 1977, when the presidents of the two organizations embraced each other as a symbol of reconciliation. According to the LMIGE, 'this was the embrace of the two Spains that previously faced each other in confrontation, but are now committed to furthering democratic coexistence'. Both organizations agreed that they had all suffered equally, that 'a civil war is always a fraud'.[38] They insisted that the war was a fratricidal conflict, and that the time had come to transcend the trauma it had left.

These very different visions of the past reflect these two groups' very different experiences in the postwar period. The way each group thought about the past was strongly influenced by the fact that for forty years they lived in different countries, with different opportunities to mourn their dead and deal with their war traumas. The exiles' obsessive commitment to destroying the dictatorship, in order to be able to return to Spain, modified their priorities and agenda for collective action. On the other hand, in the absence of personal contact with the victors, they maintained a distorted memory of them which was rooted in their experience of the war. This frozen and demonic image prevented the exiles from accepting the idea of reconciliation with the Nationalists and their heirs. When the exiles stated that the Nationalists alone were

[38] Ibid. 121.

responsible for the horrors of the Civil War, they were also blaming them for all the years they spent in exile, that is, their most evident trauma from the postwar period.

The agenda of the Republican disabled inside Spain was also shaped by their experience after the war, namely the appalling hardships and personal insecurity they faced. Thus, when they began to rebuild the LMIGE in the mid-1960s, they had little interest in political objectives but concentrated on securing very practical, essentially economic, demands. Despite the brutal and widespread repression they had faced in the immediate postwar period, this group had to live alongside the winners; this contact gave it the opportunity to modify the distorted image of the enemy that all wars create. This helps explain why the LMIGE now has a better relationship with the ACIME than the League-in-exile.

The political lesson drawn from the Civil War by nearly all Spaniards, whether of Republican or Nationalist extraction, is 'never again'. In applying this lesson, parties on both the Right and Left had to make concessions: the Right accepted the legalization of the Communist party, while the Left abandoned its Republican aspirations and admitted the legitimacy of the monarchy. The old Republicans in exile, outside Spain, rejected the Left's concessions as a sell-out.

During this same transition period, both Right and Left agreed that the bitterest aspects of the past should not be aired in public debate. The memory of the Civil War was only used, and then only implicitly, to facilitate the many social and political agreements and pacts made during this period. The principal inspiration for the consensus politics (in part based on this silencing of the past) seen during the transition to democracy was the almost obsessive desire to avoid a repetition of the war or the failings of the Second Republic, and above all the widespread social and political confrontations that had marked the period. In conclusion, therefore, whilst we do find different episodic memories of the past, there was also a common lesson derived from this. And it was this which constituted the main inspiration for the transition to democracy.

That process was not distinct from these attempts to create a 'collective memory' of disabled veterans. They, the men who bore the marks of war on their bodies and in their minds, showed viscerally what was meant by the phrase 'never again'. The status of Republican exiles, Republicans in Spain, or Nationalist veterans naturally shaped their construction of a 'social framework of memory', in Halbwachs's terms. But their common denominator was a belief in the need to point to a future for Spain not disfigured by the traumas of their own generation.

5   Children as war victims in postwar
     European cinema

Pierre Sorlin

The victims during the First World War were chiefly but not exclusively men obliged to fight and die for what turned out, very soon after the peace treaty, to have been a bad affair. What people remembered was straightforward and very sad: five years spent on the front line had marked the end of the civilized values for which soldiers, in all countries, had mobilized to defend. In their memoirs, in their poems, novels, drawings, or paintings, the survivors did not indulge in moral or patriotic reflections, they attempted to convey the rebarbative reality of the trenches and to produce stories likely to make everybody understand that they went through an ordeal that was like hell.

Things were not as clear cut in the Second World War, so that the memory of the conflict was much more ambivalent. To begin with, the unprecedented extent of casualties and destruction was seen as typical of a modernization process which was ruthlessly sweeping away the systems and societies of the past. By turning armed forces into machines for slaughter, modern warfare tended to annihilate, even in the societies which had successfully waged it, any sense that the combat had been fought, or should have been fought, for the defence of a community. Not surprisingly, emphasis was put on the killing of harmless people, especially of children – that is to say, of their own future – whom societies should have tried to protect.

However, during the same war, almost everybody, including innocent victims, realized that there were reasons for fighting. Many people had a clear, even if mistaken, idea of why they had to endure what they were enduring. The Second World War did not mirror the senseless slaughter lamented by the sufferers of the first; it was an ideological war, fought for ideological aims and even the weakest, women and children, contributed to prolonging it. It is upon these ambivalent bases that the remembrances of the Second World War were built.

Memory and images

Individual memory, our memory, is both the recollection of actual experiences and the recording of information learned from friends, picked up in conversations, or read in books. Being taken in a battle or a bombing is a pure state of affairs, a complex of feelings, fears, and hopes endured from the standpoint of one person. It is only afterwards that memory defines events by attributing a meaning to the state of affairs, by means of descriptions – usually linguistic, but also graphic – as well as through purely corporal reactions. Memory is thus a process of negotiation between individuals and the groups to which they belong. Trying to 'explore' personal memories is almost hopeless, even when people have written their memoirs, for all remembrances are shaped by a complex of data and ideas which includes rumour, lessons taught at school, monuments, and media. What is more, all kinds of remembrance are neither monolithically installed nor everywhere believed. They are in a constant state of rearrangement under the pressure of competing sources of information often in conflict with each other: produced in the course of these struggles, remembrances can always be questioned.

It is one of the tasks of historians to examine how societies, during a given period, select the 'historical' data, the data related to the past, which will be shared by their members and will frame individual memories. Beside facts, feelings have also to be taken into account since emotional norms and sanctioned affects contribute, as much as events, to reinforcing memories. For practical reasons, sentiments are often repressed during tragic epochs such as wars. In his memoirs the Austrian philosopher Paul Feyerabend, who was mobilized in the Wehrmacht, honestly acknowledges that, throughout the hostilities, he did not pay much attention to the talk about the saddest aspects of the conflict: 'the words came and went, apparently without effect' and it was later that he began to ponder the atrocities of Nazism and to confront his factual recordings with this new awareness.[1] Of course people bemoaned their relatives or friends who had been killed, but it was only after the war that it became possible to mourn the whole period and the damage it had caused.

General grief, grief about one's country, about a lost generation or a group of the dead is an abstract feeling, a representation in which things that people have seen or gone through can be subsumed. Reconstructing this grief is haphazard but it is documented by what people wanted to read, by the songs they wanted to sing and the films they wanted to

---

[1] *Killing time* (Chicago: University of Chicago Press, 1994), p. 192.

watch. These sources have their limitations. They are imaginary products which reduce to a few images long hours of misery or struggle and offer a synthesis of tragic events all the more unreal in that it has been performed by professionals used to mimicking all sorts of emotions. These shortcomings must be neither overvalued nor underrated. While being aware of the fact that novels or films do not tell the truth, readers and spectators feel strongly affected because, by restricting big conflagrations to a limited environment, by transferring from the social to the individual, fiction offers a clear, simple view on difficult problems and helps the public to understand or perceive what would be less obvious if the infinite complexity of 'the real' was taken into account. Fiction, which has no precise purpose (apart from being popular) and does not prescribe any specific behaviour, contributes to bridging the gap between personal experiences and accepted knowledge.

In an attempt to characterize the way in which Western European societies[2] grieved for child victims of war I shall use a few literary texts but shall focus mostly on films, for three main reasons. Firstly, the impact of films is easier to evaluate, at least roughly, than the impact of books. During the fifteen years following the end of the war, eighty-five films dealing with the conflict or its immediate aftermath were shot in Britain while 225 war films were screened in the cinemas of the German Federal Republic. Nicholas Pronay rightly notes that the hostilities were seldom absent from the screen for more than two or three months, at a time when the cinema was still the main form of entertainment in Europe.[3] Cinema was all the more important because, in the years that followed the war, apart from a few texts that we shall examine later, novels, radio plays – which were a very significant literary expression of the period – and theatrical plays did not expand on the effects of the conflict. It is true that there was a flood of diaries, memoirs, and autobiographical accounts written by *résistants*, soldiers, and survivors of the concentration camps, the most remarkable of which was Primo Levi's *Se questo è un uomo* (*If this is a man*, 1947). But the civilians, and especially the children, took no part in this production because what they could have told was too basic. As for novelists and playwrights they

---

[2] Why only Western European societies? First because, for linguistic reasons, I do not know the Eastern cinematographies as well as their Western counterparts. But also because the memory of the 'Great Patriotic War' was soon ritualized in the socialist countries, the fight against Nazism was given epical colours and Stalin was made its hero. Changes occurred after Khrushchev's 'Secret Speech' but the most important films of the new era, especially Tarkovskii's *Ivan's childhood* (1962), belong to a period which I do not want to consider in this chapter.

[3] 'The British post-bellum cinema', *Historical Journal of Film, Radio and Television*, 8, 1 (1988), pp. 39–54.

were more preoccupied by big issues than by trivialities. They wrote epics, like Theodor Plievier's *Stalingrad*, or reflections on ethics and politics. In what was considered the most eloquent depiction of the problems faced by a soldier returning from the front, *Eine Stimme hebt an* (*A voice is lifted up*, 1950), the German novelist Gerd Gaiser, who was awarded major literary prizes and met with a favourable response in the press, was content to explain how his character regained moral composure and did not care about trifles such as food, injuries, or lodging; while Evelyn Waugh's war trilogy *Sword of honour* and C. P. Snow's *Strangers and brothers* series were uniquely concerned with the ethical dilemmas of leading personalities. There were of course exceptions which we shall meet later but, as a whole, literature paid little attention to the weak.

The third point I want to stress is that films are important for historians because they provide spectators with images which, very often, substitute for actual memories, creating a contrived but very effective idea of the past. In their research into the recollection of the Second World War in Australia, historians have frequently encountered this 'metahistory', borrowed from screenings, which blurs actual reminiscences and, more importantly, is common to many people. Interviewing Australian women about the home front, Kate Dorian-Smith met a complex, permanently shifting interchange between the individual experience of the interviewees, history as it was told in books, and a popular television series, *The Sullivans*, which validated and perhaps even came to stand for the women's own memories of the period. Similarly, Annette Hamilton noted that scenes obviously inspired by the famous film *The bridge on the River Kwai* could be found in the recollections told by Australian POWs who had worked on the construction of the Thailand railway.[4] In the long run, the representations popularized by films matter as much as the actual facts. As a German filmmaker, Edgar Reitz, has pointed it out, films are vehicles for memory work (*Erinnerungsarbeit*) because 'the images stored up in our memories are the actual substance of history'.[5]

Reitz's most famous production, the television serial *Heimat* (1982) deals extensively with the life and pains of the inhabitants of a small village during and after the war.[6] Since 1945, countless films have evoked the same period but I shall be content with considering the

---

[4] Kate Dorian-Smith and Paula Hamilton (ed.), *Memory and history in twentieth century Australia* (Melbourne: Oxford University Press, 1995).

[5] 'The Camera is not a Clock' in Eric Rentschler (ed.), *West German filmmakers on film: visions and voices* (New York: Methuen, 1988), pp. 137–8.

[6] On *Heimat* see Anton Kaes, *From 'Hitler' to 'Heimat'. The return of history in film* (Cambridge, Mass.: Harvard University Press, 1989), pp. 161ff.

fifteen years that followed the end of the conflict. Born in the initial decades of the century,[7] the filmmakers who worked in the middle of the century had witnessed the war, had usually been mobilized, and had gone through terrible experiences. Having lost many friends and relatives, they were keen on questioning the fate of their contemporaries in order to understand why the conflict had ended as it did. Theirs was not the generation of innocent victims which was born in the 1930s and early 1940s. The eldest pitied the young for what they had suffered, but to what extent were they able to understand them? We must bear in mind the fact that cinematic images are contrived by middle-class adults who, unwittingly, emphasize the reactions of their social circle and age groups, and forget or misinterpret the concerns of other groups.

Europe reached a watershed in the early 1960s not only because her economy entered a decade of exceptional growth but also because new movements, namely the Angry young men, the French New wave, and the New German cinema, reoriented her intellectual life. The younger filmmakers had not suffered as much as the previous generation during the conflict and, with the passing of time, they could stand back and judge events more calmly. The most popular films related to the Second World War, Alain Resnais's *Hiroshima mon amour* and Rainer Werner Fassbinder's *Die Ehe der Maria Braun* (*The marriage of Maria Braun*) did not attempt to reconstruct the past but questioned the very building of memory. While acknowledging the horrors of war, Resnais and Fassbinder did not conceal its liberating aspects: their main characters were women who defied opinion in a manner inconceivable before the hostilities. A controversial Danish film, Pale Kjaerulff-Schmidt's *Der var engang en krig* (*Once there was a war*, 1966), put on stage a fifteen-year-old boy, Tim, who took advantage of the trouble provoked by the German occupation in Copenhagen to lead a difficult but emotionally exciting life. Throughout the 1960s and 1970s, novels and films played an important part in the debate about the consequences of the Second World War and the changes it had introduced. In particular, they expressed doubts about the supposed togetherness created by war and stressed the fact that the period's homogenizations were superficial and short lived. Innocent eyes, like those of children, were very convenient to observe the perpetuation of domestic frictions amidst bombings. Far from describing victimized infants as was the case previously, novels (Henry Green's *Caught*, David Lodge's *Out of the shelter*) and films (*Hope and glory*, *An awfully big adventure*) illustrated the indifference of children to whom war was a time when they escaped adult control and a

---

[7] Between 1906 (Rossellini, Radványi) and 1919 (Clément, Wicki).

wonderful experience, both deeply erotic, in a class-crossing way, and brilliantly aesthetic. This, of course, is highly interesting but it has to do with the reinterpretation of the conflict, in the context of a reconstructed Europe, not with the creation of a memory and, for that reason, I shall stop at the end of the 1950s.[8]

Children weeping among ruins

In films, childhood was an invention of the 1940s. Previously, few films had taken kids as their protagonists and, most of the time, boys or girls were mere pretexts, useful to idealize the nuclear family and legitimate the male domination. Being vulnerable, children were fit to illustrate the ghastliness of a total war and it was not rare to notice, spread across films whose characters were adults, children killed during bombings or escaping from a dust-filled shelter to watch tall buildings blazing amid crashes and sirens. The Germans have coined a word, *Trümmerfilme*, ruin-films, to point out the films in which wounded or mutilated people roam amidst collapsed houses.[9] These pictures are important for historians because they are often packed with accidental information. Getting out of his home, Joe Kirby, the fifteen-year-old main character of Charles Crichton's *Hue and cry* (1947) is shrouded in the clatter of an air-raid; he does not look afraid, and the camera, which follows him, discloses very soon a young boy who is producing with his mouth, his nose, his hands, the sounds of explosions. Side-effects of bombings, recurring fears or traumas like the obsession which affects this kid are often neglected and it is useful to have them evoked in films.[10] *Hue and cry* as well as Gerhardt Lamprecht's *Irgendwo in Berlin* (*Somewhere in Berlin*, 1947), have destroyed cities, London or Berlin, as their background and throughout the film young people go over large rubble-filled areas bordered by bombed-out buildings and even, sometimes, help to excavate and try to make the best of the squalor of ruins.[11]

---

[8] I give the original title with the English title in brackets; when the film has not been distributed in an English-speaking country, I give the translation of the title in square brackets.

[9] Manfred Bartel, *So war es wirklich. Der deutsche Nachkriegsfilm.* (Munich/Berlin: Herbing, 1986); Deutsches Filmmuseum, *Zwischen Gestern und Morgen. Westdeutscher Nachkriegsfilm* (Frankfurt am Main: Deutsches Filmmuseum, 1986), pp. 46–62; Ursula Bessen, *Trümmer und Träume. Nachkriegszeit und fünfziger Jahre auf Zelluloid* (Bochum: Brokmeyer, 1989).

[10] An aspect of war films tackled by Robert Murphy, *Realism and tinsel. Cinema and society in Britain, 1939–1948* (London: Routledge, 1989), pp. 162ff.

[11] Wolfgang Becker and Norbert Schöll, *In Jenen Tagen. Wie der deutsche Nachkriegsfilm die Vergangenheit bewältigte* (Opladen: Leske, 1995), pp. 65ff.

However, the documentary aspect of feature films is not what matters. In many cases, the images have a strong emotional impact, all the more powerful that the evocation is direct and unemphatic. The international fame of Rossellini, in the late 1940s, was largely due to the fact that he depicted in full the horrors of war but did so with restraint. There is in particular an unforgettable sequence in *Paisá* (*Paisan*, 1946) which lasts only thirty-five seconds but which is very impressive. In December 1944, partisans and American agents dropped behind the lines, who have taken refuge in the marshes of the Po delta, get some food from a farmhouse, *Casal Madalena*. Here is the above-mentioned sequence, which is made of only six shots:

- At twilight, two American soldiers, filmed in medium shot, are walking. The cries of a baby can be heard in the distance.
- A long shot reveals a few corpses lying alongside the bank, outside *Casal Madalena*. A weeping child and a dog wander among the dead bodies.
- The soldiers stop, horrified.
- A slow tracking-shot, starting from the framing of the previous shot, follows the baby who goes along the bank.
- The soldiers leave the place.
- The tracking-shot goes on and moves away from the baby who is now motionless; the cries fade away.

The poor orphan has been abandoned twice. First by the Americans. What could they do? Their situation is desperate, they are entirely surrounded by the Germans, and they will soon be captured by the enemy; their pity would be useless. But the child has also been abandoned by the spectators; the three shots showing the corpses and the baby are much too wide to represent the point of view of the Americans; they are the point of view of the public which stands outside the scene and whose experience of the soldiers' revulsion is merely that of knowledge. Spectators cannot do anything for the baby. Let us recall that the film was released in 1946, at a time when there were many war orphans and when people were so upset by their own problems that they could not care for the abandoned babies.

The fate of children without parents was surely a serious concern in the postwar period since it returned obsessively in all the cinematographies, even in the British cinema with Dan Birt's *No room at the inn* (1948), a critical evocation[12] of English children evacuated to Scotland,

---

[12] Note that the script was written by Dylan Thomas.

forced to live in filth, fed only scraps, who arouse no sympathy or pity in an indifferent local community.[13] Dan Birt exposed openly what was latent in *Paisá*: in his film, the children were neglected, even threatened by the grown-ups and one of them, the little Mary was obliged to mobilize her companions against the adults.

No room at the inn was rather traditional inasmuch as it told a finite story, from the departure of the children until their final success, and closed on a happy ending. A few Italian filmmakers, namely Rossellini and De Sica, were much more audacious, since they depicted totally abandoned children obliged to fight to survive. One episode, in *Paisá*, is focused on a little boy, Pasquale, who has no family and lives by stealing in the streets of Naples. Encountering a drunken black American soldier Pasquale robs him of his shoes to sell them; later the American finds the kid, who takes him to his shelter, a shantytown crammed with women and children dressed in rags. Pasquale is extremely convincing in his part of a prematurely grown-up boy, quick to evaluate the commercial value of objects, and the last sequence in the shacks is very impressive but here again the end is excessively optimistic: the soldier drops the boots and leaves. The approach was fairly different in De Sica's *Sciuscia* (*Shoeshine*, 1946) and Rossellini's *Germania anno zero* (*Germany, year zero*, 1947). Here the children, who have to cope alone with an hostile environment, are also obliged to reckon with the adults. Like Pasquale, De Sica's two characters, who live in Rome, are involved in the black market; allied soldiers do not pay them, or pay them badly, for cleaning their shoes and they must deal in contraband; a gang uses them to help rob a well-off lady of all her money but they are easily spotted by the lady and the police sends them to a reformatory where they are treated as hardened criminals. Rossellini's *Germania anno zero* takes place in Berlin. Edmund, who is only thirteen years old, has to support an invalid father, a brother obliged to hide to avoid denazification, and a sister. Adults employ him to sell superfluous objects to the allies but get most of the money he brings them back. Repeatedly, Rossellini shows the young boy cheated by grown-ups and he does it in his sober, impressive manner. For instance, a neighbour has instructed him to sell a scale worth 300 marks:

---

[13] The selfishness of the local community which does not care for the orphans is also the theme of Luigi Zampa's *Campane a martello* (*Children of chance*, 1950) but this Italian film, unlike its British counterpart, does not set the children against the village. It is the priest who faces the villagers and moves them. It would be interesting to see how often the fate of war victims was used for a political purpose – in this case to emphasize the positive role of the Church.

- A long shot of a street allows Edmund to enter the field; he meets other children and argues with them since they do not want to let him 'work' on their territory. A man enters in the background.
- Medium shot of Edmund with the man. The shot is framed to the dimensions of the man, which makes the boy look small and power-less. The man takes the scale to examine it but keeps it and gives Edmund two tin cans.
- Long shot; while the man goes away Edmund protests. On the screen the distance between the frail boy and the man looks impassable and Edmund's position conveys the stress and anger that he is feeling.

Of course, when Edmund goes back home, the neighbour rebukes him and takes the two tin cans: the boy has wasted his day for nothing.

Making spectators weep over the misfortunes of harmless kids is a worn-out trick abundantly used in tear-jerkers. However, children are seldom the protagonists of the novels, plays, or films which depict them; on the contrary, they may have the part of the classic victim because they are unable to play an important role. Postwar films broke new ground in the field of fiction by putting the emphasis on youth and by running the risk of having recourse to juveniles who were not even amateur actors and who seldom made a career in cinema.[14] This led them to observe some conventions. In order to justify the loneliness and hopelessness of their characters, they stressed the dramatic effects of the war. The mother of Hooker, one of the three adolescents who are the main characters of Basil Dearden's *I believe in you* (1952), explains at length that her son was a nice, clean boy until his father was killed in 1941. The background of ruins and debris, the environment of black-marketeers and allied soldiers, the atmosphere of fear and insecurity were not merely an affectation of realism, they were necessary to make it plain that the circumstances were exceptional and were the result of the conflict. As they were not professional, the young actors could not remember long lines and their dialogues were necessarily short. But it is quite obvious that they enjoyed playing and the filmmakers took advantage of their enthusiasm: the striking manner of the actors, their presence and self-assurance are impressive. Loose clothes, too wide for frail bodies, rags, fanciful headgear like the garrison cap worn by Pasquale, produced odd-looking, shabby figures and insistent close-ups of silent, pensive faces created an impression of profound sadness. These films were dark enough to engage their public in mourning, they were a direct way of experiencing various emotions, of a kind repeatedly

[14] The few exceptions were Henry Fowler (*Hue and cry, I believe in you*), Franco Interlenghi (*Sciuscia*), and Brigitte Fossey (*Les jeux interdits*).

encountered in daily life, all through the medium of sight; they did not communicate ideas marked by words but raised sentiments and feelings affecting the disposition of the spectators' minds. Emotionally intense and expressive images helped people mourn. What is more, since these pictures were fictional and featured children – that is to say visibly, weak, easily hurt beings – there could be no conflict between what the public watched on the silver screen and what it actually experienced: films were exceptionally well fitted to adapting their spectators' feelings to a very difficult situation.[15]

What did they die for?

The archetypal photograph of the First World War is of a soldier on watch in a trench. For the Second World War, it is of a baby drifting in the streets of a destroyed city. However, where Germany is concerned, another picture has to be evoked; it is a newsreel, shot in March 1945, which shows Hitler, wasted with age and worries, reviewing a squad of fifteen-year-old soldiers. Children were not only civilian victims but military victims as well in the conflict. The story is a complicated one; it has never been fully explored by historians and it is always mixed with folk-tales. All countries have their legends about young drummers who were killed while leading a charge or murdered by the enemy because they gave the alert instead of keeping silent. The mobilization of young boys, in 1944 to 1945, was a reality, but it was also a myth which helped people to ponder the meaning of the conflict.

Two boys, one fourteen and the other fifteen years of age, carry a message from a group of partisans to another group. For them it is a play but the Fascists capture and shoot them: does not that illustrate the ambiguity of resistance, asked Beppe Fenoglio in *Una questione privata*?[16] But his book was written at the end of the 1950s and, fifteen years before, Rossellini had given a totally different answer. His most famous film, *Roma città aperta (Rome, open city)*, which was released as early as September 1945, was a political plea for Italy which met with an enthusiastic response in the United States and contributed to redeeming the Italians in the eyes of the Americans. The film depicts a Rome entirely mobilized against the German occupiers under the joint direction of a Communist and a priest. All social classes, from well-off traders to workers, contribute to the fight. There are no children among

[15] Eric Santer, *Stranded objects: mourning, memory and film in postwar Germany* (Ithaca: Cornell University Press, 1990).

[16] *A private question* written in 1959–60, published after Fenoglio's death (Turin: Einaudi, 1963); see pp. 141ff.

the main characters, but kids do not stop appearing in the background and their determination is as strong as the adults'. Using words which sound odd in his mouth, a twelve-year-old boy insists that 'we have to close ranks against the common enemy'. The kids are organized like a small army, with a chief who is both the theoretician and the strategist and a second-in-command. Having collected bombs and submachine-guns, they can be very efficient, as when they blow up a train but they can also be dangerous when, unconscious of possible reprisals, they threaten to throw a bomb onto a German squad. On the whole, the film is extremely dramatic; it depicts the secret combat of the resistants as well as the investigations which lead the Germans to arrest and execute the leaders, and the public cannot but feel puzzled by the insidious presence of the children. Of course these boys reinforce the idea that every Italian was engaged in the resistance. But how can we account for the half-farcical part that they play and for the fact that, unlike the adults, they look invulnerable? We shall tackle the question later, in a comparison with other texts and films, but we may already stress the equivocation that children introduce in the movie.

If many Italian children carried messages, food, and even weapons to the partisans, very few were actively engaged in resistance. On the other hand, there was a limited but really active group of resistants to Nazism in German universities. Three German films evoked *die weisse Rose*, the White Rose, as the students called their ring, but these pictures were all shot after 1970. In the 1950s, the few films dealing with opposition to Hitler were devoted to officers who thought that they could no longer obey the Führer, especially to the failed plot of 20 July 1944.[17] If militarized youth was also displayed on the silver screen, it was when it fought against the allies. The theme must have been extremely impor-tant since it was represented three times in twelve years by Hans Müller's *Und finden dereinst wir uns wieder (And should we ever meet again,* 1947), Laszlo Benedek's *Kinder, Mütter und ein General (Children, mothers and a general,* 1954), and Bernhard Wicki's *Die Brücke (The bridge,* 1959). There were significant differences between these films. In the first two movies the boys have been transferred from their home to an evacuation camp; in the third they live in their home town until they are mobilized. In *Und finden dereinst wir uns wieder* the young, sent for safety to Westfalia where they could await the arrival of the Americans, choose, in April 1945, to go and defend Berlin against the Russians. The

---

[17] On the representation of recent German history on film in the 1950s see Bärbel Westermann, *Nationale Identität im Spielfilm der fünfziger Jahre* (Friburg am Mein: Peter Lang, 1990), pp. 73ff. and Wolfgang Becker and Norbert Schöll, *In Jenen Tagen,* pp. 79ff.

boys featuring in *Kinder, Mütter und ein General* have not been taken far from the eastern front; they are well aware of the situation and feel very scared for their mothers and family who are staying with them. The schoolboys of *Die Brücke* leave an almost normal life in a small town of Western Germany and, once mobilized, resist the American advance. In other words, in 1947 fighting Communism was a good excuse; in 1954 protecting one's family against the Reds was a reasonable explanation; in 1959 resisting an enemy, even tomorrow's best ally, was honourable. However many similarities, namely identical characters, identical situations, identical actors,[18] link the three films. In all of them the boys take their own decision; the refugees break out of their evacuation camps and the students of *Die Brücke* resolve to protect a bridge. Trying to cross Germany and reach Berlin in April 1945 is a foolish task and can only result in haphazard casualties; when they are given uniforms the boys of *Kinder, Mütter und ein General* look like dislocated puppets; as for the defenders of the bridge, once they have successfully resisted the Americans and four of them have been killed, the survivors are told that they should never have protected a structure meant to be blown up. In the three films most adults seem irresponsible and unconscious of the frailty of adolescents: a teacher incites his pupils to go to Berlin, a general agrees to enlist small boys, a commander exhorts his smooth-cheeked recruits to be ready for the final sacrifice. However a minority of adults is less inconsiderate: the mothers do their best to save their kids and, in *Und finden dereinst wir uns wieder* as well as in *Die Brücke*, a teacher tries to convince the boys that their commitment is meaningless.

There is something very puzzling in this sequence of films treating the same problem in similar terms. How do filmmakers account for the sacrifice of children torn between contradictory advice? The sense of duty is often mentioned by the boys, who say that they are ready to die a hero's death for the country. But, behind a rhetoric often borrowed from adults, it seems to me that the filmmakers, themselves adults, have in mind something else. It is striking that none of the films makes the slightest allusion to Nazism: the Germans fight for Germany and it is also for Germany that the young want to enlist. Still, given their age, since all these boys have gone through *Hitlerjugend*, theirs should be political motivations. Here, as in *Roma città a aperta*, avowed reasons are purely patriotic. Faced with adults who profess contradictory opinions, the young react instinctively, in a way which is both honourable and ill-advised. This vision of youth in war has been well expressed by Cesare Pavese in his novel *La casa in collina* (*The house on the hill*, 1949). One

---

[18] Bernard Wicki, who played the part of the general in *Kinder, Mütter und ein General*, directed *Die Brücke*.

morning the main character goes to the house where the resistants were hiding:

Half-way down the hill I met Dino [a twelve-year-old boy]. He was climbing up with his hands in pockets. He didn't look frightened.

'The Germans came in this morning in a car', he said; 'they punched Nando, they were trying to kill him.'

'Where is your mother?'

Cate had been taken too. And old Gregorio. All of them ... They had beaten Nando up in the cellar. You could hear his cries. His mother had told him to hide but he had wanted to stay behind with the others, jump up into the car as well. He had rushed forward but the Germans had stopped him.[19]

Like Marcello in Rossellini's film and like the German youngsters, Nando is unaware of danger. But, in Italy, youth had been on the 'right' side; it was not necessary to mourn them; hence the boys could go unhurt throughout the war. The German case was more embarrassing. The three films under scrutiny must be connected to the debate over moral resistance to Nazism which took place in the late 1940s. Journalists and politicians insisted that it was necessary to distinguish the German soldiers, who had behaved like gallant warriors, from the Nazis. A bright columnist, Alfred Andersch, piled up papers, talks, and pamphlets in which he opposed 'the astonishing acts of valour by young Germans in the war' to the misdeeds of 'older Germans'.[20] Films had their share in these polemics, they stressed the bravery of the young, bemoaned their tragic fate, and made clear references to the rashness of youth. According to the version of the last months of the war that they offered, getting involved in a hopeless battle had been estimable but ineffective. Nobody had to be blamed; only foolhardiness had led the boys to lose their lives. Repeatedly, film directors invited their spectators to grieve but made them understand that no remorse had to colour mourning.

A way to hope

The final shot of *Roma città aperta* is open to various interpretations. The last sequence, which depicts the execution of the priest, Don Piedro, is first filmed in a detached manner, but the children arrive[21] and the

---

[19] *The house on the hill* (English translation, New York: Walker, 1961), pp. 135–6. Note that the same situation is depicted in *Roma città aperta*. There is no need to look for influences; the German car which arrives at dawn and arrests everybody was a traumatic memory shared by many Italians.

[20] 'Deutsche Literatur in der Entscheidung, 1948' (in Gerd Hoffmans (ed.), *Das Alfred Andersch Lesebuch*, Zurich: Fink, 1979), pp. 15ff.

[21] How have they been informed, since everything has been kept secret by the Germans?

end of the sequence is seen from their point of view, in a very moving way. Once the priest has been shot, the kids go down towards Rome, which can be seen in the background. This image was chosen because it is visually very effective and, for the cinematographers, it had no precise meaning. It can be read as the end of active resistance: the leaders have been eliminated, the only thing to do is go back home. But it may also be understood as an act of faith: it is the task of the new generation to rebuild Italy. In postwar films dealing with children, sorrow and hope are often interwoven. Out of the ruins, a future can arise, thanks to the children. We have noted above the relationship between infancy and war rubble. Children, in *Hue and cry*, lead a life of their own, independent of their parents; among destroyed buildings they have colonized broken houses and redecorated collapsed walls. Two other films which emphasize the rebirth through youth, a Hungarian movie, Géza Radványi's *Valahol Európávan* (*Somewhere in Europe*, 1947) and René Clement's *Les jeux interdits* (*Forbidden games*, 1952), begin with an air raid. Expressive sharp sounds accompanied by a rapid succession of short, violent images give an impression of the end of the world. In the former film, a boy comes out of the debris, in the latter, a girl. With them, life has escaped, but they are orphans and they will have to confront a universe which has not been built for people of their age.

What strikes us in these pictures which are, in many respects, rather disparate, is the emphasis put on death. Both films use images already shown in others. *Les jeux interdits* lingers upon Paulette, the five-year-old French girl, moving away from the corpses of her parents and roaming with the dead body of her pet dog in her arms. *Valahol Európávan* depicts a gang of orphans who wander through the country, are obliged to steal, to defend themselves, and to fight a world which is afraid of them. Death in all its forms, hunger, wounds, attacks by other gangs, is for them a permanent threat which has also become a ritual: when they find refuge in an isolated castle, their first idea is to kill the owner, in order to assert their right to stay. But these films are not merely pitiful descriptions; what distinguishes them from contemporary films which were content with mourning is that they try to find a way towards the future.

The children have gone through an ordeal and, if they want to live, they have to overcome it. Paulette has no material problem, but the peasant family which has adopted her does not understand that she is trying to make sense of the loss of her parents. Her games, forbidden by the grown-ups, displace routine observances, religion, church atten-

It is one of the many inconsistencies of a film whose script was written in a hurry. The story is poor but the emotional quality is outstanding.

dance, and even funerals, to bridge the gap between death and life. The story is not based on any direct observation; it is a fantasy, open to criticism in its portrayal of childhood but interesting inasmuch as it tries to attract spectators' attention to the trauma suffered by children and to the difficulty adults have in taking it into account.

Without focusing on any precise issue like the urge to come to grips with death, *Valahol Európávan* was much more ambitious than *Les jeux interdits*. It tackled gravely questions which were also treated, but more lightly, in *Hue and cry*. Both stories evolve along similar lines: a group of adolescents is obliged to face nasty grown-ups and strengthens its unity in the struggle. In the English film, war, which has destroyed the traditional boundaries between urban districts, has induced young people from different areas to know each other and to create an informal network. Thanks to its young actors, the film throbs with vitality and uses the architecture of bombed London to great dramatic effect. The children of the Hungarian film find it difficult to live in harmony in the castle but the inhabitants of nearby villages, by assaulting their refuge, force them to get organized. Hardship transforms a mere shelter into a home where friendship will blossom. The two filmmakers have used contrasting cinematic devices to reach the same conclusion. Radványi has selected a few children and has filmed them closely, underlining thus the importance of a smile, a grimace, or a shout. In *Hue and cry*, the sequence that sticks in the mind comes at the end. It develops when Joe Kirby, the main character, summons boys of all London districts to a half-destroyed dockland where their enemies are hidden. Riding bicycles or delivery tricycles, requisitioning taxis and lorries, running, jumping, almost flying, hundreds of children cross a dead London, reviving a sleeping city. The Hungarian as well as the English films finish with an operation of self-assertion by the vital forces of youth which destroy the old order by the simple act of demonstrating that groups of kids are stronger than war.

A conflict of generations?

During the fight against their countrymen one of the children of *Valahol Európában* has been fatally wounded. His fellows take him to the village where their older friend, the owner of the castle, addresses the inhabitants. Why is it, he asks, that adults launch wars in which their children will be killed? Rhetorical though it is, this talk sums up what we have found in almost all the films mentioned in this chapter, that is to say, an open conflict between successive generations.

Extending feminist theories about the way in which films reveal the

mechanisms of pleasure and trouble at work in male-dominated societies, Marcia Landi has explored the traces of male insecurity that can be
spotted in postwar films, and she has shown that they are often provoked
by 'the disruptive character of youth'.[22] Many pieces of evidence document her assumption. After 1945, in countries like Germany, Britain,
and even Italy women outnumbered men. Since many households were
headed by widows or unmarried mothers and since children, having an
important part in the household economy, were obliged to barter, to
beg, often to steal, families suffered from dramatic crises caused by
absent or enfeebled fathers. A direct, gripping testimony can be found in
the letters that Heinrich Böll, released from a POW camp in September
1945 after seven years of service, sent to his friend Ernst-Adolph
Kunz.[23] These letters reveal a disheartened man; on 15 October 1946,
Böll wrote: 'Life is terrible. I am often torn apart by anxiety, anguish
and misery', because he was unable to find a permanent job and could
only survive thanks to casual, temporary work. Meanwhile, a young
playwright, Wolfgang Borchert, was writing a radio-play, *Draussen vor
der Tür* (*On the other side of the door*)[24] which, staged in the most
important theatres of Western Germany, was the only success of a
postwar playwright. The play tells of the plight of a returning unwanted
soldier, who finds that there is no room for him, that those of the home
front, including his own family, have arranged a new life and do not care
about what he has gone through.

It was thus commonly said that the youngest generation had got rid of
its fathers. In a short story by Wolfgang Borchert, *An diesem Dienstag*
(*This very Tuesday*), a young girl unexpectedly writes ten times in her
exercise book, in capital letters: IN WAR, ALL FATHERS ARE
SOLDIERS,[25] which means that they no longer matter. A journalist
and a professor, who had also been in the Resistance, Werner Krauss,
went so far as to assert that the young had 'put an end to the bond
between generations' and that the sons were now attacking their pro-
genitors.[26] Historians would be naive if they believed that the evidence

---

[22] *British genres. Cinema and society, 1930–1960* (Princeton: Princeton University Press,
1991), pp. 178–9 and 440ff.

[23] Herbert Hoven (ed.), *Die Hoffnung ist wie ein wildes Tier. Der Briefwechsel zwischen
Heinrich Böll und Ernst-Adolph Kunz, 1945–1953* (Cologne: Kiepebheuer and Witschen,
1995).

[24] *Gesamtwerke* (Hamburg: Rowholt, 1949), pp. 117ff.

[25] 'Am diesen Dienstag, saß Ulla abends und malte in ihr Schreibheft mit großen
Buchstaben: IM KRIEG SIND ALLE VÄTER SOLDAT. Zehnmal schrieb sie das'
(ibid. p. 213).

[26] Such was the title of one of his papers, 'Das Ende der Generationgemeinschaft', 1947,
reprinted in *Literaturtheorie, Philosophie und Politik* (Berlin: Naumann, 1984,
pp. 399–409).

given by direct witnesses constitutes a reliable description of reality. Successive age groups are always more or less in opposition and the idea of a dramatic conflict arising after 1945 was more an ideological conviction than an accurate account of what was actually happening. But the rhetorical and imaginative power of this sad vision of things has coloured a good many books and films.

Italo Calvino's *Ultimo viene il corvo* (*The crow comes last*, 1949) tells the story of a boy, 'a mountaineer with an apple face' who, being a very good shot, is welcomed by a group of partisans.[27] One morning, having spotted a German hidden behind a rock, the boy watches him and shoots every time he wants to leave. Finally the soldier, scared out of his wits, moves and is killed. One cannot but feel uneasy when reading the tale. The boy has no political idea, he does not even hate the Germans, and he is only keen on taking a potshot. What is more, the duel is unfair, the kid is content with being vigilant while the soldier gets more and more nervous. Here, it is the youth who is dangerous and the adult who is a victim.

Behind a seeming compassion, many films or novels disclose an atmosphere of panic about the young. In the postwar era the adolescents' marginal status between child and adult had made them both objects of pity and anxiety. At a time when children could ignore the law of the adults, steal, and even kill, all the structures of authority were threatened. Films have to be questioned like artefacts which historians know to be partially inaccurate but which disclose purely emotional reactions. Sometimes, a short scene, not important for the story, reveals a latent hostility, for instance when an adult, in *I believe in you*, bullies and throws to the ground Hooker, a difficult but nice boy. Even when they offer a coherent, logical point of view, films may be totally biased. Under the pretext of providing an objective account of the aftermath of war a British documentary, J. Lee and I. Dalrymple's *Children on trial* (1946), drew an impressive portrait of criminals-to-be and made it clear that, once they had gone beyond any control, youngsters could be very harmful.

Rossellini's *Germania anno zero* is the movie which best exemplifies the ambivalence of youth. Spectators should feel sorry for Edmund, who has lost everything and has no future. Defenceless though he is, the boy is able to define his private law, which makes him as powerful as an adult, and allows him to murder his father. What are his motives? Does he pity the old man who will be sent to a hospice where nobody will care for him? Does he consider that non-active people have to be eliminated

[27] English translation in *Adam An afternoon and other stories* (London: Secker & Warburg, 1983), pp. 68ff.

in a city which has become a hell? Does he want to punish the generation which accepted Hitler and a total war? Rossellini is more attentive to facts than to intentions and his sober shooting is particularly effective in the scene of poisoning. In this sequence, the filmmaker differentiates between two spaces, the room where the father lies on his bed and the kitchen where Edmund is making his preparations. The father's chat unifies both spaces and gives the sequence a flavour of quiet domestic life; there is nothing thrilling in the scene since Edmund acts in perfect cold blood. The final shot is focused on Edmund who, having put the poison into the tea-pot, enters the room, fills the tea-pot with boiling water and, calmly, brings it to his father. When the father offers to give some tea to his eldest son, Edmund, as cool as if nothing were happening, says: 'No, Papa, I made it just for you', which makes the father remark: 'You have got a good heart'. There is something very chilling in the simplicity of a domestic routine which is also an execution.

Fear can be measured by the reaction it provokes and the reaction was often harsh in postwar films. Edmund was punished by the filmmaker, who made him commit suicide. There was nothing inevitable in this conclusion since, in the film, the situation is neither improving nor worsening after the murder, with people still wandering throughout the ruins and trying to get some food. Edmund, who has done what he found it necessary to do, should wait for better days so that his death is nothing but a sanction. The harshness of some filmmakers against their protagonists was amazing. David Macdonald's *Good-time girl* (1948) seems to have been shot only to chastise a young lady. The good time was the war years. Escaping from her family, Gwen, sharp, caustic, and independent beyond her age, takes advantage of the liberties allowed by the conflict. Indulging in theft and sexual licence, going around with crooks and bad soldiers, she is eventually involved in manslaughter and sent to jail.

Stylistically, Rossellini and Macdonald are miles apart. But their films are based on an identical scheme: when families, which are of vital importance, no longer look after them, children, deprived of guidelines, become outlaws. But the films, however suspicious of youth they are, are not one-sided. We have already noted that Edmund, like many other kids, is also a victim, exploited by adults. There is even more. One day, Edmund's father makes a long confession; he mentions all that has been lost under Hitler: 'I should have protested, but I was too weak, like so many of my generation. We saw disaster coming and we didn't stop it and now we are suffering the consequences. Today we are paying for our mistakes, all of us! But we have to recognize our guilt.'

The conflict of generations, as depicted in fiction, developed around a mutual distrust and a mutual hostility. Joseph von Baky's *Und über uns der Himmel* (*And above us the sky*, 1947) cleverly set the terms of the debate. A father and his young son return from the war and try to adapt to a devastated world. The son had lost his sight, but he is cured and a skilful scene shows him *seeing*, discovering what has become of his father, now a black-marketeer. It is the look of the son at his father which is unbearable. Once he has got over the shock, the son tries to argue with the father but theirs is a dialogue of the deaf, principles against hunger and vice versa. There is a dramatic paradox here: the son referred to a code taught by his father but that his father no longer admitted. Of course, the dilemma was much too simple, as is often the case in stories. But the film suggests that, behind the conflict of generations lay something else – something that we should now try to clarify.

The discovery of childhood

In this chapter, I have treated the films made in several countries as a unique genre. Cinema was then extremely popular. Unfortunately we lack the pieces of evidence necessary to answer four basic questions: how often did people go to the cinema, what did they see, what did they think, and how, if at all, did they communicate between themselves. The only thing we may take for granted is that, because of the disarray provoked by the war, film production was limited so that most of the pictures I have mentioned circulated throughout Europe and were seen by most cinema-goers. If we except the mobilization of boys, which was specific to the defeated countries, no significant differences can be noted in the themes and issues tackled by various national studios. It may be assumed that societies turned upside down by the war used the cinema at the same time to face the urgent problem of moral and material reconstruction, and to avoid it. The only puzzle is the silence of France, which contributed only one film to the debate. Frenchmen are used to ignoring their contemporary history; it took them three decades to dare to make films on Vichy and the German occupation and little has been shot on the Vietnam War, on the Algerian War, or on May 1968. However youth was not a highly controversial matter like, for instance, collaboration or resistance. Why was it ignored? The point is, I think, that despite her symbolical intervention on the allied side, France was not a nation in arms from 1940 to 1945. Therefore, Frenchmen did not experience the contradiction between the absurdity of the conflict and the necessity of fighting which made it so difficult for the other Europeans, defeated or victorious, to understand what they had gone through.

Being attended by all age groups and social classes, cinema was important during the postwar era because it was able to represent vividly and realistically what people had endured and we have seen that, until the late 1950s, cinema-goers were regularly offered war films. Since then, television has drastically changed the function of audiovisual media by introducing immediate, direct comments about events. In the 1940s and 1950s, only a department of state could afford a series like *Why we fight*; private companies were more anxious to entertain their public by producing fiction than to inform it. But many filmmakers were obsessed by what was before their very eyes. De Sica spent much time observing shoe-shine boys in the streets of Rome; Macdonald insisted that *Good-time girl* was 'based on a true story'; Radványi reproduced in *Valahol Európávan* scenes he had actually watched. Apart from De Sica and Rossellini the directors interested in the aftermath of war were second-rate artists whose names have long been forgotten. Since they were keen on giving a fair account and cared little about aesthetics, their works were illustrated discourses conveyed via contrived stories and interpreted by actors so that, in many instances, they lacked coherence. But what matters, and what makes these films worth studying, is that European audiences appreciated them.

A very powerful image was necessary to represent all the civilians involved in the hostilities, as opposed to warriors, and children were fit for that purpose since they belonged to the same period and would soon be what adults had become before them. Mourning over them was thus an indirect manner of mourning the whole society. The conviction that the Second World War had been an ordeal for youth was so generally accepted that the images offered by films like *Paisà* or *Sciuscia* were and are still likely to impress every viewer. Far from merely documenting a dramatic aspect of the conflict, films had a soothing function: the depiction of adolescent victims of war helped to expose painful or frightening emotional realities and made them less threatening.

Understanding why films tended to magnify the sufferings of the youngest is not difficult. But how is it that a cinema built around such a pitiful vision was also critical about the part played by children during and after the war? The answer is probably to be found in the fact that youth was a metaphor for the entire society. Adults, especially in the defeated countries, used children to deal with problems which, other-wise, would have been hushed up. By hiding behind their fighting boys, adults could debate the reasons which had led their respective countries to prolong the combat and, by indirectly accusing the young, they passed over their own responsibility.

Films contributed to camouflaging unbearable tensions; they substituted suffering for guilt and contributed, together with other media, to developing the legend of a generation conflict. This fable is one of the most worrying aspects of the postwar cinema. It could have been another subterfuge if we consider that the fear of children served to cover a lack of real care for youth during the hostilities. But, without being able to prove it, I believe that something more important happened at that time. Up to that date, children had no place in fiction; they were always seen through the eyes of adults, their fate was subordinated to the concerns of their parents. In the wake of the war, kids were introduced to the silver screen and, without having had any training, they did very well. Much has been said about the irruption of teenagers upon the market during the years of the economic boom. Did they come from nowhere? As images, surely not. The ambiguous, half-hypocritical mourning of the grown-ups installed the young in fiction and obliged adults to look at them. If attention to adolescence has come to define much of European societies today, it is, to a large extent, an aftermath of the Second World War.

6   From survivor to witness: voices from the Shoah

Annette Wieviorka

'Good people, do not forget, good people, tell the story, good people, write!'[1] declared the renowned historian Simon Dubnov to his companions before his death on 8 December 1941 in Riga, killed by a Lithuanian policeman during the liquidation of the ghetto. It was the last appeal of an old man. This story may be apocryphal. But Dubnov was not alone among those who, during the Holocaust, as well as throughout the fifty years following the destruction of the Jews of Europe, tried to tell the story because to do so was an act of duty, the duty to remember.

We thus have at our disposal today a mass of testimony – perhaps in volume greater than that related to any other historical event. No single scholar can master it all: books, newspapers, audio and video recordings, alongside evidence produced privately or for personal reasons. Some are part of legal proceedings; others are pedagogic in character, related to visits of survivors or their relatives to schools. There are large-scale inquiries, frequently originating in efforts to establish a data base or oral archive.

This kind of testimony stands at the intersection of the individual and society. It affirms that every individual, every single life, each experience of the Shoah was irreducible and unique.[2] But this affirmation is in the language of the time in which the evidence is registered, necessarily creating multiple voices in the chorus of witnesses of genocide.

Translated by Jay Winter.

[1] Cited by Pierre Vidal-Naquet in 'Simon Doubnov: l'homme mémoire', preface to Simon Doubnov, *Histoire moderne du peuple juif*, trans. by S. Jankelevitch (Paris: Cerf, 1994), p. v.

[2] [Eds.: We use the Hebrew term 'Shoah' and not the English term 'Holocaust', since 'Shoah', a Biblical term which originally meant a major calamity (natural or man-made), has no associations with ritual purification, the Greek meaning of 'Holocaust'. There was absolutely nothing about ritual or purification about the Nazi extermination of the Jews.]

Testimony about a vanished world

Everybody wrote ... journalists and writers, of course, but also teachers, social workers, young people, even children. Most wrote in journals in which the tragic events of this epoch are glimpsed through the prism of the experience of individual lives. There are so many of these writings, but the vast majority will be destroyed with the extermination of the Jews of Warsaw.[3]

Thus wrote the historian Emmanuel Ringelblum who was instrumental in setting up in the Warsaw ghetto an entire organization dedicated to the establishment of a systematic archive of every single document about the ghetto. This project was entitled 'Oneg Shabbat', the Hebrew phrase for the cultural pleasures of the day of rest. Ringelblum was absolutely convinced – with reason as it turned out – that it would be preserved. The source of his project was clear: the shared belief in the urgent necessity that someday the history of these times would be written. It was a belief shared by historians like Dubnov and Ring-elblum, and also Ignacy Schiper, killed at Majdanek. Schiper told Alexander Donat that:

everything depends on those who will transmit our testament to the generations to come, to those who will write the history of this epoch. History is written generally by the victors. All that we know of vanished races is what their killers have wanted to say about them. If our killers will win the war, if they will write its history, our annihilation will be presented as one of the most beautiful pages of world history, and future generations will render homage to the courage of these Crusaders. Every one of their words will have the significance of the Gospels. They could also decide to blot us out completely from the memory of the world, as if we had never existed, as if there had never been Polish Jewry, the Warsaw ghetto, and Majdanek ...

But, if we will be those who write the history of this period of tears and blood – and I am sure that we will do so – then who will believe us? No one will want to believe us, since the disaster is the disaster of the whole civilized world.

We will have the thankless task of proving to a world which will refuse to listen, that we are Abel, the murdered brother.[4]

To the official archives of the ghettos, and principally in Warsaw[5] and Lodz, other chronicles were added, such as that edited by Emmanuel Ringelblum in Warsaw,[6] or that of the Lodz ghetto, a collective news-

---

[3] Emmanuel Ringelblum, *Chronique du ghetto de Varsovie* (Paris: Robert Lafont, 1980), p. 21. For the English translation, see Ringelblum, *Notes from the Warsaw ghetto*, edited and translated by Jacob Sloan (New York: McGraw-Hill, 1958).

[4] A. Donat, *The Holocaust kingdom*, as cited by Rachel Ertel, *Dans la langue de personne. Poésie yiddish de l'antéantissement* (Paris: Seuil, 1993), p. 23.

[5] The archives of Oneg Shabbat were buried in three separate lots, each encased in a milk bucket.

[6] Ringelblum, *Chronique*.

paper, edited by a range of people of different ages, education, and origin.[7] Between ten and fifteen intellectuals worked openly in the department of the archives of the ghetto, while clandestinely building up the secret chronicle.

But personal diaries remain the most vivid documents of the need to preserve the traces of events which defy the imagination. These diaries are by no means uniform. Some are written in a lapidary style, in which events and facts are noted. Thus, Adam Czerniakow, head of the Jewish Council (Judenrat) in Warsaw, always carried little notebooks in which he jotted things down, with an occasional reflective comment or citation. Most – though not all – such documents are a bit like telegraphy, without literary embellishment. Czerniakow's notebooks were spirited out of the ghetto by his widow. They were published much later, only in the 1980s, in English and Hebrew.[8] In the immediate postwar period, only the 'heroes' were celebrated, and the Jewish Councils were definitely not heroic: they were stigmatized as collaborators. In this context, the publication of Czerniakow's notebooks drew very little notice.

Other diaries and notebooks were also published in English and French. There were the Warsaw ghetto diaries of Chaim Kaplan,[9] Abraham Lewin,[10] and Mary Berg.[11] Among thirty or so notebooks written in Auschwitz-Birkenau, three are extant: those of Leib Langfus, Zalman Lewental, and Zalman Gradowski.[12]

The publication of these works at diverse dates interested only a very small public. None was a best-seller. The exception was John Hersey's *The wall*, based in part on the archives of 'Oneg Shabbat', whose principal character was precisely the ghetto chronicler. Hersey's book was indeed widely read and discussed on both sides of the Atlantic.

The transformation of the story into literature facilitated its transmission. This was the view of a number of those writing during the

[7] This chronicle was a collection of texts – stories, news, and so on – published in the United States under the title *The chronicle of the Lodz Ghetto, 1941–1944*, ed. L. Dobrosyscki (New Haven: Yale University Press, 1984) and in *Lodz Ghetto. Inside a community under siege*, ed. A. Edelson and R. Lapides (New York: Penguin Books, 1989).

[8] *The Warsaw diary of Adam Czerniakow*, ed. R. Hilberg, S. Staron, and J. Kermisz (New York: Stein and Day, 1982).

[9] Chaim A. Kaplan, *Chronique d'une agonie. Journal du ghetto de Varsovie, découvert et presenté par Abraham I. Katsch avec une preface par Jean Bloch-Michel* (Paris: Calmann-Lévy, 1966).

[10] Abraham Lewin, *Journal du ghetto de Varsovie. Une coupe de larmes*, ed. Abraham Polonsky (Paris: Plon, 1990).

[11] Mary Berg, *La Ghetto de Varsovie*, ed. S. L. Schneiderman (Paris: Albin Michel, 1947).

[12] These texts are in Bernard Mark, *Des voix dans la nuit: la résistance juive à Auschwitz-Birkenau*; preface by Elie Wiesel; trans. from Yiddish by Esther and Joseph Friedmann and by Liliane Princet (Paris: Plon, c. 1982).

catastrophe. Abraham Cytryn was one of them. He was born in 1927 and grew up in the Lodz ghetto. He wanted to write down facets of the life of the ghetto through news, short stories, poems.[13] Simha Guterman wanted to write a book, and not just personal testimony. It was discovered by accident in 1978 by two Polish masons in Lodz in a bottle hidden under the stairs of a house. It is an account written in January to March 1942 about the city of Plock from the outbreak of the war in 1939 until the liquidation of the ghetto in March 1941. The narrative is 'a text, constructed, divided into chapters, organized around key people and scenes. A book for the living, the ultimate act of resistance in the face of forgetting and death. He wrote so that one day, perhaps, in a world he would never see, others would discover his suffering and that of his people.'[14]

Am I a murderer? by Carel Perechodnik, is in the same category.[15] After the liquidation of the ghetto of Otwock, Perechodnik was hidden in the 'Aryan' quarter of Warsaw. There he wrote a book – a 'second child' – dedicated to the memory of his two-year-old daughter, whom he himself had brought to the *Umschlagplatz*, the point of deportation, in his role as a member of the Jewish police of the ghetto. This is what he said: 'Since our daughter is not longer alive, I shall care for this second child whom I will protect until that day when no force can kill her ... I sense immortality in me; since I have created an immortal work, I have been immortalized.' Here the mission is clear. It is a protest against death and a desire to leave a trace that life had once existed here. But this is the only confession we have of a Jewish policeman, full of violence, cynicism, cruelty, psychological insights, all born out of the author's certainty that he would not survive.

Many bore witness precisely because so many more could never do so. Primo Levi observed that we have no evidence of those inmates who were functionaries in the camps.[16] Nathan Beyrak, who directed one of the attempts to interview concentration camp inmates who had survived and were in Israel, remarked, 'we haven't managed to interview people who belonged to the Jewish police, or those who were not particularly nice'.[17]

[13] Abraham Cytryn, *Récits du ghetto de Lodz* (Paris: Albin Michel, 1995).
[14] Nicole Lapierre, in Simha Guterman, *Le livre retrouvé* (Paris: Plon, 1991), p. 19.
[15] Carel Perechodnik, *Suis-je un meurtrier?* (Paris: Liana Levi, 1995). Published in English translation as, *Am I a murderer?: testament of a Jewish ghetto policeman*, edited and translated by Frank Fox (Boulder, Colo.: Westview Press, c. 1996).
[16] Primo Levi, *Les naufragés et les rescapés. Quarante ans après Auschwitz* (Paris: Gallimard, 1989), p. 18.
[17] Nathan Beyrak, 'To rescue the individual out of the mass number: intimacy as a central concept in oral history', in Maurice Cling and Yannis Thanassekos (eds.), *Ces visages qui nous parlent* (Brussels: Fondation Auschwitz et Fondation pour la Mémoire de la Déportation, 1995), p. 141.

It is apparent that the first accounts, those of the period of the ghettos, the extermination, were the accounts of people who did not survive. They shared the same wish: that the people whom the Nazis wanted to remove from the face of the earth would not be removed from history.

The aftermath

Accounts of the Shoah continued to appear well after the defeat of the Nazis. Two forms predominated. The first was in Yiddish poetry, 'a kind of account of the human voice uttering what is irreducibly human', writes Rachel Ertel.[18] But also, there was the appearance of edited memorial volumes, 'Yizkor books',[19] discussed in the Israeli context by Emmanuel Sivan in chapter 9.

From the moment of Germany's defeat, historical committees tried to retrieve the accounts of survivors and to establish a chronology of the massacre. The editors quickly moved back to the history of life before genocide. And inevitably so, since the term 'genocide' entailed not primarily an astronomical number of victims, but the destruction of an entire world. It wasn't solely the professional chronicler – rabbi or erudite Talmudic scholar – who started to write. Everybody did. 'Everyone wrote', noted Ringelblum with respect to the Warsaw ghetto. And after the liberation, all the survivors wrote. Their having lived in Jewish communities, their having escaped from the genocide was enough to legitimate their evidence, both oral and written. These accounts were gathered together in works designated 'Yizkor books', thereby locating them at the intersection of two traditions: that of the martyrology of communities – *Memorbuch* – and that of Jewish historiography of the post-1918 period.

The term used for genocide in these books is the *dritter hurban*, the third destruction, 2,000 years after the second destruction of the Temple. This third catastrophe had created a new situation – the destruction not only of a community, but also the annihilation of a collective, a culture, a way of life, what they termed *Yiddishkeit*. All the tools of recovery had been smashed: a language, a history, a physical space, a network of sociability, indeed, all the forms of what Halbwachs termed the social framework of memory. These books of collective

---

[18] Ertel, *Dans la langue de personne*, p. 28.
[19] On 'Yizkor books', see Annette Wieviorka and Itzhok Noborski, *Les livres de souvenir. Mémoriaux juifs en Pologne* (Paris: Archives-Gallimard, 1983); Jack Kugelmass and Jonathan Boyarin (eds.), *From a ruined garden. The memorial books of Polish Jewry* (New York: Schocken Books, 1983).

memory had as their aim the resurrection of a vanished universe. They traced by tales and photographs the outline of what had been lost, and thereby did the work of collective mourning for a catastrophic loss.

These works directly engage in the construction of collective memory. This is what gives over 400 such books their homogeneity. They, the surviving collective, sketched the lived experience, sometimes turned into myth, of a vanished collective. They reached out to a reservoir of knowledge, gestures, habits, forms of organization, which have meaning only because the older generations, passed away in their time, had transmitted their culture, their *patrimoine*, to new generations.

To be sure, the survivors had their own private cultural lives, in which Yiddish played a central part. But there was so much that had been lost of their collective culture that the notion of transmission of their codes of behaviour and modes of life to a new generation became very problematic. It is in this sense that these authors tried to save the dead from oblivion. Memorial books, with their portraits and litany of names, retrieved the dead from oblivion. Their authors and editors created a Covenant not with God, but between the living and the dead. Through these artefacts of remembrance, the recovery of the vanished face of individuality led to the retrieval of the collective and its culture.

These Yizkor books faded from the memory even of the descendants of their authors. Part of their aim of generational transmission, therefore, has not been realized. The grandchildren of the victims grew up largely blind to their grandparents' fate. Jews without a heritage, 'imaginary Jews' in Alain Finkelkraut's phrase,[20] they sensed that the cultural transmission of generations had been reduced to the ashes of the crematoria. The links between generations had been broken, either through the death of the grandparents, or through their mute survival. The grandparents spoke French poorly; the grandchildren were ignorant of Yiddish. In these Yizkor books, that indissoluble bond between those born before and after genocide was reaffirmed. But nonetheless something had been destroyed, which precluded the revival of a collective identity. Amnesia was a reality for those who stumbled on the edge of the void created by genocide. It was for this reason that Yizkor books remained unvisited cemeteries.

Yizkor books highlight vividly the problem of the language of testimony. This was a problem the poet Avram Sutzkever wrestled with *en*

---

[20] Alan Finkelkraut, *Le Juif imaginaire* (Paris: Le Seuil, 1983). See also Henri Raczymow, 'Fin du peuple ashkénaz', in Jean Baumgarter, Rachel Ertel, Itzhak Niborski, and Annette Wieviorka (eds.), *Mille ans de cultures ashkénaz* (Paris: Lian Levi, 1994), and Nicole Lapierre, *La silence de la mémoire. A la recherche des Juifs de Plock* (Paris: Plon, 1989).

route to testifying at the Nuremberg trials.[21] He was the sole survivor of the Shoah to testify at the trials. His testimony was in Russian. The issue here is not primarily one of the linguistic skill of the witness. It is more a question of his point of view: where does he come from? Of what precisely does he speak? Is he there to tell of the world of the concentration camps? Or of the death of a people? Xavier Léon-Dufour, in a study of the uses of the word 'witness' in the New Testament, observes that 'the true witness is the witness of blood'; as in Revelation, it is testimony after which blood is spilled. 'The witness is forever tied to the destiny of that which he witnesses.'[22]

In this context, consider the remark of Rachel Ertel about Yiddish. It is, she argues,

the only language which shared the fate of its speakers. Even if it survives in pockets here and there, it died in Auschwitz, in Majdanek, in Treblinka and in Sobibor with the people who spoke it. Yiddish writers and poets are the only ones who speak at one and the same time of the death of their people and the death of their language. They write in an unhearing world, fully aware of being without connection, of writing in a language of no one. The death of a language is irreversible. If the literature of the Shoah is like none other, as Elie Wiesel said, it is not because it is more authentic than any other, but because it speaks of a double disappearance.[23]

It was in this spirit that Elie Wiesel wrote his first book, ten years after his liberation from Buchenwald. *And the world was silent*, published in French, later became, in a very different form, *Night*. For this man, one of the pioneers of the literature of witness, Yiddish remains the only language through which one must speak of the Shoah:

We need to emphasize the fact that in no other language can we evoke it. The literature of annihilation without Yiddish is a literature without a soul. I know that much is written in other languages, but they are not comparable. The most authentic testimonies of the Shoah, in prose and in poetry, are in Yiddish. Is it because most of those killed spoke that language and lived their lives through it?

As for me, I know only one thing: if I had not written my first book in Yiddish, if my memories were not in Yiddish, my other books would have foundered in muteness.[24]

Wiesel's book had a cathartic function. As Ertel noted, 'it gave him a voice, for he had to escape not only from physical extermination but also

21 See his memoir *Où gîtent les étoiles* (Paris: Seuil, 1988), and his article 'Le ghetto de Vilna', in Ilya Ehrenburg and Vassili Grossman (eds.), *Le livre noir* (Paris: Actes-Sud, 1995), pp. 499–590.
22 Xavier Léon-Dufour, *Dictionnaire du Nouveau Testament* (Paris: Seuil, 1996).
23 Rachel Ertel, 'Ecrit en yiddish', in Michael de Saint-Chéron (ed.), *Autour de Elie Wiesel* (Paris: Odile Jacob, 1996), pp. 21–41.
24 Elie Wiesel, 'Rand Makhhovès vegn Yiddish', in *Di Goldene Keyt*, 98 (1987), p. 26, as cited in Ertel, 'Ecrit en yiddish', p. 23.

from the death of his language'.[25] His ability to write in French of this world of which he was one of the few survivors probably explains his role as a leader of the effort to retrieve the collective memory of the world he lost. All his points of reference are imbedded in the Yiddish world that was destroyed. He has translated them into another language, and thereby has reached his readers.

No one can deny that there is a memory of the Shoah transmitted to us by the survivors of that Yiddish world. But this collective memory is, as it were, sealed-off, unable to invigorate society at large. Some of the survivors felt that their memory was one their neighbours and colleagues were neither able nor willing to share. The historian Jacob Shatzky was born in Warsaw in 1893, and fought in Pilsudski's Polish Legion in the First World War. He was a Polish delegate to the Paris Peace Conference in 1919. In 1922 he submitted his thesis on 'The Jewish question in the Kingdom of Poland during the period of Paskiewicz (1831–1861)'. In 1925 he left Poland for New York, where he founded the American branch of YIVO, the Jewish Scientific Institute. Later this organization would receive the bulk of the archives and library of the original YIVO, located in Vilna. Between 1947 and 1953, Shatzky published three volumes of his history of the Jews of Warsaw, bringing the story up to 1897. This was a monumental achievement, but one Shatzky could not complete. Why? Because of his despair over the decline of the secular Jewish culture rooted in the Yiddish language. In 1947, he wrote to his wife while on a lecture tour of Brazil: 'The Jews are far from Yiddish culture, or culture of any kind. They are for Palestine or for the Soviets. The dream of a Yiddish culture in the United States has vanished, and I see all too clearly how futile my life has become.' This blocked his research, as he noted at the 29th annual YIVO conference in 1955:

What meaning does research have on the subject of the ancient communities of Europe? Detailed study of political and economic themes has lost all relevance. There is no part of that heritage which can be transmitted there to Jews living today. Only intellectual history remains, the study of Jewish culture in the broadest sense of the term.

But above all, the completion of his third volume of the history of the Jews of Warsaw had broken him: 'Why am I working like a slave? Why do I work and on what do I write? My people are dead. My subject is a dead subject, and I am tired to death.' After suffering depression in 1954–5 Shatzky died of a heart attack the following year, without having completed his fourth volume.[26]

[25] Ertel, 'Ecrit en yiddish', p. 27.
[26] Robert Moses Shapiro, 'Jacob Shatzky, historian of Warsaw Jewry', *Polin*, 3 (1988), pp. 200–13.

Shatzky's reflections touch on two problems. The first is the difficulty of writing about a vanished world. Certainly the Jews of Poland were gone, but along with them went a social framework in which their lives were inscribed. After the Warsaw ghetto uprising, the whole area had been demolished. Both the Jews of Warsaw and Jewish Warsaw were gone. The same was true, to different degrees, throughout Central and Eastern Europe. How then was it possible for an historian to establish a link between that world and his own? 'In this world, there are no more Jews. This people no longer exists. It will never be again', wrote Marek Edelman, the sole survivor of the leadership of the Warsaw ghetto uprising, of the victims of the Shoah.[27]

In the immediate postwar decade, the survivors did not emerge as a collective. This was true wherever they landed. Their associations were simply foci for sociability and mutual aid. Any efforts to engage in collective remembrance in public were fruitless. Plans to erect a memorial in New York got nowhere in the 1940s and 1950s.[28] The exception was in Paris, where in 1956 the tomb of the unknown Jewish martyr was dedicated, at about the same time as the Knesset set up Yad Vashem, the Holocaust memorial in Jerusalem.[29] The Paris monument remained the only one of its kind for some time.

Consequently, individual memory inscribed in a closed ethnic group, and constructed in terms of family stories, took the place of collective remembrance. Such individual efforts of retrieval went against the grain of the time; they had hardly any political echoes. It was only when political conditions changed in the 1960s and 1970s that the collective remembrance of the *Hurban* could become not a private matter but a social phenomenon of great significance.

The emergence of the witness

The Eichmann trial was a critical moment in the emergence of the collective memory of the Shoah in France, in the United States, as well as in Israel. With the Eichmann trial we enter a new period, one in which the memory of genocide became a fundamental part of Jewish identity, and in which that identity demanded public recognition.

This was the intention of those running the trial. Little was left to chance. For Israel, there were both domestic and international consid-

---

[27] As cited in J. M. Rymkiewicz, *Umschlagplatz. La dernière gare* (Paris: Laffont, 1990).

[28] Rochelle G. Saidel, *Never too late to remember. The politics behind New York City's Holocaust Museum* (New York: Holmes & Maier, 1996).

[29] Annette Wieviorka, 'Un lieu de mémoire et d'histoire: Le Mémorial du martyr juif inconnu', in Foulek Ringelheim (ed.), *Les Juifs entre la mémoire et l'oubli* (Brussels: Complexe, 1987), pp. 107–32.

erations behind the decision to seize Eichmann and bring him to trial. The world had to be reminded of the Nazis' objective and of the silence or indifference of the world when they tried to realize it. The world had to be made to feel shame. Support for the Jewish state had to follow from this fact. But in addition, it was necessary to educate a young generation, to give them a history lesson. Here we see for the first time the combination of teaching and transmission, a combination that has dominated forms of collective remembrance ever since. It is present in educational programmes, in the erection of museums and memorials destined for the young, in the construction of film and sound archives out of which multimedia tools have been made.

It all started in the Eichmann trial. For the prosecutor, Gideon Hausner, a trial is not only a forum for dispensing justice: 'every trial contains the possibility of a return to order, of a hope of an example being set. It tells a story, draws a moral.' To tell this story, to draw out its implications, Hausner decided to construct the trial on eye-witness testimony. It was his decision to do so, and not that of the survivors to be heard. Sufficient time had passed after the events of the Shoah to give the survivors a forum. And now there were other supports for their testimony: radio and television made possible the diffusion of words and images without the need for the written page.

For Gideon Hausner, the foil, the alternative to be avoided, was the Nuremberg trials. There the American prosecutor, Justice Robert Jackson, conducted his case on the basis of documents, supported by a minimum of testimony. Certainly Hausner saw the force of documentary evidence: the case against Eichmann was buttressed by a formidable dossier of documents. 'Written proof is irreplaceable', noted Hausner. 'Its eloquence is there, in black and white. It was no longer necessary to rely on the memory of a witness who had aged a decade since these events. The defense lawyers can't unsettle a document as they can a witness. The document speaks quietly: it doesn't explode, but it refuses to go away.' It is true that the Nuremberg trial was conducted efficiently, but 'it didn't touch the heart of men'. After all, the point was not just to get a guilty verdict. There was enough documentary evidence 'to convict Eichmann ten times over'. There had to be more than a verdict, there must be the public expression, the 'telling in letters of fire of a national disaster, a human disaster without proportions'. Only through living voices could this be done. This is why Hausner decided to rest his case on 'two pillars and not on one alone: on documentary proof and on the depositions of witnesses'.[30]

---

[30] Gideon Hausner, *Justice in Jerusalem* (New York: Holocaust Library, 1968), p. 382. All references are to the French edition.

For Hausner, as much as for those collecting video testimony in later years,

the only way to touch the truth is to call as many survivors as possible to the bar and to ask of each a small fragment of what they had lived. The narrative of a certain chain of events presented by one sole witness is insufficiently tangible to be visualized. But, taken together, successive depositions of very different people who lived through very different experiences created an image sufficiently eloquent to be registered. In this manner I hoped to give to the phantom of the past an additional dimension, that of the real.[31]

This is why Hausner sought out new witnesses, who would enable him to establish diverse facets of the process of extermination. 'Above all, I wanted people to tell what they had seen with their own eyes and lived in their own flesh.'

Gideon Hausner tells how he worked with Michel Goldman, a police investigator and a survivor, to choose those who would testify. They read through hundreds of recordings made of survivors' testimony for the Yad Vashem oral archive, under the direction of one of the leaders of the Warsaw ghetto uprising, Rachel Auerbach. It is not the case that those who spoke at the Eichmann trial did so for the first time. They were chosen in the light of their already recorded or written testimony. Then Hausner went over the ground with these witnesses, and chose those he wanted to appear at a trial with huge media coverage. It was a casting operation for a media event.

Not surprisingly, many were reticent about appearing and speaking. 'This hesitation to testify', Hausner noted,

was due in part to a deliberate effort to forget events which, whatever they did, followed them in their dreams. They did not want to relive them. But there was another, still stronger, reason: they were afraid that no one would believe them. The day the survivors emerged from the forests, the camps, the hideouts, they experienced a need to tell their story. But when they started to speak of things so unheard of, so much beyond comprehension, the person to whom they spoke had a moment of doubt and astonishment. Often, this sense of estrangement existed only in the imagination of the speaker; but for many of these people, still injured and sensitive to the slightest nuance, that was enough to send them into a protective silence. They buried in their hearts everything they knew, and decided never to speak of it.

Such a reticence to bear witness was not universal. A large number of volunteers came to offer their stories. In effect, Hausner's choice was sociological: 'I wanted', he wrote in his memoirs,

to make known what happened in all corners of the Nazi occupation and I wanted that that [sic] story be told by a range of people – professors, housewives, artisans, writers, farmers, businessmen, doctors, civil servants, labourers. That

[31] Ibid. p. 384.

was the source of the diversity of testimony. They came from every social group, demonstrating that the catastrophe had fallen on the entire nation.[32]

How was it possible to avoid errors in the evidence 'of people who were asked to tell of facts twenty years old'? To handle this problem, Hausner chose 'to call people who had put their recollections in writing in Yad Vashem or who had collected their own memoirs, published or not, since their memories would be more easily refreshed from their notes'. In truth, this was not the case. The story told became the memory itself. As Primo Levi has noted: 'after 40 years or so, I tell all that through what I have written: my writings play for me the role of artificial memory'.[33]

Among those who gave evidence was Leon Wieliczker-Wells. He came from the United States, where he had lived since 1949 as a distinguished scientist. Wells had been among the detachment whose job was to open the mass graves, to sort out the bodies, to put them in pyres, to burn them, to grind down the bones, and to extract anything of value in the remains. This was not the first time he had testified. He had appeared at the Polish war crimes trials in Lodz in 1946.[34]

For the historian, the value of the written text is incomparable. But the physical presence of this witness, 'the strangest man whom I had ever seen in my life', according to the Israeli poet Haïm Gouri, who covered the trial as a journalist was more striking. Wells's comportment, the tone of his voice, added to his factual testimony. He spoke in a heavily accented English, Gouri recalled. It was a language without adjectives, 'as if he really was somewhere else and the man who spoke at that moment was but the spokesman of the man belonging to death commando 1005'.[35]

George Wellers testified too – as he had done in his memoirs written upon his return from Auschwitz – about the arrival at the transit camp at Drancy of the Jewish children deported after the round-up in Paris of 16 and 17 July 1942. These children had been held in the 'Vélodrôme d'hiver', a hall for sporting events, then moved to camps at Loiret, Pithiviers, and Beaune-la-Rolande. They were separated from their mothers before being sent to Drancy for further deportation. There again, though the words were the same, the juridical framework, radio, television amplified the evidence, and gave to it a much more powerful resonance than that of a book of modest circulation.

---

[32] Ibid. p. 389.
[33] Primo Levi, *Le devoir de mémoire. Entretien avec Anna Bravo et Federico Cereja* (Paris: Mille et une nuits, 1995), p. 22.
[34] See Leon W. Wells, *Pour que la terre se souvienne* (Paris: Albin Michel, 1962), and in English L. W. Wells, *The death brigade. The Janowska road* (New York: Holocaust Library, *c.* 1978).
[35] Haïm Gouri, *La cage de verre* (Paris: Albin Michel, 1964), p. 50.

The final example is one repeatedly used in television accounts of the Eichmann trial. It is the testimony of KaTzetnik, whose real name was Yehiel Dinour. He too wrote memoirs immediately after the war. They were published in Yiddish, and then became a best-seller in the United States under the title *The girl's house*. After appearing briefly at the trial, the witness fainted and later withdrew from public life. His absence is a part of the film record of the trial shown time and again in later years.

The Eichmann trial marked the emergence of the existential witness, the man of memory who embodies the past and demonstrates that it is present still. These people helped turn the genocide into a succession of individual experiences with which people today could identify. We have moved beyond the time of Nuremberg, with its exposure of the tyrants, their supporters, the criminals beyond the law and their plans for war, to another period, when the searchlight is fixed on the victims. If Nuremberg was about writing the history of this terrible period – albeit an imperfect history – then after the Eichmann trial, the task was different: to constitute a collective memory. The diverse functions of the witness needed in the Eichmann trial changed thereafter. They became witnesses in another sense, not discussed during the trial itself.

The era of the witness

At the end of the 1970s, there began a massive effort to collect individual testimony in audiovisual form. One source of this interest was entirely banal: the stage-managed and commercial exposure first on radio and then on television of people speaking of their psychological and personal problems. By the 1990s programmes appeared in Europe as well where individuals spoke about their anguish to strangers in a television audience. This insertion of private meditations in public space marks the emergence of what the sociologist Dominique Mehl called the 'television of intimacy'.

At the end of the 1970s, after the broadcast of the dramatized television series *Holocaust*, there began the systematic taping of the memories of all American 'survivors'. Now the term had a normative as well as a descriptive sense. The first centre for these records was at Yale University. By 1995 the Fortunoff Video Archive for Holocaust Testimonies had 3,600 such individual tapes, incorporating nearly 10,000 hours of interviews conducted in America, Greece, Bolivia, Slovakia, France, Germany, Israel, Argentina, Serbia, Poland, Byelorussia, and the Ukraine.

Other initiatives followed. Museums, memorials, and commemorative associations have begun similar work. The most ambitious is Steven

Spielberg's Visual History of the Shoah Foundation. In 1995 alone this foundation collected 20,000 testimonies; 50,000 interviews, covering hundreds of thousands of hours of evidence, will be collected by the year 2000. These voices will be available to anyone with a computer, and especially to young people whose interest can be focused by an index of subjects and themes. Multimedia linkages will make it possible to add much more information to each testimony. How far we are from the clandestine writings in the ghettos themselves, written in a vanishing language, frequently hidden underground, and the survival of which was a matter of chance. Now that the process of transmission has been revolutionized by computers, what image of the Shoah will be formed by the young? Today it is difficult to say.

In place of the needs of war crimes trials and the demands of the prosecutor, today we have the social imperatives of collective memory. The survivors must still perform an act of remembrance. They are still summoned to tell the story, to preserve for history their evidence for the generations to come after their deaths. 'To be deported and a witness' is the way it was put in a colloquium addressed by Anne-Lise Stern, survivor of Auschwitz-Birkenau and psychoanalyst.

The nature of testimony itself has changed. There is no longer an internal logic which impels the survivor of the deportations to tell her story in front of a camera. Now what matters is a social imperative. The collapse of Communism made it much easier for survivors and others to visit the sites of extermination and imprisonment. The young come to Auschwitz and other sites more and more in the presence of those who had been deported to them. Now recognition of what happened can occur in the presence of the 'real', the real location of the crematoria, the real person who had been deported. Now the witness is less the bearer of knowledge about the destruction of the Jews, than a man or woman who embodies an experience. Here the witness resembles the model of the early Apostles who brought the word of the Gospels to the people. And the young who hear the story from the survivors, they themselves will become 'witnesses', apostles of a story they too can spread after the first 'witnesses' have vanished from the earth.

What impels these arduous efforts to collect video testimonies by the tens of thousands? On the one hand, there is a professional question of preserving a record of contemporary history on a theme of universal importance. This is part of the impulse behind the creation of the Holocaust Museum in Washington. On the other hand, there is the desire to draw the individual survivor out of the mass, to give to simple people the platform, to preserve the words of those unwilling or unable to write down their story. At this point we hear echoes of the effort of those who created the Yizkor books. We also hear the voice of those like the Israeli author and concentration camp survivor Aron Applefeld, who has noted, 'Literature says: "let's give him a place; put a cup of coffee in his hand" ... The strength of literature lies in its ability to convey intimacy ... the kind of intimacy that touches your own.'[36] Nathan Beyrak, director of the Israeli branch of the Fortunoff Archives concurs: the concept of intimacy is the central theme of the work in which he and thousands of others are engaged.[37]

Two facets of this effort are worth noting. The first is a constant in Jewish remembrance of the Shoah: the need to give a name, a face, a story to each of the victims of mass murder. This was the impulse behind earlier memorial books, as well as Serge Klarsfeld's 1978 publication *Le Mémorial des Juifs en France*, in which are inscribed the names and details of Jewish men, women, and children deported during the war. Here we are dealing with the dead; but the second facet of Holocaust testimonies in recent years concerns the living. In video archives, the survivors appear, though frequently in quest of their loved ones who perished in the war. As Nathan Beyrak put it:

I have no details of the murder of my relatives, my grandmother and her mother, sons and daughters – my mother's two brothers and sister – which probably took place in the death pits near Slonim. I always felt compelled to know, to learn the most intimate details of what they experienced, moment by moment. I think the nearest I go to satisfying this curiosity was when I taped the testimony of a man who was taken to the very same death pits, possibly together with my family, and described the experience in great detail. Unlike my relatives, he fell into the pits without being hit by a bullet, and later managed to climb out.[38]

This notion of intimacy is at the heart of the movement to collect testimony and is evident too in the appearance of survivors in television interviews. Dominique Mehl notes that this phenomenon arises out of 'the crisis of expertise and the questioning of the pedagogic credentials of scholars and specialists'. When an instructor brings a survivor or a filmed interview of a survivor to a class, it is an admission of the teacher's incapacity to bring to his students a narrative of genocide. Instead of a written or spoken narrative, he prefers to present a discourse based on the emotions and the voice of witnesses. The technique of filming is the same as in television broadcasts and in video archives of deportees: 'The film director lies in wait for postures which reveal emotion. A look, a gesture, hand movements are signals to the techni-

---

[36] Aron Appelfeld, *Beyond despair: three lectures and a conversation with Philip Roth*, trans. Jeffrey M. Green (New York: Fromm International, c. 1994).
[37] Beyrak, 'To rescue the individual'.
[38] Ibid.

cian. In intimate broadcasting, the eye of the camera searches for the eye of the witness.'[39]

The act of testifying before the camera, and of then being able to show the cassette to his grandchildren, assumes great importance to the survivor. 'For many of us', noted Primo Levi, 'to be interviewed was a unique and memorable occasion, the event for which one had waited since liberation, and which even gave meaning to our liberation.'[40] To speak of what had been his life during the Shoah validated an experience which, to many survivors, soon after the liberation appeared so unreal that they feared no one would believe their account of what indeed had happened.

The more that experience is brought into the public space through trials, through the appearance of survivors in schools, or still more on television, the greater the chances that survivors would 'complete the formation of a social identity' which requires notice, that is to say, the sanction of society itself. At this point a mode of being – that of the survivor – requires socialization in order to become a constituent part of the personality of the survivor and a sign of his individuality. The alternative, Mehl argues, is that the experience becomes 'a sign of stigma or oddity. Recognition [in a literal sense] by society legitimates one's right to take on and to claim a specific identity, because visibility is a prerequisite for the location of a personality in the world.'

This assertion of identity through testimony is problematic when the historical narrative fragments into a series of individual stories. Here we confront, in the words of Richard Sennett, 'an ideology of intimacy: social relations take on reality and credibility only when located in individual psychology, thereby transforming all political categories into psychological ones'.[41] In effect, the witness speaks from the heart and not from reason. He invites compassion, pity, indignation, even revolt. The witness and his hearer form a 'compassionate pact', similar to the 'autobiographical pact' between the author of an autobiography and his readers.[42]

Thus, Nazism and the Shoah are only present because they devastated the lives of individuals, individuals who have triumphed over death. The witnesses are there to testify, and they speak of the future by invoking their children and more often their grandchildren. Yet the witness never highlights this issue when, in his retirement, he makes the rounds of schools in the United States or in France to offer his testimony. The

[39] Dominique Mehl, *La télévision de l'intimité* (Paris: Seuil, 1996), pp. 11–12, 13, 28.
[40] Levi, *Le devoir de mémoire*, p. 75.
[41] As cited in Mehl, *La télévision*, p. 154.
[42] Philippe Lejeune, *La pacte autobiographique* (Paris: Seuil, 1975).

witness always gives to his story a finality, a significance which goes beyond it.

That significance changes over time. In the immediate postwar period, as we have noted above, it was to prevent the rebirth of a Germany 'intrinsically Nazi'. Today it is to fight against the negation of the Shoah and against the resurgence of 'Fascism'. At times the struggle against other 'genocides' is evoked. In other ways the story becomes stereotyped, brought into line with conventional political messages superimposed on the testimony.

Anyone offering testimony tries to construct, perhaps to reconstruct, it freely and with a meaning she herself assigns to it. But those who are in the business of retrieving, storing, and preserving in large collections such testimonies would do well to reflect on some of the possible flawed uses of this vast array of testimonies offered by the survivors of the Shoah. Among such problematic uses are the conversion of the political into the solely psychological, and the isolation of individual voices, the partitioning into one-person units of the collective memory of the survivors, whose testimony, one at a time, or taken as a whole, is said to constitute the 'true' history of the catastrophe.

7   Landscapes of loss and remembrance: the case of Little Tokyo in Los Angeles

Dolores Hayden

> How many people are buried here?
>> Question from reporter at site of camp cemetery,
>> Manzanar, California, 1973

> A whole generation. A whole generation of Japanese who are now so frightened they will not talk.   Reply by former camp inmate[1]

War disrupts and reconfigures attachments to cultural landscapes on an unprecedented scale. The process of mourning for the losses of war often involves memories of treasured places, and human connections within those places. Mourning also involves memories of hated or feared places such as the front line or the concentration camp. This essay explores the ways in which cultural landscape history can be used to frame the connections between places, memories, and public history. It looks at the possibilities of individual and community-based spatial histories for processes of collective remembrance. It focuses in particular on how spatial histories have been used in Little Tokyo in Los Angeles, first, by former inmates of War Relocation Authority (WRA) camps as part of an exhibit at the Japanese American National Museum, and second, in historic preservation and public art for the First Street Historic District (of which the museum is part).

The production of space

Every society in history has produced a distinctive social space that meets its intertwined requirements for economic production and social reproduction. Space is a material product of the political economy. As Henri Lefebvre has written, 'Space is permeated with social relations; it is not only supported by social relations but it is also producing and produced by social relations.'[2]

---

[1] Arthur A. Hansen, 'Oral history and the Japanese American evacuation', *Journal of American History*, 82 (Sept. 1995), p. 628.

[2] Henri Lefebvre, *The production of space*, trans. Donald Nicholson-Smith (Oxford, and Cambridge, Mass.: Basil Blackwell, 1991), p. 286.

The social activities of inhabiting, naming, occupying, and appropriating make spaces into places. People make connections to places that are critical to their well-being or distress, and 'place attachment' has been described as a psychological bonding process analogous to an infant's attachment to parental figures.[3] Place attachment includes biological, social, material, and ideological dimensions, as individuals develop ties to kin and community, own or rent land, and participate in public life as residents of a particular community. How might the production of space and the process of place attachment be affected by war?

In wartime, the production of space often proceeds at an extremely rapid pace. War requires that societies gear up for armed offence and defence; arrange to feed and house bureaucrats, war workers, and combatants; intern prisoners; bury the dead, organize displaced civilians; and manage occupied territories. All of these activities involve rapid spatial change. Territorial constraints already existing in society may be intensified or lessened by the requirements of production and reproduction in the new spatial circumstances of war. Occupational and residential segregation may be tightened, or loosened, depending on the need for a wartime labour force and its location.[4] Intersecting patterns of segregation by race, ethnicity, class, age, and gender, are sometimes transformed in the crisis.

As the production of built space increases in intensity and scale during wartime, conflicts over territory are constant. Wartime changes the process of social reproduction rapidly, and introduces new barriers and incentives in the use of all kinds of space, from private to public. The space of social reproduction ranges over different scales, including the space in and around the body (biological reproduction), the space of housing (the reproduction of the labour force), and the public space of the city and the nation (the reproduction of social relations). To look at just one example, changes in housing and the reproduction of the labour force might include the establishment of concentration camps and the related destruction of residential neighbourhoods. A spatial history of this process would involve many aspects of the upheaval, from the first plans for forced relocation, to the development of camps, to the physical circumstances of exile, and, perhaps, of return.

---

[3] Irwin Altman and Setha M. Low (eds.), *Place attachment* (New York: Plenum Publishing, 1992); Peter Marris, *Loss and change*, rev. edn (London: Routledge and Kegan Paul, 1986).

[4] Margaret Crawford, 'Daily life on the home front: women, blacks, and the struggle for public housing', in Donald Albrecht (ed.), *World War II and the American Dream: how wartime building changed a nation* (Cambridge, Mass.: MIT Press, 1995), pp. 90–143.

Place and memory

Paradoxically, in times of anxiety and fluctuation, place-bound identities often become more rather than less important – homeland, neighbourhood, and hearth seem more precious when groups are forced to leave them behind. Memory also becomes more important when losses accumulate. The inability to forget traumatic experiences may become as much of a problem as wanting to remember positive ones. For the victims, experiences of being caged in concentration camps might be juxtaposed with memories of houses, gardens, businesses, and neighbourhoods now lost, amplifying the pain.

Because place attachment encapsulates the human ability to connect with the cultural landscape, and people perceive places with all five senses, the encoding of long-term memory connected to places is particularly strong.[5] Many different societies have used historic places to help citizens define their public pasts. Places trigger memories for insiders, who have shared a common past, and at the same time places often can represent shared pasts to outsiders who might be interested in knowing about them in the present. Places also permit people who have lived in them to re-experience their pasts while simultaneously experiencing the place in the present. They may stimulate individual memory while mirroring current circumstances.

Commemorations of war sponsored by the state or by wealthy patrons often attempt to solidify place memory through architectural designs such as the Trench of the Bayonets, from the First World War (oddly enough, not located over the real trench it commemorates)[6] or the Holocaust Museum in Washington, D.C. The architect of the Holocaust Museum, James Ingo Freed, has been praised for his use of narrative architectural elements within a brand new building to evoke the past. But spending a lot of money on architecture does not guarantee an evocative place. An expensive building or sculptural monument may have little ability to trigger place memory, if it lacks much connection to the context of everyday life during the war or in the present. Humble, battered buildings and natural landscapes often evoke more direct responses than elaborate structures because they are closer to the experiences of most people.

Body memory is also difficult to evoke in a museum context. It

---

[5] Alan Baddeley, *Your memory: a user's guide*, 2nd edn (Harmondsworth: Penguin, 1994; Edward Casey, *Remembering: a phenomenological study* (Bloomington, Ind.: Indiana University Press, 1987), pp. 186–7.

[6] Jay M. Winter, *Sites of memory, sites of mourning* (Cambridge: Cambridge University Press, 1995), pp. 99–102.

connects people into places because the shared experience of dwellings, public spaces, and workplaces, and the paths travelled between home and work, give body memory its social component, modified by the postures of gender, race, and class. In a munitions factory, a foxhole, or a fighter bomber, people acquire the characteristic postures of certain occupations. Philosopher Edward Casey argues that body memory 'moves us directly into place, whose very immobility contributes to its distinct potency in matters of memory.' He suggests that 'What is contained in place is on its way to being well remembered.'[7] Thus one particular place can trigger an avalanche of specific memories – an effect exploited in the famous scene in the post-Second World War film, *The best years of our lives*, when the veteran air ace climbs up again into the cockpit of his old aircraft, now located in a scrapyard, and relives his war. Recalled to the present, he asks for, and gets, a job in the scrapyard.

The authors of the chapters in this book have agreed to move beyond looking at physical 'sites of memory' and exhibits of artefacts to study the process of remembrance and identify its agents in civil society.[8] An emphasis on process leads to the question of how projects of remembrance can be designed to use place memory effectively. Some projects might involve the participation of victims in reliving spatial histories, but of course, this could mean re-experiencing the trauma rather than exorcizing it. Activities designed to trigger place memory for individuals are best organized in the context of a supportive community process of both personal and public remembrance.

In any such process, there are bound to be conflicts between victims and observers, between insiders and outsiders, between members of older and younger generations, as well as between various individuals. Public discussion of the forced exclusion and incarceration of persons of Japanese ancestry during the Second World War is now reaching a climax after three and a half decades of silence and about fifteen to twenty years of the redress movement. Oral histories of the victims have been developed to the point that this may be the best-documented subject for oral history in American archives.[9] Now some of the spatial components of the experience are being explored and recorded in new ways at the Japanese American National Museum in Little Tokyo in Los

[7] Casey, *Remembering*, pp. 214–15.
[8] For recent reviews of the 'memory' scholarship see David Glassberg, 'Public history and the study of memory', *The Public Historian*, 18 (Spring 1996), pp. 7–23; James Fentress and Chris Wickham, *Social memory* (Oxford: Blackwell, 1992); 'Collective memory and remembering' special issue, *The Quarterly Newsletter of the Laboratory of Comparative Human Cognition*, University of California, San Diego, 9 (January 1987).
[9] Hansen, 'Oral history', pp. 625–39.

Angeles. These projects are rooted in a sophisticated understanding of the Japanese American community before, during, and after wartime. They offer the possibility of reconnecting important spatial memories for the culture as a whole, as well as for the victims.

Japanese Americans in Little Tokyo

Close to City Hall, in the heart of downtown Los Angeles, stands Little Tokyo, a district that has been home to Japanese immigrants to the United States since the late nineteenth century. By 1915 there were over 7,000 Japanese Americans in Los Angeles, the largest Japanese settlement in mainland United States, a distinction it retains today. By 1930, 35,000 persons of Japanese descent lived in Los Angeles County, most of them close to Little Tokyo.[10] They ran grocery and produce shops, sold bamboo, cultivated vineyards, citrus groves, and commercial flower fields, and owned labour-contracting firms, clothing stores, boarding houses, billiard parlours, cafés, nurseries, florists, and a local newspaper.

Smaller Japanese American communities developed in Boyle Heights, West Los Angeles (Sawtelle), Hollywood, and Gardena, but Little Tokyo was the centre which pulled these residents together, a place for community and connection. Little Tokyo also drew Japanese Americans working in the fishing industry on Santa Monica Beach or Terminal Island near San Pedro, as well as families working in agriculture in the San Fernando valley. There Japanese Americans of all classes and occupations could attend religious services, learn traditional sports, or take classes in kimono etiquette and flower arranging. There, too, Nisei Week parades transformed the city streets with Japanese pattern and colour, starting in 1934.

During the Second World War, Japanese Americans lost Little Tokyo completely. Following the bombing of Pearl Harbor on 7 December 1941, selected Japanese American community leaders were arrested and interned in Department of Justice camps. By 19 February 1942, Executive Order 9066 authorized the forced exclusion and incarceration of all West-coast Japanese Americans, 40,000 Issei (first-generation immi-

---

[10] Ichiro Mike Murase, *Little Tokyo: one hundred years in pictures* (Los Angeles: Visual Communications, 1983), p. 11; William M. Mason and John A. McKinstry, *The Japanese of Los Angeles, 1869–1920* (Los Angeles: County of Los Angeles, Museum of Natural History, 1969); Carey McWilliams, *Southern California: an island on the land* (Salt Lake City: Peregrine Smith Books, 1983); John Modell, *The economics and politics of racial accommodation: the Japanese of Los Angeles, 1900–1942* (Urbana: University of Illinois Press, 1977); Yuji Ichioka, *The Issei: the world of the first generation Japanese immigrants, 1885–1924* (New York: Free Press, 1988).

grants) and 70,000 Nisei (second-generation immigrants, many of whom had never been to Japan). No similar action was taken against Italian Americans or German Americans. Executive Order 9066 followed the pattern of earlier anti-Japanese legislation. (California in 1913 passed the Alien Land Law which kept Issei from owning land. The federal government in 1924 ended all new Japanese immigration to the United States.) Executive Order 9066 was publicized in haste and resulted in frantic packing. Many families lost businesses and homes, as well as personal property. All persons of Japanese ancestry were forced to wear white tags with family identification numbers and assemble for transportation with limited baggage, often bundles hastily wrapped in sheets.[11]

Under the direction of the War Relocation Authority (WRA), West-coast residents affected by 9066 were forcibly moved twice. First came relocation to fifteen so-called 'assembly centres'. Little Tokyo residents were assigned to the Santa Anita Racetrack, where horse stables provided inadequate temporary quarters for 18,709 people between 7 May and 27 October 1942.[12] Then the detainees were moved to so-called 'relocation centres', ten crudely built prison camps. Eight occupied unirrigated desert sites – Manzanar and Tule Lake, California; Minidoka, Idaho; Topaz, Utah; Poston and Gila River, Arizona; Heart Mountain, Wyoming; and Granada, Colorado. Two were situated in undrained swamps – Rohwer and Jerome, Arkansas. (There were also internment camps run by the Immigration and Naturalization Service of the Department of Justice which interned aliens and people considered political organizers or troublemakers.) Travelling to these destinations by slow trains which took up to ten days, with blackout shades covering the windows, the exiled ethnic Japanese were occasionally let out to stretch on station platforms patrolled by armed guards.

This mass incarceration was described by the United States government in language designed to obscure the identity of the people affected

---

[11] Donald Teruo Hata and Nadine Ishitani Hata, *Japanese Americans and World War II: exclusion, internment, and redress*, 2nd edn (Wheeling, Ill.: Harlan Davidson, 1975); Roger Daniels, *Prisoners without trial: Japanese Americans and World War II* (New York: Hill and Wang, 1993); Roger Daniels, Sandra C. Taylor, and Harry H. L. Kitano, *Japanese Americans: from relocation to redress*, rev. edn (Seattle: University of Washington Press, 1991).

[12] Murase, *Little Tokyo*, p. 16. Also see Roger Daniels, *Asian America: Chinese and Japanese in the United States since 1850* (Seattle: University of Washington Press, 1988); Ronald Takaki, *Strangers from a different shore: a history of Asian Americans* (New York: Penguin, 1990); Sucheng Chan, *Asian Americans: an interpretive history* (Boston: Twayne Publishers, 1991); Gary Y. Okihiro and Joan Myers, *Whispered silences: Japanese Americans and World War II* (Seattle and London: University of Washington Press, 1996).

by 9066, the processes people were subjected to, and the places they were forced to reside. Government documents spoke of 'non-aliens' as opposed to citizens, and discussed their 'evacuation' rather than forced removal and incarceration. These euphemisms Raymond Okamura has compared to the 'emigration and evacuation' rhetoric used by the Third Reich for the Jewish population, although the WRA camps were not the death camps of Hitler's 'final solution'.[13] The WRA, with unwarranted cheerfulness, referred to 'colonists' or 'residents' in 'relocation centres', and provided addresses such as block number, barrack number, apartment number, when in reality there were no apartments, since entire families had one minimal room with no bathroom or kitchen.

Upon arrival at the camps, families were crowded into military barracks hastily built of wood and tar paper, partitioned with blankets, lit by kerosene lamps. The compounds provided almost no privacy. There were communal kitchens, dining halls, laundries, and latrines. At the barbed wire perimeter of each camp were guard towers, manned by guards with guns and searchlights. On occasion, internees were shot – in December 1942, a riot at Manzanar resulted in the deaths of two residents by military police gunfire.

Japanese Americans were at first forbidden cameras to document the spatial dimensions of their incarceration. A number of talented exiled artists, including Mine Okubo, Hisako Hibi, and Henry Sugimoto, created drawings and paintings of the places.[14] A few managed to sneak in lenses to build box cameras or even film equipment to make home movies. (Outsiders could photograph camp conditions – illustration 1 is by Dorothea Lange, who worked at Manzanar.[15]) Japanese American writers and poets also created poignant accounts of their incarceration.[16] Many exiles occupied their time making furniture, building better walls and windows, and creating small gardens.[17] Despite the high level of skill many possessed in commercial agriculture and horti-

[13] Raymond Y. Okamura, 'The American concentration camps: a cover-up through euphemistic terminology', *Journal of Ethnic Studies*, 10 (Fall 1982), pp. 95–109.

[14] *The view from within: Japanese American art from the internment camps, 1942–1945* (Los Angeles: Japanese American National Museum and the Wight Art Gallery, University of California, Los Angeles, 1992); Deborah Gesensway and Mindy Roseman, *Beyond words: images from America's concentration camps* (Ithaca, NY: Cornell University Press, 1987).

[15] Maisie and Richard Conrat, *Executive order 9066* (Los Angeles: UCLA Asian American Studies Center, 1990).

[16] Jeanne Wakatsuki Houston and James D. Houston, *Farewell to Manzanar* (New York: Bantam, 1973); Lawson Fusao Inada, *Legends from camp* (Minneapolis: Coffee House Press, 1992).

[17] Deanna Matsumoto, 'The built environment of America's concentration camps: 1942–45', unpublished paper, 24 May 1990; Kenneth Helphand, 'Defiant gardens', *Journal of Garden History*, 17 (April–June 1977), pp. 101–21.

1. War Relocation Authority Center, Manzanar, California, 3 July 1942, photograph by Dorothea Lange, National Archives #210-G10-C839

2. First Street, Little Tokyo, Los Angeles, showing reassembled barracks building from Heart Mountain, Wyoming, with contemporary addition, guard tower, and fence; part of exhibit, 'America's Concentration Camps', 1995–6, Japanese American National Museum, photograph by Dolores Hayden

culture, the sites of the camps were so barren that skill did not always bring success in the dust or the swamp.

Much discussion of citizenship and civil rights went on. WRA authorities wanted 'Loyalty Oaths' signed by their victims. There were many who counselled quiet accommodation to the usurpation of their civil rights and tried to present themselves as '200 per cent American', and others who resisted.[18] Some accounts of the internal struggles have been written; others are in progress. At this point one can be sure that some incarcerated American citizens of Japanese ancestry sued in court for their civil rights and that others among the incarcerated thought that their hope for the future might lie with the Japanese.[19] The formation of the 442nd Regimental Combat Team, a much-decorated Nisei unit serving in Italy, publicized Japanese American patriotism in 1944.

By 1945, the exiled were on their way back to their old neighbourhoods. But, of course, war had totally reorganized the uses and ownership of those spaces. During the war, the empty buildings of Little Tokyo in Los Angeles became 'Bronzeville', home to African Americans from the South who had migrated there in search of wartime jobs in booming defence industries. The Japanese Union Church became a black community centre. Jazz clubs thrived where small Japanese American businesses had once flourished.

Because many former businesses run by the first-generation immigrants had been devastated, many younger members of the community needed to obtain employment elsewhere. While younger Japanese Americans dispersed in the search for jobs, Little Tokyo remained the best location for the elderly, for cultural organizations, and for stores emphasizing traditional Japanese products. Public history was not a priority or even a possibility for many years. As one resident put it, 'It wasn't to our advantage to be a visible minority in the past.' Most Japanese Americans turned away from remembering the loss of Little Tokyo and the humiliating experience of the internment camps. Silence prevailed. The late Amy Uno Ishii said: 'Women, if they've been raped, don't go around talking about it ... This is exactly the kind of feeling that we as evacuees, victims of circumstances, had at the time of

[18] Edward H. Spicer, Asael T. Hansen, Katherine Luomala, and Marvin K. Opler, *Impounded people: Japanese Americans in the relocation centers* (Tucson: University of Arizona Press, 1969). The authors were anthropologists employed by the WRA to write this report in 1946.

[19] Peter Irons (ed.), *Justice delayed: the record of the Japanese American internment cases* (Middletown: Wesleyan University Press, 1989) records the legal battles. Brian Masaru Hayashi is at work on a study of the spectrum of 'Japanist' and 'Americanist' views among residents.

evacuation. A lot of Nisei and Issei are actually ashamed ... that they were in a concentration camp.'[20]

Networks and the process of remembrance

In 1969, Sue Kunitomi Embrey and a group known as the Manzanar Committee organized pilgrimages for victims and their descendants to the site of the camp, and began to explore the possibility of preserving the remains of the Manzanar camp. (The state designated it as a California Registered Historical Landmark in 1973.) By 1976, a national redress movement was well under way, and as part of the Bicentennial, President Ford apologized to Japanese Americans, revoking 9066. A campaign for financial restitution culminated a dozen years later when President Reagan signed the Civil Liberties Act, and in 1990 cheques for $20,000 arrived for survivors, along with a written letter of apology signed by President Bush. Political scientist Leslie T. Hatamiya has analysed the legislative process undertaken by various congressmen and senators of Japanese American backgrounds, as well as the lobbying activities of citizens groups, including the Japanese American Community League (JACL), which resulted in passage of the act and the necessary appropriations. It was a complex process, and Hatamiya has shown that 'skillful leadership, lack of coherent opposition, and a moral appeal to "right a wrong"' all contributed to this civil rights legislation.[21]

By 1990, the Census recorded 866,160 persons of Japanese American background (about 60 per cent native born). Japanese Americans are about 0.34 per cent of the total United States population. They are scattered across the country but still concentrated on the West coast. Sometimes called a 'Model Minority', Japanese Americans have higher incomes and lower unemployment rates than African Americans, Hispanics, or Chinese Americans, but are still twice as likely to be poor as non-Hispanic whites.[22]

When, in the 1980s, the Presidential Commission on the Wartime Relocation and Internment of Civilians held hearings and authorized reparations to victims, many witnesses came forward to testify about their experiences and the entire Japanese American community had to deal with the bitter past in a public way. Several younger Japanese Americans commented: 'These hearings took place during a time when

[20] Hansen, 'Oral history', pp. 627–8.
[21] Leslie T. Hatamiya, *Righting a wrong: Japanese Americans and the passage of the Civil Liberties Act of 1988* (Stanford: Stanford University Press, 1993).
[22] Hatamiya, *Righting*, pp. 53–5.

many of the Issei generation were passing away and many Nisei were nearing retirement age. Increased sentiment has grown to preserve their history ... The physical structures of Little Tokyo were the place from which the reality of the experience sprang, a way for the "stories" to be validated and grounded in reality.'[23] As a result of public discussion among several generations of Japanese Americans, two goals emerged as part of a larger strategy of affirming ethnic identity and the importance of public history: creating a Japanese American National Museum, and preserving some remaining pre-war buildings in Little Tokyo in Los Angeles.

The Japanese American National Museum

On 15 May 1992, the Japanese American National Museum opened its doors in a former Buddhist temple in Little Tokyo. The building includes a Legacy Center where visitors can engage in interactive programs about ethnic history. They can learn how to request files from the federal government under the Freedom of Information Act, or obtain more information about WRA camps where they or their relatives and friends spent time. Visitors can also learn how to develop a family tree. Artists and writers of many different ethnic backgrounds read or perform their work in the museum on a regular basis. The museum seems to have benefited from the long years of organizing done in the redress movement: it enjoys broad support from Japanese Americans, and forms coalitions with other ethnic museums and arts groups readily.

In the autumn of 1994, curator Karen Ishizuka created a remarkable exhibition for the museum, entitled 'America's Concentration Camps'.[24] Ishizuka's career began in gerontology, moved to visual anthropology, and then on to curating and documentary filmmaking. The opening of her exhibit was preceded by a strange construction that appeared on the corner of First Street and Central Avenue, opposite the museum and adjacent to the historic district (illustration 2). First a fence, then a military watchtower, and finally a ragged tar-paper barracks went up. This latter building, sheathed in rough black paper and wooden battens, balanced on rough concrete blocks, had a weathered appearance that suggested it was neither warm nor dry. It was a WRA camp dormitory.

---

[23] Christopher Doi, Tom Fujita, Lewis Kawahara, Brian Niiya, and Karen Umemoto, 'Little Tokyo redevelopment: The North Side of First Street', unpublished paper, 20 June 1986, p. 31.

[24] James Hirabayashi, ' "Concentration camp" or "Relocation center": what's in a name?' *Japanese American National Museum Quarterly*, 9 (Oct.–Dec. 1994), pp. 5–10.

It was not a complete structure, but enclosed space on three sides, a gigantic billboard to the city of Los Angeles announcing that the lost world of the camp experience had been temporarily returned to the city. By bringing the physical structure to the city, Ishizuka was declaring that everyone would now have to deal with this place and its existence in a public way. Ishizuka had developed a process of remembrance integral to this act: the museum recruited formerly incarcerated persons and their children who travelled to Heart Mountain, Wyoming, site of one of the WRA camps, to disassemble a surviving barracks given to the museum. They brought the building back to Los Angeles, reliving the journeys of many years before, and reassembled it next to the museum. Many former inmates agreed to serve as docents, bringing visitors to the remnant of the building and leading tours about its history. Pilgrimages to the actual incarceration sites continued to be sponsored by the museum as well.

The main exhibit was in the museum itself, and here Ishizuka created other activities involving spatial memories. In the exhibit, designed by Ralph Appelbaum Associates, the ten WRA camps and the one family camp run by the Justice Department were represented by eleven long tables covered with detailed site plans. When formerly incarcerated persons arrived at the opening, they were asked to name their barracks, and given a small scale model of the building to place on the site plan. During several hours, each camp became three dimensional, as survivors placed the missing buildings on the plan, and row upon row of bleak structures, miniatures of the building from Heart Mountain across the street, formed the model of the whole camp. (Non-inmates watched the process of forming the whole from the individual parts.)

Former inmates were also asked if they would like to be photographed in front of a large photograph or a model of their camp. Most said yes. Their images, and their handwritten testimony of their memories of the places, began to fill 'Camp Albums', loose-leaf notebooks organized by site. Here the scale of the tragedy becomes clear as thousands and thousands of individual faces, names, camp addresses, current addresses, and phone numbers appear. Over and over again, survivors wrote that they had materials they would like to donate to the museum. Again, the books form the whole from the parts. (As Hanna Krall observed about an exhibit of photographs of Polish Jews, 'You can't have compassion for millions, for all those zeroes. The best thing we can do is to give back individual faces to all these people.'[25]) Abstraction cannot

[25] Jane Perlez, 'Poland turns out for glimpse of a lost world', *New York Times*, 19 May 1996, p. 8.

convey the losses as well as faces, in this case, tens of thousands of Japanese American faces.

Robert Y. Hasuike built a model of a barracks at Manzanar, the size of a large doll's-house, about 6 feet long, now located in the lobby of the museum, to show the typical improvements made to barracks over the years by many residents – partitions, furniture, closets, installed to make the environment more bearable. *Something strong within*, a new, award-winning documentary film was made by Ishizuka (producer/writer) and Robert A. Nakamura (director/editor), composed of footage from home movies taken by both victims and sympathizers who filmed the forced removal. (It was shown at the museum and internationally, one of three films based on home-movie footage they have made.) Artist Nobuho Nagasawa created a replica of the bronze camera constructed by photographer Toyo Miyatake, a Little Tokyo commercial photographer sent to Manzanar, who carried a forbidden lens in his baggage. He took pictures of the camp, and at night his photographs are shown as slides on the exterior wall of the museum.

All of these visual and spatial representations of the camps, and the written and oral discussions of the experience, created wide interest in the city of Los Angeles and in the nation. People from many different backgrounds attended the exhibit and filled comment books labelled 'THIS TOO IS OUR STORY' with their connection to the forced removal of Japanese Americans. One wrote: 'Very interesting and moving, never again, such racisms', and identified himself as the son of a Holocaust survivor. Some were younger-generation Japanese Americans who had never fully understood what their parents and grand-parents had endured:

Mom, Dad and Nanny – I never really understood camp life. You spoke of it so much as I was growing up. I can fully understand your experience. However I cannot even begin to imagine your feelings and hardships. Now that I am a mother, I can't fathom my children enduring this. Nanny, this must have been so painful. My biggest breakthrough in this museum was [what] someone wrote of my uncle who drowned in Heart Mountain. He was only 13. It all hit me on really how you must have went through [*sic*]. I am so proud of your strength . . . I visit here on my birthday. What a special gift to myself.

Another man simply noted, 'I cried.'[26] (I saw no negative comments on the exhibit in the comment book.)

The Japanese American National Museum has become an important agent for a widening set of processes of remembrance, first focused on

---

[26] From the comment book, 'This too is our story', Japanese American National Museum, undated, 'son of Dachau survivor', Lynn Shibata Goodman, Sacramento, Calif.; 'Robert'.

the particular experiences of the victims but now generalized to larger questions of cultural landscape history and civil rights. It shows how the memories of places can be used to stimulate a process of remembrance which begins in a personal way but links private memory to public history and politics. The written materials accompanying the exhibit emphasize these connections: 'The lesson here is that the abrogation of rights for any citizen is an abrogation of rights for all citizens.'[27]

In the museum's comment books are testimonies from Americans who agree: native Americans whose ancestors lost their lands; Mexican Americans whose grandparents were repatriated to Mexico during the depression years, who lost the barrio of Chavez Ravine to urban renewal in the 1950s, or who fear Proposition 187 denying any social services to illegal immigrants; and African Americans who wrote about residential segregation in South Central Los Angeles. Most of all, the public space next to the chain-link fence and the guard tower, outside the transported barracks across from the museum, invited informal, contemporary conversations about civil rights and the conflicted ethnic territories of the city. These went on, one or two at a time, night and day, whether the museum was open or closed, until the barracks was removed in the summer of 1996, augmenting the attendance at the exhibit of approximately 51,000 official visitors. As John J. Miyauchi notes, the museum provides a place where 'old people can go to remember; where young people can go to learn, lest they grow up in ignorance of their own past; it will be a place to teach other people about the Japanese American people.' Another resident put it even more simply, calling the museum 'the family album of the Japanese American community'.[28]

Context: the First Street Historic District

The presence of the museum in the First Street Historic District activates a whole urban block. At the same time as the museum has developed, the historic district has emerged as the result of work over many years by hundreds of residents and dozens of organizations, including a group of Japanese American Second World War veterans, the Little Tokyo Citizens' Development Advisory Committee, the Japanese American Cultural and Community Center, the Los Angeles Conservancy, the Los Angeles Community Redevelopment Agency

---

[27] Hirabayashi, ' "Concentration camp" ', p. 8.
[28] John J. Miyauchi, 'We're here', brochure of the Japanese American National Museum, quoted in *Cultural and ethnic diversity in historic preservation*, Information series No. 65 (Washington D.C.: National Trust for Historic Preservation, 1992), p. 19; 'Things that make us unique and yet so American', *L.A. Architect* (June 1992): p. 11.

(CRA), and The Power of Place. This is an important urban area whose historic significance is finally recognized. In 1976 and 1977, a county survey had deemed the area ineligible for National Register status, and in 1986 the California state historic preservation officer deemed it of state rather than national importance. Times change – in 1993, the National Park Service nominated it for National Landmark Status. The rescue of the district is particularly significant since it began during a time when much demolition had occurred and bitterness about the past existed. Little of thriving, pre-war Little Tokyo remained to reflect the demand for public history expressed in the 1980s. Urban renewal had taken its toll, as well as incarceration.

The city demolished part of First Street for a new police station in 1950 and relocated a thousand people. Then the Community Redevelopment Agency began a redevelopment project in Little Tokyo in 1970 and introduced many high-rise projects which created dramatic conflicts of scale as commercial investment from both Japan and the United States overlaid the pre-war blocks of modest housing and small businesses. With the new buildings came higher rents that forced many small shops to close and poorer tenants to move. Redevelopment in the 1970s and early 1980s made any type of preservation difficult to negotiate.[29] The showdown between the community and the CRA finally occurred in the mid-1980s with the remaining buildings on the North Side of First Street. The CRA proposed a major office development right behind them, and co-sponsored an architectural competition with the Museum of Contemporary Art for the design, although many members of the Japanese American community felt cut off from this process. In October 1986, through the combined efforts of the Little Tokyo Citizens' Development Advisory Committee and the Los Angeles Conservancy, thirteen buildings on the north side of First Street, between San Pedro Street and Central Avenue, were nominated as a National Register Historic District.

The preserved block reflects the scale of the neighbourhood in the 1920s and 1930s. At the San Pedro end stands the Union Church, a Japanese American church built in a neoclassical style in 1923, resulting from the merger of three Christian Japanese congregations. For many years it served as a social and community centre. It was also used as an assembly centre for the forced removal to the camps. At the opposite end, on Central Avenue, stands the former Nishi Hongwanji Buddhist Temple, a brick building from 1925 planned with some commercial

[29] Mike Davis, 'The infinite game: redeveloping downtown L.A.', in Diane Ghirardo (ed.), *Out of site: a social criticism of architecture* (Seattle: Bay Press, 1991), pp. 77–113.

space on First Street to generate revenue for the congregation. It, too, was an assembly centre for the victims, and now houses the museum.

Between the two was the San Pedro Firm Building, constructed in 1924 by shareholders from the Southern California Flower Market. Among its tenants was the courageous photographer, Toyo Miyatake, who smuggled a camera lens into the Manzanar detention camp to document conditions. Also in the block was the Kawasaki Building, the only continuously Japanese American owned building in the district, built on land purchased by Yajusiro Kawasaki in the name of his three American-born daughters in 1933. In the same building was the Futaba Nisei Beauty Shop. Fugetsu-do, a Japanese confectionery store, sold traditional bean cake and rice-paste candy next door. Then came the Asahi Shoe store, specializing in small sizes and Japanese footgear. In the same building was Moon Fish. The Dai Maru Hotel was once Tokyo Baths. A noodle shop and a Japanese restaurant rented the commercial space attached to the Temple. A German American black-smith's building and a Chinese restaurant completed the block.

In 1989, Susan Sztaray, a UCLA graduate student in Urban Planning, fluent in Japanese, worked with me and an organization I founded called The Power of Place, which organized public history and public art projects in Los Angeles.[30] Sztaray's 'A proposal for public art: Little Tokyo's Historic District' drew on the rich historical research provided for the National Register nomination to suggest the possibilities of public art contributing to spatial memory here.[31] She recognized that retaining the existing small-scale businesses in this historic block posed a difficult economic problem, since the scale of real-estate development usually promoted by the CRA was not supportive of old-fashioned family businesses. Certainly it would be preferable to support the survival of these traditional shops, as a living dimension of the cultural landscape, than to rely on public art to recall recently lost businesses. However, effective public art might call attention to both the history of small businesses on the street and the distinctiveness of businesses that were surviving, despite the years of clearance and large-scale redevelopment in surrounding blocks.

Sztaray proposed that public art be created in the form of a new sidewalk to unify the block and represent the commercial and political history it embodied. Using Japanese publications similar to Chamber of

---

[30] Dolores Hayden, *The power of place: urban landscapes as public history* (Cambridge, Mass.: MIT Press, 1995) contains an account of this larger work in the city.

[31] Susan Sztaray, 'A proposal for public art: Little Tokyo's historic district', unpublished paper, 12 March 1989. She is also the author of *Little Tokyo: a walking tour sponsored by the Los Angeles Conservancy* (Los Angeles: Los Angeles Conservancy, 1992).

Commerce directories, she traced the histories of the small businesses in the block and illustrated their specialized Japanese products such as sweets or kimonos. Upon her graduation, Sztaray worked on the proposal with planner Gloria Uchida at the CRA. By 1990 the CRA had formed a Little Tokyo First Street public art initiative, based on Sztaray's detailed programme. A competition was held. Artist Sheila de Bretteville submitted the winning proposal, and was asked to work in collaboration with two Japanese American artists, Sonya Ishii and Nobuho Nagasawa. De Bretteville's design for a new terrazzo and concrete sidewalk wrapping the block, combines residents' personal statements about remembering Little Tokyo with the names of the small businesses that had flourished there, and the imagery of traditional Japanese wrapped bundles. The sidewalk, *Omoide no Shotokyo* (Memories of Little Tokyo), was constructed in July 1996. It carries memories of Executive Order 9066 and of many layers of neighbourhood activity, before and after 9066, in both English and Japanese.

Beyond silence, after remembrance: insiders and outsiders

Breaking decades of silence to create resonant public history in Little Tokyo has involved all kinds of organizations as well as individuals from school teachers to US presidents, civil rights lawyers to artists, anthropologists to poets. Amy Uyematsu writes in 'The shaping of pine':

> I was forced into desert camps
> where you didn't hear me counting what was stolen
> and afterwards when I returned in silence
> you even praised me
>
> . . .
>
> I am talking now, inside our silence,
> after forty years of waiting
> a nisei mother's public statement
> the poems which could not be thrown away
> and the grandfather who could never
> take me back to Manzanar
> where he rebuilt his garden
> loud with sand, rock, and pine
>
> I am talking to us now.[32]

In Little Tokyo itself, the sensitive planning done by Susan Sztaray and Gloria Uchida, and the public art by Sheila de Bretteville, Sonya Ishii,

---

[32] Amy Uyematsu, *30 miles from J-Town* (Story Line Press, Ashland, Oreg., 1992), p. 41.

and Nobuho Nagasawa, reach out to a wide audience by making the connections between urban physical history in the block of storefronts and individuals' particular memories of that block. But there is a limit to how much planners or artists who do not have access to large numbers of camp survivors can do. Karen Ishizuka's access to thousands of victims, and her insights about how to link the private world of place memory with public processes of remembrance, make her work particularly unusual for its breadth and depth of spatial history.

Ishizuka is above all a process-oriented person, and she has said, 'Rather than authorities, we at the Museum are catalysts. We seek to join you and ask you to join us in the ongoing process of coming to grips with the incarceration, learning more about its many issues and nuances, and applying its lessons now and in the future.'[33] She has choreographed performative exercises (such as pilgrimages to disassemble the camp building, or rituals of survivors rebuilding the site models at the opening of the exhibit) that use place memory in a unique way. She has also orchestrated the participants' use of models of buildings, home movies, and personal spatial histories to explore the larger issues of political oppression and make them tangible. She makes these abstractions more bearable for the participants who have been victims, because of her emphasis on their courage, dignity, and community building efforts. At the same time, she educates the rest of us, who will find it hard to forget, once having seen such poignant spatial representations.

Is it possible to transfer some of the techniques developed in Little Tokyo to deal with the Japanese Americans' cultural landscape of war, forced removal, incarceration, and redress to other contexts? The curators, planners, and artists creating these projects have recognized the delicate relationships between people and places, and dealt with the complex character of place attachments. Are they distinctively gendered projects? They do build on and extend women's traditional roles in maintaining ties to kin and community. They emphasize social and spatial connectedness. The process of remembrance here involves far more active participation than costly commemorations that rely on a single monumental building or sculpture. And these projects are much

[33] Karen L. Ishizuka, 'From the Curator of "America's concentration camps: remembering the Japanese American experience"', *Japanese American National Museum Quarterly*, 9 (Oct.–Dec. 1994), p. 2. Two reviews of the exhibit are David Yoo, 'Captivating memories: museology, concentration camps, and Japanese American history', *American Quarterly*, 48 (December 1996), pp. 680–99; Lon Yuki Kurashige, 'America's concentration camps: remembering the Japanese American experience', *Journal of American History*, 83 (June 1996), pp. 160–2. The exhibit will be at the Ellis Island Immigration Museum from 30th March 1998 to 8 January 1999.

more subtle than others that simply rebuild a building or a neighbour-hood destroyed by war, brick by brick. (To recreate a physical place without new representations of peoples' traumatic experiences of it may simply constitute denial.) The projects in Little Tokyo reweave the past and the present, the social and the spatial. They address the possibilities of healing, as personal memories of loss are braided in new public activities of remembrance, redress, and resistance.

Acknowledgements

The Harry Frank Guggenheim Foundation has sponsored two confer-ences discussing 'War, victimhood, resistance, and remembrance.' I would like to thank the foundation, and the conference leaders, Jay Winter and Emmanuel Sivan, for suggesting that I write this paper, and Gail Dubrow, Peter Marris, Sibyl Harwood, Karen Ishizuka, and Diane Okawahira for their advice.

8   The Algerian War in French collective memory

Antoine Prost

From November 1954 to March 1962 French troops fought in Algeria, in order to keep Algeria a part of France. This was a conflict which, in France, was not officially termed a war at all. The end result was the independence of Algeria under the control of the FLN (National Liberation Front), and the departure for France of 1 million French people who thought life would be impossible in Algeria under the new regime.

This war was arguably the longest war of decolonization, and although French forces undoubtedly were better equipped and more numerous than the Algerian *fellaghas*, it still cost 35,000 French soldiers their lives. However, it has disappeared from collective memory. No agency of remembrance did work to commemorate the memories of this war. Jean-Pierre Rioux pointed out this fact effectively in a paper published in 1990: 'Since 1962', he wrote, 'there is no French national memory of the Algerian conflict; this un-named war never received the honours of memory.'[1] This chapter deals with the reasons why in France there is no public memory of the Algerian War.

The Algerian War

Algeria was an integral part of France. During the Second World War, de Gaulle's provisional government moved from London to Algiers, where it was on French territory. It was divided into three *départements* and had roughly the same administration as others in metropolitan France. When needed, bureaucrats and teachers were appointed to Algerian selection boards and schools as well as to metropolitan ones by committees in the central administration. Many civil servants began their career there and later went back to France.

---

[1] Jean-Pierre Rioux, 'La flamme et les bûchers', in Jean-Pierre Rioux (ed.), *La guerre d'Algérie et les Français* (Paris: Fayard, 1990), p. 499. This important book arose out of a colloquium organized by the Institut d'histoire du temps présent, 15–18 December 1988.

During the early 1950s, approximately one out of a million people living in Algeria were French full citizens; they were termed the *Pieds noirs*. They were settlers, workers in the public services, teachers, merchants, and so on. Some of them were wealthy and arrogant *colons*, but many of them were lower-middle-class people, very ordinary people. Their families had migrated to North Africa during the nineteenth century or later. Some came for political reasons, after the Paris Commune for instance, or for reasons of national sentiment, as in the case of Alsatians arriving after German annexation in 1871. Some of them had Spanish or Italian origins, but it did not matter much, because they were all French-speaking people and they had exactly the same rights as people living in France. They participated in the legislative elections as French citizens and sent MPs to Paris.

Alongside the *Pieds noirs*, there were nine million people who were termed 'Frenchmen of North African origin'. These natives spoke Arabic or Berber rather than French, and only about one in five had been to school. Most of them were Muslims. They understood French and spoke a kind of French. Some of them were fully educated and constituted a native elite: there were native lawyers, doctors, chemists, teachers, civil servants. However, even this elite was not given equal citizenship; for local affairs, the local council was composed of two parts, one elected by the *Pieds noirs*, the other by the native-born. For the national legislative elections, the voters were similarly divided in two parts, electing the same number of MPs. But since the government illegally manipulated the results of the native electoral college, this dual regime gave full power to the *Pieds noirs*. Attempts to reform this inegalitarian and undemocratic system had been tried, but they had been unsuccessful. The *Pieds noirs* opposed them in order to preserve their own control of public affairs and their social superiority. Here are the main sources of the emergence of an Algerian nationalist movement. It was heavily repressed and had no hope of achieving its political goals except by violent confrontation with the French police and army.

The Algerian War began in November 1954, when small groups of Algerian partisans made attacks on several areas of the Algerian country-side and killed eight people.[2] For French public opinion, the appropriate policy was to send police forces to Algeria and to maintain order. However, the nationalist rebellion expanded, and it was necessary to

---

[2] The best history of the war remains Bernard Droz and Evelyne Lever, *Histoire de la guerre d'Algérie* (Paris: Editions du Seuil, 1982). A much shorter account is given by the well-known specialist, Charles-Robert Ageron, in his article 'Guerre d'Algérie', in Jean-François Sirinelli (ed.), *Dictionnaire historique de la vie politique française au XX siècle* (Paris: PUF, 1995), pp. 462–70.

send military units into Algeria in 1955. The legislative election of January 1956 was won by a socialist–radical coalition after a campaign for ending the Algerian War. The socialist Guy Mollet, the leader of the party, had said that he would make peace in Algeria. But he went to Algiers and was confronted by a *Pied noir* demonstration which impressed him so much that he changed his policy and gave 'pacification' priority over 'negotiation'. Hence, he decided to send conscripts to Algeria.

From 1956 until the end of the war, in 1962, there were permanently 500,000 young conscript soldiers from France in Algeria. These conscripts were not as strongly committed to the cause of French Algeria as were the officers. Active officers were convinced that the Algerian rebellion was a Communist one, inspired and supported by Nasser. They applauded the Suez expedition in November 1956 and opposed any French government which they supposed eager to negotiate with the FLN. Hence the upheaval of 13 May 1958, which led to de Gaulle's coming back to power and to the advent of the Fifth Republic.

However successful, the military conflict against the FLN did not open the way to a political solution. De Gaulle progressively withdrew from his policy of keeping Algeria French. He moved to the policy of self-determination (September 1959), and later to negotiations with the FLN which resulted in the Evian treaty (18 March 1962) and to the recognition of an independent Algerian republic.

To French public opinion, the Algerian War was a much more important matter than the Vietnamese War which had ended with the Geneva agreement of 1954. First, Vietnam was quite far from France, and French vital interests were not at stake there; very few people from France were living there, and French people with family in Algeria were much more numerous than those with kin in Vietnam. Algeria was just the other side of the Mediterranean Sea, and it was viewed as a part of France; it was impossible not to help the *Pieds noirs*, these not-so-distant cousins, against the threat of the Algerian 'rebels' who were fighting for a new Algeria, free from colonial – that is, French – control.

However, French public opinion was reluctant to support fully the *Pieds noirs*' stance in Algeria; in a confused manner, French people felt that the *Pieds noirs* were responsible for the Algerian situation and that 'French Algeria' was very difficult to maintain. Defending the status quo would lead to a deadlock but no alternative policy was clearly conceivable; hence, from very early on, there emerged, amid the perplexities and hesitations of public opinion, the thought that negotiations with the FLN would necessarily occur.[3]

[3] Charles-Robert Ageron, 'L'opinion française à travers les sondages', in Rioux (ed.), *La guerre d'Algérie et les Français*, pp. 25–44.

There was a second reason why French opinion, although indecisive, was concerned with the Algerian conflict much more than with the Vietnamese one. The Vietnam War had been fought by an expeditionary force, including many troops from the French Empire, and Moroccan and Algerian Muslim soldiers; only volunteers had gone from metropolitan France to the Vietnamese battlefields. General Giap's army was actually an army, with guns and heavy weapons; against it, the French army had fought a war similar to ordinary wars, with battles such as that of Dien Bien Phu, with winners and losers. On the contrary, the Algerian War was fought by conscripts from France against small groups of rebels, and not against an army. The FLN *fellaghas* never became an army, with heavy weapons and large battalions. The 'un-named' war was termed an 'operation to maintain public order'. It consisted of a succession of small-scale fights with dozens of rebels, not battles in the full meaning of the word. Rather than a war, it was a series of guerrilla clashes.

Actually, in Algeria the crucial issue was to keep a tight control of the Muslim civil population, an objective which made it necessary to have French troops in almost every village. For this *quadrillage*, a huge number of soldiers was needed. The French government sent to Algeria the whole of the conscript army, month after month, and for the entire span of their military service, which was lengthened from eighteen to twenty-four, and later to twenty-seven, months.

During the six years which the war lasted, there were permanently nearly 500,000 soldiers from France in Algeria. In total, almost 3 million young Frenchmen crossed the Mediterranean Sea to campaign in the Algerian *djebels*, far from their family and their loved ones. They belonged to all sections of French society: they were white-collar workers, workers, peasants, students; they had postponed their personal projects, left their jobs, their young brides, or their fiancées, sometimes newborn children. They suffered losses, injuries, separation from their families, and so on. Inevitably millions of French people worried about their fate.

This is the context in which to place France's very strong concern for the Algerian War. Many highly emotional issues were intermingled: considerations of national prestige, solidarity with the *Pieds noirs*, worry for sons, husbands, and friends fighting in Algerian *djebels*. These reasons made it difficult to envisage either an independent Algeria or a never-ending war.

It seemed to French public opinion that only a few activists were involved in the rebellion on the *fellaghas*' side, and it was inconceivable that a powerful army would be unable to win a war against so weak an enemy. But it was clear too that it was impossible to maintain the privilege of the *Pieds noirs*. Time was needed for the idea to surface that there was no alternative to entering into discussions with the FLN, leading to an independent Algeria. Potentially, ex-soldiers and *Pieds noirs* had the possibility to present themselves as victims of the Algerian War. We will discuss later the reasons why they did not fulfil this prospect.

Let us begin briefly with a third group of potential victims, of whom we have not spoken: the *harkis*. The *harkis* were soldiers from the native Muslim community of Algeria, enrolled as complementary forces to supplement the French army. They did not form regular units enrolled in the French army; they rather formed a kind of civil militia with light weapons for night patrols around the villages. The *harkis* helped the French army to flood the countryside, in the tactic they called *quadrillage*.

At the end of the war, the *harkis* were in a critical position. They were volunteers, committed to the French and the perpetuation of colonial domination. They were deemed traitors by the FLN, and it was clear that many of them would be murdered after independence. Actually, between 55,000 and 75,000 of them were killed.

Notwithstanding contrary orders, some officers thought it was impossible to abandon them when they left Algeria, and approximately 85,000 of them came to France.[4] Unfortunately, it was difficult to integrate them into French society. They had no family in France, no relations; most of them were unskilled, and only some of them were educated, French-speaking people. When in France, they were put in camps. Progressively, their conditions of living and housing became better, their children went to French primary schools, they found casual employment.

But the difference between them and Algerian immigrants was not evident, and in France they encountered the same difficulties as immigrants in renting a flat or finding a job. They were perceived as a burden to the army and to French society as a whole. They did not even form a sub-sections of veterans' associations. They remained second-class Frenchmen. They did not count in the public debate until recent years, when mass unemployment precipitated nationalist, racist, or xenophobic movements. Then, the sons and daughters of the *harkis*, more educated than their parents, no longer saw being unemployed and socially excluded as acceptable, suffering at one and the same time for their fathers' commitment to France and their own Algerian origin.

---

[4] Benjamin Stora, *La gangrène et l'oubli, la mémoire de la guerre d'Algérie* (Paris: La Découverte, 1992), pp. 200–3 and p. 261.

Some of them joined in violent demonstrations in several small towns of southern France. They won some improvements, but they were insufficiently numerous to create more than local difficulties.

Much more puzzling is the case of the other two groups: neither the *Pieds noirs* nor the ex-soldiers found ways to commemorate collectively their experience and their losses. They never formed a community of victims. Why?

The *Pieds noirs*: a restricted memory

The first reason was the division of these two groups. Had they united their forces, they could have been more successful. But the fact is that they were divided. The relationship between the ex-soldiers and the *Pieds noirs* had been ambiguous during the war. A recent study in oral history among ex-non-commissioned officers shows the resentment of these young Frenchmen from France against the *Pieds noirs*. Although they came to fight the Algerian rebellion and protect the *Pieds noirs* at great personal risk, they were not given a very warm welcome by the *Pieds noirs*. They felt that the *Pieds noirs* thought it was natural that French soldiers would protect them, and that the locals did not value highly enough the sacrifices they had made.

Small anecdotes still vivid in these ex-officers' memories illuminate their sense of frustration and deception. One of them says they were never invited to dance with the daughters of the *Pieds noirs*.[5] Another remembers that once a *Pied noir* settler asked him to pay for a glass of water. A poll among 533 soldiers coming back to France in 1959 presented similar evidence. Such little incidents, and their significance to French soldiers, are revealing. They help account for the fact that in this 1959 poll 61 per cent of the respondents expressed more antipathy against the *Pieds noirs* than against the 'Arabs'.[6]

On the other hand, the *Pieds noirs* resented the distinction made by many non-commissioned officers and conscript soldiers from the other side of the Mediterranean Sea between the interests of France as a nation-state and the interests of the *Pieds noirs*. They found that at times the French army did not share their point of view. This friction turned into open opposition when renegade French army officers formed a clandestine organization, the OAS (Secret Army Organization), dedi-

[5] Benoît Kaplan, 'Une génération d'élèves des Grandes Ecoles en Algérie. Mémoire d'une guerre', mémoire de maîtrise d'histoire, Université de Paris I, 1994, published as winner of a prize: Fédération de l'Education Nationale, *Cahiers du Centre fédéral*, no. 18 (November 1996), p. 110.

[6] 'De jeunes militants dans le contingent: l'enquête des organisations de jeunesse de 1959–1960', in Rioux (ed.), *La guerre d'Algérie et les Français*, p. 90.

cated to keeping Algeria French. The OAS directly confronted the army, and so did the *Pieds noirs*. French soldiers opened fire on *Pieds noirs* demonstrating against the French government; several demonstrators were killed. The fusillade on the rue d'Isly in Algiers on 26 March 1962 was the climax of this kind of internal war. In the light of such events, one can understand why it was very difficult for ex-soldiers and *Pieds noirs* to constitute any kind of community after the war, let alone act as a 'fictive kinship group'.

The one million *Pieds noirs* living in Algeria were full French citizens. After independence, most of them had the right to live in Algeria, with joint Algerian and French nationalities. However, there was a clear and overwhelming consensus within Algerian public opinion and among officials that their only choice was between leaving or being killed. They chose to go – for some to return – to France, abandoning in Algeria everything they could not take with them.[7] They lost their land and property, their houses, their furniture, and sometimes their savings. As they were numerous and had suffered heavy material losses, they had grounds to claim reparations from the French state.

After a few months in France, the *Pieds noirs* formed specific associations of *rapatriés* (people returning to their homeland) in order to express their demands for compensation from the state. The main association, with perhaps 200,000 members in the late 1980s, is the ANFANOMA (National association of Frenchmen from North Africa, from overseas and of their friends). This organization had been founded in 1956 after Tunisia and Morocco had declared independence. After 1962, it was there for the *Pieds noirs*. Many other associations were formed in later years: RECOURS (Rallying point and unitary coordination of *rapatriés*); and FURR (Federation for the unity of *rapatriés*, refugees and their friends), among others.[8]

These associations operated as pressure groups urging Parliament and the government to pass laws to compensate *rapatriés* for all that they had lost. But, as such indemnification would have been costly, the government was very reluctant to do so. The law of indemnification was passed only in 1970, after the events of May 1968. Payments were spaced over a long period after claimants submitted documentation often

---

[7] 930,000 *Pieds noirs* came to France from Algiers in 1962. See Stora, *La gangrène et l'oubli*, p. 256.

[8] See Joëlle Hureau, 'Associations et souvenir chez les Français rapatriés d'Algérie', in Rioux (ed.), *La guerre d'Algérie et les Français*, pp. 517–25. As these associations' names are meaningful in French, let me explain their acronyms. ANFANOMA means Association Nationale des Français d'Afrique du Nord d'Outre-Mer et leurs Amis; RECOURS means Rassemblement et Coordination Unitaire des Rapatriés et des Spoliés; FURR means Fédération pour l'Unité des Rapatriés, Réfugiés et de leurs amis.

difficult to obtain. This unsatisfactory and deceptive law was modified in 1974 and further improved in 1987, but many *Pieds noirs* still believe that they have never been compensated for the losses they suffered.

The *Pieds noirs* movement was and still is weakened by political rivalries. Many associations opposed the Gaullists in the presidential or legislative elections, since de Gaulle remains in their opinion the man who abandoned and betrayed them. RECOURS alone supported Jacques Chirac. The resentment against the Gaullists, responsible for the Algerian disaster, opened the way for more radical tendencies. The nationalist Front National of J.-M. le Pen is very active in some associations such as the JPN (Young *Pieds noirs*). By and large, as the *Pieds noirs* were not united politically, the associations they founded are politically diverse.

However, claiming benefits is only one of the functions of these associations; they have cultural and emotional aims too. Besides the major associations, there are smaller ones grounded on local affinities of origin or of destination – *Pieds noirs* from the city of Jemmapes, or of Beni-Saf, or living in the Val d'Oise *département* for instance. Other associations have cultural objectives, keeping alive songs, folklore, and theatre. There is a *Pieds noir* culture, with its jokes, its tales, its particular argot, its traditions. The memory of lost Algeria is still alive in these small local groups, as it is alive in the very large families where cousins, aunts, uncles, and their kin meet together regularly for baptisms, weddings, funerals, or sometimes for birthdays or feasts.

This *Pieds noirs* memory is built on the divide between before and after.[9] What matters are the good memories of Algeria before the war. These are memories of particular places: the landscape, the orange trees and the vineyards, the light and warmth of the sun, the aromas of the market places and of the wine cellars. Memories of a homeland where life was simple, easy, and cheap. Memories of a kind of community with the 'Arabs': the children playing football together, with their parents on good terms in business or in the neighbourhood. It conjured up a kind of sociability which made it impossible to understand why the story ended in a tragic way. The memory of the loss of their Algeria is that of a paradise lost, from which their exclusion remains an inexplicable misfortune. This nostalgic reverie is still strong and vivid among the *Pieds noirs*.

However, it is not a set of memories expressed or directed to French society as a whole. They never argued that France had a 'duty of

[9] See the excellent analysis of some *Pied noirs'* interviews by Anne Roche, 'La perte et la parole: témoignages oraux de pieds noirs', in Rioux (ed.), *La guerre d'Algérie et les Français*, pp. 526–37.

remembrance' about lost Algeria; it is only 'their' memory, a memory restricted to the initiate population.

What are the reasons for this restriction? A first reason is the physical location of the *Pieds noirs*: they did not form homogeneous communities. Most of them migrated to southern France where the land, the climate, and the kind of agriculture were similar to that of Algeria; others went to the Paris region or elsewhere. But, even in the Garonne valley or in Provence, they never built new villages or settlements. They were living amongst a long-settled population, and had to cope with local customs and get along with native-born people. More than this, they wanted to become Frenchmen like anyone else, not to distinguish themselves from the population at large. After 1962, they worked passionately to be integrated into French society.

This was no simple task, for they had to find jobs and homes, to form new friendships and bonds within their neighbourhood. Many of them had no money, no support. They helped one another very frequently, but their success depended upon their constant effort and the fortuitous conditions of a booming economy. Working so hard to become integrated into the French community prevented them from claiming that they were victims of this very community. These aims were contradictory.

From this point of view, their cultural institutions or traditions, such as theatrical companies, choirs, and so on, can be seen as a means of integration, for other groups, from various provinces of France, of from various countries, have similar activities. These ethnic associations are more integrative than distinctive. Hence it is difficult to avoid the conclusion that the *Pieds noirs* are a progressively vanishing community. Their cultural difference remains, but it does not operate as a framework for a kind of outward political or social movement. Their restricted memory is for internal use only.

On that point, two qualifications must be made. One could ask whether hostility to immigrants in contemporary France is fed by the *Pieds noirs'* trauma. Possibly, some *Pieds noirs* think that since they had been forced to quit their beloved country and their familial environment thirty-five years ago, now they want to keep this country as their own. One can understand their propensity to take an active part in the nationalist movements such as the Front national of J.-M. le Pen, himself a former activist in the cause of French Algeria.

A second qualification concerns Jewish *Pieds noirs*. Was not the new strong Jewish identity of French Sephardi Jews, whose fathers were not threatened by the Nazi genocide, a kind of substitute for an alternative identity, that of victims of Algerian independence, a population in exile, forced to leave their homes and go to metropolitan France? These victims could choose their victimizers. Supporting this statement, one could underline the double relationship between the *Pieds noirs* and the Jews of Israel, and between the Algerians and the Palestinians.

The ex-soldiers: an impossible memory

The second group of potential victims of the Algerian War were the ex-soldiers. Like the *Pieds noirs*, although for different reasons, they too were unable to convert personal memories of that war into a collective memory. First, they were deeply divided politically. Their veterans' association, the FNACA (National Federation of *Anciens Combattants* of Algeria), was controlled by the French Communist Party. This made it impossible for more conservative veterans to enrol in that association. Hence the Rightist association of *anciens combattants* of the First and Second World Wars, the UNC (National union of combatants) organized a particular sub-section for Algerian veterans. These two associations opposed each other on every issue, especially on symbolic ones. Therefore it was impossible, for instance, to find an agreement on the date on which to commemorate the end of the war. It would make sense for people of this forgotten generation who participated in the Algerian War to have a day in the year devoted to rituals of remembrance, parades, talks, banquets, and so on. However, for one ex-soldiers' association, the Leftist FNACA, the appropriate day is 19 March, which is not exactly the date of the treaty between France and the FLN (18 March), but the day when the struggle ceased; for the rightist association, this is unacceptable, for this treaty is considered as a kind of betrayal. They tried to make 16 October the date for commemoration because on that day, in 1977, one unknown soldier of the Algerian War was buried in the cemetery of Notre-Dame de Lorette.[10] This conflict over dates made commemoration impossible. Commemoration enforces unity but it first needs some unity.

The second reason is more profound. This war was meaningless for the soldiers who fought it. The conscripts hated it. Armand Frémond, a geographer who himself went to Algeria as a non-commissioned officer, underlines this point. The untranslatable slogan: 'La quille, bordel!' was the strongest, the most profound, and the most popular epithet of this period. 'Said with anger, violence or derision, it sums up fairly well the attitude of nearly all the conscripts. They did not accept the task they had to fulfil, even when they did their duty. The death of every one of them was seen as a double scandal: dead aged twenty; dead for

[10] See Claude Liauzu, 'Le contingent entre silence et discours ancien combattant', in Rioux (ed.), *La guerre d'Algérie et les Français*, pp. 509–16.

nothing.'[11] They never thought that French national interests were at stake: the Algerian War was not the beginning of something; only the end of colonial times. It was a closure, not an opening.

A final reason is probably the most important of all: it arises out of the absence of a generally accepted sense of the legitimacy of the Algerian War itself. This war was not legitimate from many points of view. The French army committed many crimes, including torture and killings in Algeria. One of the best-known cases was that of Maurice Audin, a junior lecturer in mathematics at Algiers University, who was a Communist. He was arrested by French paratroops, led to the villa Susini, the well-known headquarters of the investigation section of the army, tortured by French officers whose names are known, and finally killed. Torture was an ordinary practice, and one general, General Paris de la Bollardière, was dismissed for not accepting it. These facts were covered by an amnesty; hence they have not been discussed in the courts. It is possible to charge Mr Papon for the role he played as general secretary of the Gironde prefecture in 1942–3 in the deportation of Jews, but not for what he did when he was prefect in Constantine during the Algerian War, or later in October 1961 when he was responsible as the Prefect of Police in Paris for the killing of hundreds of Algerians demonstrating in the streets against an illegal curfew.

Papon's case is interesting because it leads to my central point: the link between the non-remembrance of the Algerian War and the remembrance of the Second World War. On the one hand, the illegitimacy of the Algerian War was due to the methods and practices of French army. But on the other hand, the entire war was illegitimate in itself; its goals were not acceptable. Opposing Algerian independence was not legitimate, as the United Nations said openly. The Algerian people had the right to become an independent nation-state. The French government claimed that Algeria was France, and a part of the French nation supported that position. They said that this war was not a war, but only an operation to maintain order, with the legal consequence of excluding ex-soldiers of that non-war from war benefits. However, in their soul and conscience, most French people knew perfectly well that the kind of domination imposed on the Algerian people had to come to an end.

Confusedly, French society did not feel that this war was a fully legitimate war. This lack of legitimacy was rooted in the obvious, although impossible, comparison between the Algerian situation and that of France occupied by the German army from 1940 to 1944. Undoubtedly, there is a myriad of differences between those two

---

[11] Armand Frémont, 'Le contingent: témoignage et réflexion', in Rioux (ed.), *La guerre d'Algérie*, p. 84.

historical situations. But there are similarities too. French soldiers fighting the *fellaghas*: were they entirely different from German soldiers fighting the *résistants*? Were their methods so different? The debate over torture posed the question anyway: was the villa Susini different from the Gestapo's cellars? It was impossible to avoid the parallel; even if confronted openly, such a debate would have been devastating.

However, French soldiers in Algeria still had the question in mind. Some of the ex-officers interviewed by B. Kaplan say it openly: 'We were doing *quadrillage* as the Germans did. Others [the *fellaghas*] were fighting guerrillas as the maquis were. We knew that very well; we had seen the maquis, we had seen the Germans. It was memories of our childhood. And we were the Germans, with our heavy weapons. They, they were the maquis, and we were the German occupation troops.'[12] For these soldiers, the Algerian War was and remained a dirty war; the indisputable legitimacy of the Resistance against the Nazis undermined the legitimacy of the Algerian War.

Hence, as B. Stora has suggested, the soldier's memory of the war remained a merely private memory. 'Soldiers without victory, without good causes, and without enthusiasm cannot become positive figures.'[13] Many books were published about the war – more than one thousand reflecting every angle of opinion. However, most of them were only narratives of individual experience, given and read as such. There was no collective work of remembrance, and the memory of the Algerian War was submerged by that of other events. This un-named war was and still is an un-remembered war. And for the same reasons.

The Second World War: resistance and national unity

This is precisely what makes the memory of the Second World War a necessary memory. The principle of legitimacy is fully alive here: it works to support and deepen the memory of this war. However, such principles tend to bend memories in some respects.

The victims were many. Prisoners of war, for instance, numbered 1,800,000 in 1940. No doubt they were victims of the war, but not entirely legitimate ones. They had not fought enough. According to the military system of values which was shared by the older cohorts among

---

[12] Kaplan, 'Une génération d'élèves', pp. 176 ff. Many years later, Claude Bourdet who had been one of the leaders of the *résistance* movement 'Combat' and an ex-deportee to Buchenwald, stated the point: 'I saw what the Nazis did. Was it worth it to defeat the Nazis by doing the same things as they did?' Cited in Stora, *La gangrène et l'oubli*, p. 110.

[13] 'Des soldats sans victoire, sans cause juste ou sans enthousiasme ne peuvent devenir des figures positives', Liauzu, 'Le contingent entre silence', p. 515.

the French population, mainly by First World War veterans, surrendering was shameful.[14] The POWs were not welcomed by the existing associations of *anciens combattants de '14*, which contested their status as combatants. Was not surrendering the opposite of fighting? Hence the POWs were obliged to create their own association in order to claim benefits. They meaningfully entitled it the 'Federation of combatant prisoners'.[15] It is now the largest association of veterans (300,000 members) and it succeeded in making the prisoners legitimate victims of the war. But when it achieved this goal, it was too late: the individual prisoners had succeeded too in achieving their own goals – to recover their civilian condition, their occupation, and their family life. The time when the ex-prisoners were accepted by French society as legitimate victims of the war was the time when they ceased suffering the consequences of the war. They did not constitute or perpetuate a sense of the kinship of victims of war.

The most legitimate victims, at the very end of the war, were the *résistants*, especially those who had been deported by the Nazis to the concentration camps. The predominant legitimacy of having fought the Nazis had many consequences. The major crime was collaboration with the Nazis: this was the main focus for the work of memory. Pétain and the Vichy officials were tried for having offered aid and assistance to the enemy. Otherwise, their judgment would have been a political, not a national event. Hence the original features of the *Epuration* – the cleansing of collaborators – in France.

Some people have argued recently that the *Epuration* in France was relatively mild. They are wrong: on the contrary, France had a very broad and tough *Epuration*. The civil courts opened more than 300,000 files for inquiry; 150,000 cases were judged; more than 25,000 civil servants were punished; nearly 10,000 people were executed.[16]

However, it is true that the main point was whether the person charged had had some kind of relation with the Germans or not. When the general secretary of the anti-Jewish office, Xavier Vallat, was prosecuted before the High Court, he said in his defence that he was proud that his own anti-Semitism was purely French and existed long before the Nazi regime. In the circumstances of 1945, being an anti-Semite

---

[14] Antoine Prost, *In the wake of war: 'les Anciens Combattants' and French society* (Providence/Oxford: Berg publishers, 1992).

[15] Christophe Lewin, *Le retour des prisonniers de guerre français* (Paris: Publications de la Sorbonne, 1986), tells the story of the formation of the Fédération nationale des combattants prisonniers de guerre.

[16] Henry Rousso, 'L'Epuration, une histoire inachevée', *Vingtième siècle, revue d'histoire*, no. 35 (January–March 1992), pp. 78–105; François Rouquet, *L'Epuration dans l'administration française* (Paris: CNRS Editions, 1993).

through personal initiative was less culpable than being one in response to Nazi orders.

This paradox is still alive. Paul Touvier was sentenced in 1994 for having sent to death seven Jews in 1944. According to French law, it is impossible to try someone fifty years after the deed, except in the case of crimes against humanity. But the definition of such a crime implies collaboration with the Nazi genocide. Hence the court justified its pronouncement stating that Touvier had obeyed Nazi orders, although it was perfectly evident in the proceedings that the Gestapo had nothing to do with these seven murders, which were the sole responsibility of Touvier himself. A just sentence is founded on an unjust argument.[17]

Conceived on these premises, the *Epuration* had the function of uniting the French people: the evil was outside. That made it impossible to face the fact that this war had been a civil war in some respects. The work of remembrance was made of lies, pious lies, well-meaning lies, but lies nonetheless. For instance, let us consider the case of Jean Zay. He was a very young and brilliant, talented politician, and the Minister of Education from 1936 to the war. He was murdered by the French *miliciens* (French collaborationist police) on 20 June 1944, because he was a freemason, a left-wing member of the hated Radical party, a minister of the Popular Front and supposedly a Jew. On his gravestone, one reads: 'killed by the enemies of France'. Before the door of the high school which has been named after him, there is written: 'victim of Nazi barbarity'. Both statements are wrong: the right one would have to be: 'victim of Frenchmen who thought themselves more French than he was'. The work of remembrance has tried to hide the fact that Frenchmen murdered other Frenchmen. Remembering was a way of preserving this kind of secret. The victims were rightly identified; the executioners were not.

Eight years later, it became somewhat difficult to preserve this hypocrisy. In 1953, the Court of Bordeaux had to judge the German SS soldiers who had burnt the little village of Oradour, near Limoges, in June 1944, burning inside the church most of the inhabitants of this village, including women and children. This martyred village was and is a strong symbol. It was a good case for remembering: the victims were French, and the executioners German. Unfortunately, it appeared that among the SS soldiers prosecuted, fourteen out of twenty-one were not Germans, but Alsatians, conscripted into the German army. Undoubtedly, they had contributed as much as the purely German soldiers to the slaughter. Meanwhile, Alsace was now part of France again, and there

---

[17] See Eric Conan and Henry Rousso, 'Touvier: le dernier procès de l'Epuration', in *Vichy, un passé qui ne passe pas* (Paris: Fayard, 1994), pp. 109–72.

was an outcry in that part of France when it became clear that the Alsatians were guilty and would be sentenced. The government suspended the proceedings and found a compromise: they were sentenced first and immediately received full pardons.[18]

This attitude toward resistance and collaboration had two consequences for ensuring that the Algerian War would be un-remembered. As noted above, the legitimacy of the resistance made the *fellaghas'* fight somewhat justified, and undermined the legitimacy of the war on the French side. Furthermore, the incapacity to face what had been a kind of civil war inside the world war made it quite difficult to acknowledge that part of evil which was in the behaviour of the French army, if not of all French soldiers in Algeria. The distinction has to be made, for torture is spontaneously spoken of by many veterans of the Algerian War, although no one says he was actually involved in the torture business. Everybody knows something which nobody did.

The emphasis put, after the world war, on fighting the Nazis as the basic principle of remembrance had a second consequence: only those who had actually fought the Nazis were real, legitimate victims. Those who had not, were not worth remembering.

Such was the case of the few Jews (2,500 out of 75,000) coming back from the concentration camps. As they had not been deported for fighting the Germans, but 'only' for being Jews, they were not true victims. This point is widely documented. For instance, former minister Simone Veil (then aged 16) was evacuated from her camp to Birkenau at the end of the war. A few days after entering Birkenau, she heard voices speaking French in a shed. She entered and tried to take part in the conversation. After she had said she was a racial deportee, something was broken; she felt the political deportees despised her and she gave up.[19] Another example of that attitude is to be found in the main agencies of remembrance, the associations of ex-deportees. They accepted as members only Resistance deportees, not racial ones. There were painfully few racial deportees who had come back from the camps. The survivors were obsessed with reintegrating into the French community, and as many of them were ill and depressed, they did not succeed in making themselves a community of legitimate victims. They were not seen as a distinctive group. More books about the deportation of the Jews were published between 1945 and 1950 than during the

[18] Henry Rousso, *Le syndrome de Vichy de 1944 à nos jours* (Paris: Editions du Seuil, 1987). See also 'La Seconde Guerre mondiale dans la mémoire des droites françaises', in Jean-François Sirinelli, *Histoire des droites en France*, vol. II: *Cultures* (Paris: Gallimard, 1992), pp. 549–620.

[19] See Annette Wieviorka, *Déportation et génocide, entre la mémoire et l'oubli* (Paris: Plon, 1992), p. 249.

twenty-five following years, but they were not read. As Annette Wieviorka put it, Buchenwald hid Auschwitz.

Things changed one generation later, around 1968 to 1970. There were many reasons for this change: the Middle Eastern wars and the Eichmann trial; the coming to the fore of the generation of deportees' children, such as Serge Klarsfeld; a new intellectual mood, inspired by 1968–1970 and the Foucauldian spirit of demystification. Undoubtedly, some agencies of remembrance were at work, as Annette Wieviorka's essay in this volume attests. The results are clear: the issue of genocide has become the crucial one for the memory of the Second World War. The specifically French question of collaboration with the enemy has been replaced by that of co-operation in genocide.

Thus there has emerged progressively, forty years after the war, a community of victims of genocide. This community was constructed less by the victims themselves, survivors of the camps, but by their families and sometimes by people whose family had not been threatened by the Nazi genocide.

And here we have to cope again with the *Pieds noirs*: the Sephardi Jews from Algeria contrast their condition to that of the victims of genocide. The Ashkenazi Jews deported from France to the death camps have a legitimacy as war victims which the Algerian Jews never had as victims of the Algerian War. Here is another link between the very weak collective remembrance of the Algerian War and the much stronger remembrance in France of the Second World War. One could not win on every table: the memories of the *résistance* occluded, indeed precluded, remembrance of the Algerian War. The memories of the good, noble war, hid the memories of the dirty one, which remains un-named.

Here we see how the social framing of individual memories is a decisive element. Individuals can form groups with the aim of transforming their collective memories into social action only when these memories are compatible with social norms and values accepted by the larger community. On the contrary, it is as implausible for ex-soldiers as it is for the *Pieds noirs* to claim their rights as victims of war. The war itself lacked the legitimacy necessary for this claim.

Victims are victims only when being in no sense guilty of complicity in their suffering. Suffering and losses are necessary but not sufficient conditions for victimhood. Innocence is needed too.

9   Private pain and public remembrance
in Israel

Emmanuel Sivan

> Even my loves are measured by wars:
> I am saying this happened after the Second
> World War. I'll never say
> before the peace '45–'48 or during
> the peace '56–'67.
> Yehuda Amichai[1]

I

A budding Israeli novelist, Amos Oz, in the introduction to a 1968
booklet commemorating his cousin, fallen in the Six Day War, describes
a meeting of friends and relatives during the ritual week of mourning:

Words. Commonplace words and unforgettable words. Tearful words. And also
unspoken words . . . and between the words – silences. It is impossible,
ineffable. We cannot explain. There were things, moments, deeds; yet we're
unable to name them. There once was a boy in Jerusalem, we loved him, we still
love him, we cannot let go of him. How little we can say about him. We
remember moments, laughs, conversations. Beloved smithereens of never-to-
return days.

They talk in confusion. Cutting into each other's words, repeating themselves.
Dazed by the dazzling sword of death . . . Here, now, what can we say. Now
there will be a commemorative booklet.[2]

Oz takes us into an intimate, typically Israeli scene, a sort of vigil; a
wake in which comrades-in-arms, friends, and family gather and recollect, tell stories, sing songs of praise and lamentation, one after another.
Together they conspire somehow to keep the beloved man around a
little longer, fixing him vividly in language, before memory fades. Oz
depicts an act of remembrance, part of a process of coping with death,
interlaced with a rehearsal of memory traces. Unlike wakes in other

---

[1] Y. Amichai, *The great tranquility*, trans.G. Abramson (New York : Harper & Row, 1983),
  p. 31.
[2] *Yizkor – Yigal Wilk* (Jerusalem: privately printed, 1968), pp. 4–5.

177

cultures, the Israeli one is likely to end up in a written and edited product. The memory artefact produced thereby – the commemoration (*Yizkor*) book (or booklet) is presented as a virtually inevitable product; as though the mourners were programmed by their society to express their grief thus while also creating an artefact, several specimens of which are to be found in virtually any Jewish-Israeli home (ultra-Orthodox ones excepted).

The therapeutic potential of the activity primes it all – as evidenced with particular poignancy in letters to the dead soldier (by mother, wife, etc.), or excerpts from diaries of family and friends, included in the booklets, which ponder the question of coping with grief. Yet almost as important is the remembrance aspect of this activity. It is best encapsulated in a terse poem contributed by a farmer to a book in memory of his son (and five of his comrades) killed in the Lebanon war (June 1982):

> You also were felled.
> It's spring, Memorial Day approaches,
> almost two years to your death,
> the passing time doesn't blunt the pain
> your twenty years erased
> as though they had never existed.
> Only your name
> drawn in the cement path, in our yard,
> testifies you had been on the earth.[3]

One notes indeed a nagging fear running through all the generations participating in the production of this folk historiography – namely, the fear that memory, personal, familial, and particularly social, is fallible, that the fallen may very easily be forgotten, unless some rearguard battle against forgetfulness is fought. 'Why write about him? For whom? For what?' notes another bereaved father, one of the heads of the Israeli intelligence service, in his diary, soon after the 1948 war.

I do not want this figure to sink like a stone in the Sea of Galilee, leaving a few ripples and that's all. He was my son and thus, thanks to kinship, I may have understood this unique human being better than others. I've learnt from experience that one cannot sketch out an authentic description of a great figure without an intimate affinity. This affinity suggests, nay even commands me, to try to do just that for my son.[4]

Both fathers echo the conviction that to forget is all too human. Indeed did not William James suggest that forgetting may well be essential to the health and vitality of the mind? The upshot is that the perpetuation of memory requires 'memory work', or remembrance. And

---

[3] R. Rosental, *Sayeret Beaufort* (Tel Aviv: privately printed, 1983), p. 41.
[4] S. Avigur, *'Im Gur* (Tel Aviv: Am Oved, 1981), p. 181.

in this particular case, memory work is intertwined with grief work. Fear of oblivion propels these two fathers, among a multitude of other relatives and friends, towards an effort against the tide of oblivion; that effort is bereaved commemoration.

The singularity of the Israeli case, due perhaps to the fact of its being a small, democratic society, is that the bulk of the effort is carried out through spontaneous activity of civil society rather than by the state. Parents, relatives, friends, army comrades – separately or together, usually in *ad hoc* groupings – but also sports clubs, youth movements, kibbutzim, schools, and the like, produce the booklets which have been dedicated to about one in two of all fallen soldiers.

This form of commemoration through civil society is even more popular than monuments. The booklets still occupy pride of place in the library of most Israeli homes. It is thanks to these books that the children born after a war (or too young when it takes place) are exposed to the war experience and its human costs. Moreover, this folk literature constitutes a unique attempt to catch and preserve the individuality of the fallen, going beyond the mere mention of their names (and the circumstances of their deaths). Each soldier – or group of soldiers (members of the same kibbutz, graduates of the same high school, members of the same platoon, etc.) – has many pages consecrated to him; his biography is composed by family, friends, teachers, or comrades-in-arms, often illustrated with photos; parts of diaries or letters are published; other creative mementoes, such as drawings, add their own singular touch.

Booklets are not costly (in money terms, albeit not in terms of time and effort). Yet even monuments, a much more onerous artefact to produce, are due, in virtually half of the cases, to the initiative of cells of civil society with no, or little, help by public subsidy. The same goes for other artefacts generated by remembrance: concerts or sporting matches held on the anniversary day of death, library inaugurations, scholarships granted, or Torah scrolls consecrated. All these practices can be traced back to a voluntary grouping, whether permanent or evanescent. Like the booklets, they attempt to commemorate the fallen in their individuality (vocations, hobbies, beliefs) – thereby constituting yet another effort against the current, in the age of mass, industrialized warfare.

Hence, perhaps, the deep sense of loss that the booklets (and even monuments) evince. There is little triumphalism in their mood, even in the wake of the 1967 war. As such, their long-term, unintended contribution has been to put in relief the human price of war and thus mitigate the tendency towards its glorification which five decades of warfare might have produced in Israel.

Another unintended, perhaps ironical, consequence of that plethora of initiatives was that whole generations of the fallen (1948, 1967, 1973, and 1982) were implanted in collective memory. The myth of the Israeli Fallen Soldier was rooted there; less due to official commemoration than to efforts of civil society of its own will and on its own terms. The irony of this consequence arises from the fact that it is intertwined with non-consequent intentions, those of grieving relatives and friends. The individual soldiers who died – the objects of all this intense activity – are or ultimately would be forgotten beyond their immediate circle, with the exception of a few dozen emblematic war heroes or particularly gifted individuals (poets, musicians, scientists). What remains is the memory trace – the price paid by ordinary people for the state's existence. The myth of the fallen soldier became from 1948 onwards an integral part of the Zionist-Israeli foundation myth. This narrative merged with the two former ones: the historical right of the Jewish people to the land and the pre-1947 pioneering effort.

The act of memory retention as well as the density of the recall may have been facilitated by the emotional nature of the event(s) and their unique characteristics; all the more so as they are linked to and etched on autobiographic memory.

This etching is why the moment of death or discovery of the body (for comrades-in-arms) or the moment of being notified (for parents and others) is so traumatic and, hence, saliently recurs in their accounts. The blow delivered by notification was not much cushioned by the fact that it was usually done in person by army representatives accompanied by a doctor. That traumatic moment was certainly emotional, but it was also a unique event; for parents to bury grown-up sons is a rare phenomenon in the modern age with the lengthening life span. It is rare and particularly wrenching due to a long period of attachment suddenly smashed, parenthood status suddenly ended, and the rising fear of impending ageing alone, with no children or grandchildren as solace and assurance of continuity. This applies to parents (and relatives); among comrades and friends who usually encounter for the first time the death of a young man of their age-group, and a well-liked one on top of that, one detects – through the private Yizkor books – the syndromes familiar to us from the two world wars' experience: guilt feelings at the fact of one's survival, anger and hatred towards the enemy, and thirst for vengeance. In the case of comrades-in-arms, who may have been suffering from cumulative fatigue, stupor, and dullness of feeling due to combat conditions, the sudden and violent disappearance of someone close shattered the dullness and created a gaping wound.

Again, personal experience (whether direct or mediated) is etched on autobiographic memory and rehearsed. At times this happens internally; at others, in public – in preparatory meetings during the planning of the Yizkor book (or other artefacts). It also occurs later in the yearly meeting of relatives and friends talking about the dead soldier (or group of soldiers).

Such meetings are an Israeli civic, secular ritual. They also gave birth to a widely popular Yizkor book, *Comrades talking about Jimmy* (Tel Aviv: Hakibbutz Hameuchad, 1955), which spawned many imitations. The conversation, whether transcribed or tape-recorded, has the quality of overlapping voices, a quality caught so well by Oz. Yet the conversation also creates a dramatic story, or a sort of song created and shared by the chorus of memory. As Jerome Bruner has suggested,[5] this story with many loose ends enables the mourners – and beyond them the 'community of memory' to encompass contradictory feelings and story lines with no need for the resolution that an expository representation would have required.

In order to understand the mechanisms involved in these forms of civil society commemoration and its social impact, we shall concentrate upon Israel's two major wars: the Independence War (1948), which was by far the bloodiest (5,900 war dead or one-third of Israel's total fatalities during a half-century of conflict); and the Yom Kippur War (1973), the second most costly (2,660 dead) and by far the most intensive (three weeks versus fifteen months of the War of Independence).

II

It was 1948 which created the 'booklets of commemoration' and some lesser forms of remembrance. Commemoration during the Yishuv period (1882–1947), when there was low intensity conflict with the Arabs, was largely official and institutional. Large-scale commemorative activity by civil society appeared during the 1948 war, and continued virtually unabated for the following five to seven years. It then levelled off, but never died. Some books about soldiers killed in 1948 have been published even in the 1990s. Revised versions of commemorative booklets have also appeared, prepared by siblings after their parents' deaths, which contain shocking stories on the circumstances of death, which they had censored in the 1950s so as not to exacerbate the parents' grief.

The shock of 1948 was due not only to the scale of casualties (1 per cent of the Jewish population of Palestine), but also to its distribution: in

---

[5] J. Bruner, *Acts of meaning* (Cambridge, Mass.: Harvard University Press, 1990).

the most heavily hit age-group (19 to 21 years old) more than 8 per cent of the males were killed. Furthermore, the overall figure showed a quantum leap in the number of losses suffered by the Yishuv during the seventy years preceding the war. Even if one adds to those killed in violent conflicts with the Arabs (about 800 until 1947), the Yishuv volunteers killed in the ranks of the British army during the Second World War, the total is only a quarter of those lost in the War of Independence. The 1948 war still casts a heavy shadow over the life of the nation, especially in the realm of collective memory and social imagination.

The emergence of the 'booklets of commemoration' highlights the Israeli cult of the fallen and the centrality of the 1948 experience. Patterns of this cult were shaped in the years just after the War of Independence and spread throughout society, helped by the impact of some Yizkor books which became best-sellers. While the genre underwent various changes, most characteristics of this 'literature of commemoration' – as it is termed in Hebrew – have remained constant. It is still the most authentic expression of the way civil society deals with the human losses resulting from the Arab–Israeli conflict.

This literature records reactions to the death of a soldier as shock, leading to expressions of loss and grief, among his relatives and friends. The first phase is individual and intimate. How do these feelings coalesce into commemoration as a social act, celebrated in public? (We are not referring here to those patterns of commemoration which remain in the private domain, such as hanging a picture of the dead son on the wall of the parental home or keeping his room as it was; our subject is public recollection.)

The conventional psychological study of mourning[6] locates this linkage of the private and the public, of intimate feeling and public behaviour, in the conventional 'third stage' of the grieving process, following disorientation and self-imposed isolation. The bereaved tries to recuperate, learning to distance themselves slowly from the dead, and to reactivate (or relearn) social norms of behaviour. Commemoration may serve the bereaved in two senses: first, as a social activity which requires cooperation with others, including those who share, in differing degrees, their sense of grief, providing them with social backing predicated upon affective sympathy. Secondly, commemoration may represent the objectification of the dead – in a monument or a booklet – and may help the mourners to distance themselves from them and to form

---

[6] G. Gorer, *Death, grief and mourning* (Garden City, N.Y.: Doubleday, 1965).

new relationships, while neither repressing their love for the dead nor denying the very fact of their demise.

If commemoration is part and parcel of an effort to rehabilitate the bereaved, it is a rehabilitation of a special kind, in that it intends to contribute to society at large while at the same time endowing the death in question with meaning. It does not seek to divert one's mind from the dear departed or to provide substitutes for them (in activities, new relationships, etc.). It rather endeavours, by objectifying their individuality, to transfer their memory to a wider social circle. What they have represented for their intimates is sought to be transmitted to others, from an in-group into out-group(s). A personal-familial memory may be integrated thereby into a collective memory.

It is no coincidence that most 'booklets of commemoration' appear on the first anniversary of the soldier's death. The Jewish traditional calendar of bereavement – followed even by most secularized Israelis – dovetails with the conventional insights of psychology. There is the practice of mourning in the week after death, the rest of the first month, then the following eleven months, corresponding roughly to the three stages of the grieving period during which there is a lessening of the rigour of ritual obligations and a growing integration of the bereaved into the normal life of the community. The first anniversary is the ideal point for the completion of a rite of passage – or rather near-completion – for future anniversaries may enable the bereaved to deal with the lingering sense of loss. (Half of the booklets on the 1948 war appeared on the second to fifth anniversaries; the majority of private monuments were erected during these years.)

In order to objectify the private memories of the bereaved, and thus contribute to collective memory, a vast amount of social activity is called for: preparatory conversations, the establishment of an informal committee, fund-raising (rather limited in scale in the case of most booklets), the collection of documents, the soliciting of articles, and the writing down of oral testimonials (sometimes at a special gathering). If one counts copy-editing, typing, production, and distribution (usually to a privately drawn-up list of addresses), each booklet involves the help of at least a dozen people, all associated in some way with the fallen soldier, shocked by his sudden violent and untimely death, and trying, according to their varying degrees of intimacy with the departed, to cope with their sense of loss, while attempting – through this very social activity of writing and publishing – to enlarge the social circle for which his death may have meaning. The dynamics of the support group and of group therapy are quite evident in these booklets, especially the reliance of parents on the help of comrades-in-arms (or friends) of their sons, and the collaboration between parents whose sons fell in the same battle.

Interviews conducted many years later with editors of commemorative books, as well as remarks interspersed in the booklets themselves, indicate that the idea of commemoration was usually broached during the first month after death (sometimes during the first week), that is, prior to the ritual visitation of the tomb, which in the Jewish bereavement process marks the end of the first year. The decision to edit and to publish is taken either at that stage or during the months immediately after. The book form was and is, more often than not, the only or, if there were later moves to have a multiple commemoration, the first option discussed. The idea is usually first discussed at the moment when the definitiveness of the soldier's death pervades the mind: the traumatic moment of viewing his body or – more typically – when the parent or friends stop writing in their diary, 'I still cannot believe he is dead.'

The guilt feeling among comrades-in-arms born out of their survival, due to sheer chance, is present in a different guise in the parents' generation. (Very few grandparents were involved in 1948, for they were not numerous in Yishuv families, founded for the most part by people who had immigrated young and without their own parents.) As one might perhaps expect in the highly ideologized society of the 1950s, parents – but also former teachers, who are frequent contributors to booklets – evince a deep sense of responsibility for the soldier's death, an event viewed in a way as the end-result of having brought their children up to serve the nation. In a broader context, death is seen as the upshot of their very immigration to Palestine. When parents recount their own life-story in a booklet, they begin, as a rule, with their immigration; life in the Diaspora is, typically, disregarded. In what was then a strongly conformist society, and in the context of a war deemed a 'good war', fought in self-defence and for the undisputed ideal of national independence, none of these issues gives rise to doubts as to the sense of this death, but they do provoke a feeling of deep personal responsibility that needs to be resolved, and endowed with meaning, in order to mitigate grief. An appeal to history and reference to an historical context could be a means to that end, hence the urgency of contributing to history-writing through the activity of commemoration.

At times editors and writers (especially of the parents' generation), however conformist, attest to their own anxieties that the Zionist dream may be turning sour – given certain Israeli realities of the 1950s (the decline of the pioneering ethos, party squabbles, corruption). They see the activity of commemoration, therefore, as a response to the social ills which have developed: social amnesia about the values on which the state was established, values for the sake of which they believe their sons had fallen. This complex of feelings is summed up by a telling metaphor – the 'sacrifice of Isaac by Abraham'. It was first used in a Zionist context in 1930 by the poet Yitzhak Lamdan to describe the pioneering effort, and it was adopted by bereaved parents during the 1948 war. Through them it passed into current usage through the Yizkor books. In the Biblical story, both father and son agree to obey the order; and even in the post-Biblical Midrash commentary, only the father has some doubts (which he overcomes). Indeed, the 1948 war was not a contro-versial war, as the Yom Kippur and Lebanon Wars would be. But gnawing doubts and anxieties remained; and certainly grief never disappeared, as all booklets testify. Healing is never assured.

Commemoration, it was hoped, might help to resolve this predica-ment within the context of the support group (family, friends, youth group, kibbutz, neighbours) which organized the commemoration and in a way stood for society at large. Resolve somewhat, but never completely, particularly as far as parents were concerned. There was justification but no sign of real (or enduring) solace. Here is the testimony of a mother:

It is difficult to acquiesce in this loss. Why is it that this being, so full of life and animation, lies still, his glowing eyes dimmed, his fresh body turning into earth. Why is it that there will be no more joy at my home, no worry for his future any more. I'll never hear his pals whistling for him. But why do I say this, I who have educated him to be a dedicated patriot, and even fight if necessary? Why do I say this, I who at your open grave declared that I am proud you fell for our homeland? Why?[7]

This does not explain why Israelis chose the publishing of booklets as a preferred method of commemoration. Booklets were obviously much less costly than monuments – their closest competitor. Many were published with the aid of a stencilling machine and required a short preparation time. There was no need to call upon a sculptor or ask for permission from the land-surveyors or zoning authorities. Monuments, on the contrary, had to be left usually to the initiative of the state, large army units, towns, or municipalities. What is more, as against the mere mention of a name engraved upon a slate, the booklet could present some of the individual traits of the departed – meeting a need felt perhaps with particular intensity in a small, intimate society like that of Yishuv (630,000 in May 1948). Other available alternatives did express this individuality, usually in a cultural project such as a library, com-munity centre, or scholarship. Yet these were often more costly than a booklet. A fourth alternative, the planting of a grove of trees or a special

---

[7] *Micah Fisher, Alim Le-zichro* (Tel Aviv: privately printed, 1952), p. 52.

garden, had the advantage of fitting in with the future-oriented pioneering ethos (leaving one's mark upon the landscape, etc.). Yet, here again, all that could be left was a mere name, with no individual message for posterity, no hallmark of who was the name's carrier, or what his life had been like.

Traditional religious forms of commemoration – for instance, the introduction to a synagogue of a Torah scroll named in honour of the dead – did not appeal to what was then an overwhelmingly secularized society, and account for barely half a dozen cases in the 1950s. They will emerge in the late 1960s, with the growing number in Israeli army ranks of 1950s immigrants (and their children) coming from Islamic countries, and imbued with a more traditionalist outlook; a development amplified by the growing, post-Six-Day-War respectability of religion even among Ashkenazi Jews.

In the wake of the 1973 war, civil society commemorated 52 per cent of the war dead (as against 32 per cent of those who were killed in 1948). The booklet mode still has pride of place, but it is followed by synagogue-oriented commemoration (dedication of a Torah book, chanting of psalms on the anniversary day of the death in battle, donation of chandelier or air-conditioning to synagogues), which accounts for one-quarter of the cases. The secularist nature of commemoration in the 1950s and 1960s is evident in the fact that even monuments and memorial plaques in cemeteries are rarely to be found (except in religious kibbutzim). In the eyes of Yishuv society, monuments sanctify the soil on which they are built, and not the other way round. No wonder that in the commemoration booklets themselves God's name is rarely mentioned; the name of God appears in a significant number of booklets only after the 1967 war, and even then only in a minority of them.

Respect for learning, long cherished among Jews, no less than considerations of cost and individuality, most probably contributed to that predilection for books as artefacts of memory. Most of the 'special commemoration projects', such as libraries, were and are related to books and book-learning.

Yet the phenomenon goes deeper than what is covered by the bland formula of 'people of the book'. It has roots in the Jewish tradition of commemoration, a tradition recently transformed and reinvented in the wake of the 1948 bloodletting.

These roots are to be found in the Yizkor (remembrance) books which appeared in thirteenth-century Germany and later spread to Central and Eastern Europe. These were chronicles of specific communities, updated from time to time by their notables, which depicted the history of the community: its major rabbis and prominent individuals, the persecutions it had suffered (especially since the First Crusade, that watershed of Jewish life in Christian Europe) and, most particularly, its list of martyrs, a list recited in synagogue four times a year within the framework of the special Yizkor prayer instituted in the early twelfth century. This prayer and the martyrs' names were the major motivation for the persistence of the literary genre and its conscientious updating. Historiography here was a sort of ancillary practice to ritual – that is, a way of conserving the collective memory by means of the perennial 'chain of martyrology' which was perceived as the Jewish people's lot in Exile, the martyrs sacrificing themselves in obedience to the just demands of the Lord. Collective memory was thus conveyed in a religious interpretive mode, especially through sacred liturgical texts. Each new wave of persecutions was taken to be a re-enactment of former ones.

The growing secularization of the Jewish people in the nineteenth century filtered down in the early twentieth century from elite historiography to the level of collective memory, and reshaped the martyrology. It is not fortuitous that this happened primarily in the two most lively centres of Jewish collective activity – Eastern Europe and Palestine.

In Eastern Europe the recasting of the tradition took place in the folk historical literature written in the 1920s under the impact of the pogroms which had taken place during the Russian civil war and the Russian–Polish war. The typical artefact is the community notebook (*pinkas*) which contains a description of the pogroms in a specific locality (Vilna, Pinsk, etc.), a list of the dead, the fluctuations of community life during the First World War, as well as a sketch of its life prior to 1914. These very sketches, sometimes quite long, reflected the change in outlook as compared to traditional Yizkor literature: in describing the community they did not limit themselves to rabbis and notables, but depicted all avenues of social and economic activity and dwelt upon emigration to the New World. Demographic transformations as well as pogroms are explained by this-worldly factors and not by a medieval-type theodicy.[8] This new, or rather reinvented, framework for collective memory, created a new form of Yizkor book, in which European Jews, during the Second World War and much more intensively after it, would register their collective response to the Holocaust (see chapter 6 of this book). Its artefacts constituted that spontaneous literature of Yizkor books and *pinkasim* commemorating those communities which had been obliterated, and published by *Landsmannschaften* of the survivors

---

[8] See articles by N. Wachtel and L. Valensi in *History and Anthropology*, vol.2 (1986).

in Europe, but above all in North and South America as well as in Israel. Here the aim of the survivors, or of relatives amongst earlier immigrants, is to cope with their grief and make it into a tool for crystallizing a historical consciousness. There is very little theodicy, because of the secularized character of most *Landsmannschaften*. The stress is upon the detailed description of the pre-war community and the horrors of its extermination, so that both will leave their indelible mark on the collective memory. The identity offered to the survivors does not refer to the deity but to the dead – a historical relationship predicated upon the continuity of an ethnic, secular affiliation. The centrepiece is the local community, and the individual is measured by his contribution to the latter. There is little trace of the ritualistic-liturgical context.

An analogous secularization of the Yizkor literature took place in the pre-1948 Jewish community in Palestine, starting with the Yizkor book to the memory of Second Aliyah members killed by Arabs (published in Jaffa in 1911), which produced numerous offshoots over subsequent years. As in Eastern Europe, the thematic framework is that of a profane grief. Bereavement is integrated into a consciousness of historical continuity, but lacks a transcendental presence. The entity overarching the individuals is that of the nation, not the local *shtetl*. The individual 'martyrs', who are accorded in Palestine, from the very beginning, much more detailed attention than in the East European books (perhaps because of the smaller numbers involved), are measured by their contribution to the pioneering project of the nation.

Still, it is significant that these booklets were self-consciously given the title of Yizkor books and that they made ample usage of the traditional martyrological discourse, reinterpreted according to the needs of the new ethos. Even modern societies, when facing war and the existential challenge of mass violent death, do need some anchoring in tradition (see chapter 2). That this happened even in a revolutionary, future-oriented society such as the Yishuv only underscores this argument; all the more so as the 'commemoration literature' is suffused not only with secularism but also with agnosticism and atheism. God is absent from the great majority of these books. Emblematic of this profane state of mind is the poem written by a father addressing his dead son:

> Standing before your closed book shelves
> as before the Ark of the Law [in synagogue];
> Ark with no curtain.
> Your father and mother shed tears there.
> Tears with no prayers.[9]

9 E. Kalir, *Mikerev* (Tel Aviv: privately printed, 1950), p. 37.

The encounter with death presents the true mirror of a society. And here we have one which even in an existential crisis makes no appeal to religious transcendence; it does, however, feel an urge for tradition.

This new martyrological ethos subsumed by the Yizkor literature of the Yishuv puts its subject, those who died a violent death (usually at the hands of Arabs), in a special, higher category among those who lost their lives for the sake of the Zionist endeavour (more 'sacred' than those who died of malaria, for instance). Here is the origin of the distinction still maintained by Israeli society between fallen soldiers and civilians killed by terrorist action.

The historical framework which endows their sacrifice with meaning is that of those who fell fighting for Jewish sovereignty, beginning with the Hashmoneans (second century BC), and those who rose in revolt against the Romans (first and second century AD), a tradition renewed, after a hiatus of nineteen centuries, with the First Aliyah. Jewish martyrology in the Diaspora is rarely, and at best erratically, mentioned. Unlike the traditional martyrology which cherished passivity, accepting the fate laid down by the Lord, the Yishuv martyrology had a distinct activist edge. Even when commemorating those killed in the Arab attack on Tel Hai in 1920 – an event transformed into a General Custer-type 'epic of defeat' – the emphasis was on the 'last stand' as an inspiration to continue the struggle, to take the initiative, to imitate the model of a heroism which does not resign itself to Fate (whether imposed by Providence or by the nation's enemies). Heroism consists of revolting against Fate.[10]

This secular, collectivist, and activist ethos was also geared to express the individuality of the fallen. In pre-twentieth century Yizkor books, only rabbis, notables or particularly heroic martyrs received such attention. The secular Yizkor and *pinkasim* literature of the 1920s or the post-Holocaust era concentrated on a wider gamut of prominent individuals (in culture, economics, social life) of an increasingly secularized *shtetl*. In Palestine, even when the numbers of dead during periods of riots were in the hundreds (1929, 1936–9), the 1911 formula was adhered to: a biography (usually accompanied by a photograph) of each of the dead, followed by testimonials, evaluations, memoirs, documents, literary, or artistic bequests.

While the first initiatives were entirely due to the leadership of the labour movement and, above all, to its mentor Berl Katznelson, the genre soon spawned a more spontaneous literature produced primarily in the kibbutzim, which possessed an institutional infrastructure, such

[10] See E. Sivan, *Dor Tashach* (Tel Aviv: Am Oved, 1991), ch. 8.

as a 'culture committee' and a stencilling machine. From the late 1930s on, the genre began to spread little by little beyond even the confines of the so-called 'labour (pioneering) sector' into long-established right-of-centre colonies or groups of friends in towns. Some semi-commercial publications followed suit. Other forms of commemoration (monuments, groves) did not proliferate to the same extent.

III

The commemorative literature on the War of Independence represents not merely a quantitative leap – almost ten times as many booklets were published in the 1950s as in all the pre-state days. What was still in Yishuv days to a large extent a semi-institutional literature, mostly beholden to the labour movement, now became a widespread social phenomenon, the product of a plethora of private initiatives. It should be noted, though, that the Ministry of Defence in 1955 published its own official Yizkor book, with quarter-page biographies of all the fallen, as it continued to do for subsequent wars.

Parents, friends, comrades-in-arms, neighbours, fellow residents, and professionals created *ad hoc* grassroots associations for publishing such books and booklets, side by side with kibbutzim, schools, etc.

The spread of the Yizkor literature as a socio-cultural mode of action had a direct impact upon what Roger Bastide calls the 'organization of memory'.[11] People remember as a part of a social group. Personal memories exist in relationship to the memories of other people who are relevant to the individual. Personal memories intermingle, influence each other and thus create a collective memory, feed it, and maintain its continuity. A collective memory enables groups to attain a consciousness based upon a sort of 'network of complementarity'. Collective memory is, thus, not an abstract entity over and above individuals. It is the product of these exchange relationships to which each group member contributes his or her own memories. Obviously the weight of the various memories is not equal. The group's organizational structure moulds the organization of its memory. The contribution of elites carries more weight. Whoever articulates his or her memories in public leaves a deeper imprint than one who does it merely in private or not at all.[12]

If we apply these analytical tools to the Israeli case, we perceive immediately that the 'organization of memory' gave a distinct advantage

---

[11] R. Bastide, 'Mémoire collective', *L'année sociologique* (1970), esp. pp. 76–96.
[12] M. Douglas, *How Institutions Think* (London: Routledge, 1986), chs. 6 and 7.

to certain social groups in the early years of the state. For instance, a comparison of the distribution of the fallen commemorated in booklets shows that sabras are substantially over-represented among the commemorated (four out of ten as against three out of ten among the bulk of fallen soldiers of the 1948 war). The longer an immigrant was in Palestine the greater his chances of being commemorated. Soldiers who had come before the Second World War were over-represented; those who had come after 1940 were under-represented by half; those who had arrived during 1948 barely figured at all. This applies even more acutely to those who were given what one may term 'intensive' commemoration – that is, in a booklet as well as in a scholarship, grove, youth group, or who were the subject of an individual booklet rather than part of one consecrated to a whole group. Sabras and veteran immigrants had an even greater advantage. This inequitable commemoration is all the more noteworthy, given the fact that war casualties were evenly distributed among all social categories, a fact due perhaps to conscription operating from the early months of the war.[13] What accounts for this commemorative imbalance?

Social integration is crucial here. Commemoration is carried out above all by families, by friends, by fellow soldiers, or by voluntary associations. Given that the median age of the fallen soldiers was twenty-two, if they had arrived in Palestine before the Second World War, they would have passed at least half their lives there, or at least had part of their schooling there. Moreover, those who had immigrated after 1940, and *a fortiori* after 1945, were Holocaust survivors, and hence much more likely to arrive as orphans, without any other immediate relatives in Palestine.

Due to their short sojourn in the country, immigrants who arrived in 1946–7 (more than a quarter of the fallen) were less likely to be members of youth movements or other voluntary associations, so vocal in what one may call the chorus of collective memory. Those who came in 1948 – usually from Displaced Persons camps in Europe or Cyprus – a few months or weeks prior to their death, were totally uprooted, hence rarely commemorated.

As one poet, a veteran of the war, was to put it years later, writing about new immigrant soldiers:

> We should try to remember them
> but this is not easy . . .
> In whose memory would a [newcomer] live?

[13] The statistical data and method used here and in what follows are set out in my 'The life of the dead', in J. Frankel (ed.), *Reshaping the past* (New York: Oxford University Press,1994) , pp. 172–4 (esp. figs. 1 and 2).

He has no parents to visit his grave
through the seasons, and water his roots.
He has no room to fit his photo,
no friends to talk about him, no widow
to confer his name upon her son.[14]

While social integration is a major factor, in what was (and still is) an immigrant society, in the 'organization of memory', it operates in tandem with the location of the individual in the gamut of articulation and social activism. The more educated the soldier, the greater the chances that his family, friends, or fellow group members would have access to commemorative modes: a knowledge of Hebrew (there are virtually no booklets in other languages); a newspaper (likelier in a kibbutz, a youth group, or a well-established neighbourhood); contacts with printers. No less crucial was the sheer fact of having relatives, friends, or associates who could invest the time and who possessed the editorial capacity to collect (or write down) testimonials and memoirs. It is hardly surprising that the higher the educational standard of the fallen, the more he featured as the subject of a booklet. He was also more likely to be given 'intensive commemoration'. Being an officer was an extra advantage, as it presupposed a high level of education (the same is true of the sabras and veterans). The collective profile of the commemorated thus tends to be somewhat slanted in favour of elite groups.

This characteristic begins to change from the 1973 war onwards, as the immigrants of the 1950s or their offspring gained access to secondary education and became integrated into social networks, for instance, synagogues, sports clubs, and the like.

Moreover, the better organized a social sector and the higher its collective consciousness (and sense of history), the more likely it is to devote effort and resources to commemoration. In the wake of the 1948 war this gave a distinct advantage to the kibbutzim, most of which had weekly or monthly newspapers, not to speak of the publishing facilities of the four major kibbutz movements. The upshot was that three out of five kibbutz members who died were commemorated (as against one in three of all fallen soldiers). Their share declined from the 1970s on, but still remained substantial. Even the rising representation of the national-religious during the past twenty-five years is due above all to commemoration by religious youth movements and yeshivas.

So strongly did integration combine with articulation to determine the organization of civil society commemoration in the 1950s and 1960s that the collective profile of those who are the subject of books is

---

[14] *Ma'ariv* (Tel Aviv), 8 May 1981.

dominated by sabras and those who had migrated in early childhood, officers and NCOs, the better-educated, kibbutz members, and members of youth movements in Palestine rather than members of such movements abroad.

Who, then, are those who are forgotten and left un-commemorated? Primarily 1948 immigrants and those with less than full primary schooling (who received a third of the share of the commemoration to which they were 'entitled'). They were followed by other new immigrants and lower socio-educational groups, who are under-represented by 50 per cent. New immigrants were obviously at a double disadvantage: they were less integrated socially and had a significantly lower level of education as a result of interruption of schooling in the war years. The vast majority came from Central and Eastern Europe.

And indeed to this very day Israeli society tends to remember the '1948 generation' as one made up of Sabras (or virtual Sabras, Palestine-educated veterans), articulate young males, preferably kibbutz (or labour-movement) affiliated – a sort of Israeli variant of the image of a lost, elite generation in Europe. This representation disregards the sizeable share of uprooted, barely educated, isolated, and perhaps alienated Holocaust survivors, who make up almost one-third of the population of fallen soldiers as a whole. Indeed, these people comprised about one-third of all those drafted in the 1948 war.

This is not to say that this folk literature was the only factor which created the image of a myth of the Sabra generation in the 1948 war. No less important was the role played by the poetry and fiction dedicated to the 1948 war experience. This creative effort was dominated by writers in their twenties and thirties; members of the older generation, standing in awe of the sacrifice of younger men, felt themselves, on the whole, disqualified from dealing with it. The young writers (the so-called 'Palmach generation') were, with few exceptions, Sabras or old-timers, preferring to write about those they had known best as comrades-in-arms and school friends. They were oblivious of the newcomers, insensitive to their past and present predicament, if not arrogant towards them.

The up-and-coming novelists and poets of the 'Palmach generation' (with its offshoots in the theatre and the media) were arguably the most powerful of the social actors shaping the collective memory of the 1948 war. Historians, for one, were almost totally absent from this arena. Yet how could such a distorted picture of the 'lost Sabra generation' be depicted without any protest from a civil society which had undergone the war experience? One way to account for this is through the fact that myth-making paralleled the spontaneous production of memory in civil society itself. At the same time they created an image of a war, the burdens of which were carried by Sabras and old-timers, a war in which a huge educated elite was sacrificed, thus creating a sense of qualitative social loss. This sense of loss was authentic but exaggerated, as was the role attributed to Sabras, though in qualitative terms (through their large representation in the officers' ranks) they did make a unique contribution to the war effort.

That the Sabras' and old-timers' claim to hegemony in Israeli society was thereby legitimated, was an unintended consequence of this parallel effort. One finds no trace of deliberate manipulation by the elite. This does not mean that those active in the field of memory-shaping, who tended by virtue of integration and articulation to come from these very social groups, were not comforted by this extra degree of legitimacy. For it did fit in with their own exalted self-image; an image shaped by, among other things, the way they remembered the war experience, and dwelled on those close to them who had fallen. The social and political rewards of their dominance of collective memory would not be refused by people so sure of their superiority as members (or descendants) of the 'pioneer generation', and at the same time so bruised personally by the sacrifices made by their social milieux in the 1948 war.

In the course of the (intended) passage from commemoration within the social group to the community at large, selective storage/retrieval and reconstruction (nay even distortion) of memory traces occurred. Collective myths were generated through the interplay of unintended consequences and non-consequent intentions (see chapter 1, p. 30 and above).

Yet what was the shelf-life of the remembrance of the 1948 war? The half-life of intense in-group (and some out-group) activity was, in this as later wars, approximately five years. During this period, a memory artefact is created which had a life of its own in the out-group (readers of the booklets, visitors of monuments, audience of a commemorative concert, etc.) and in the society at large. The in-group continues its activity (e.g. annual meetings of friends, camp fire chats, visits to the monument, etc.), though the pace tends to slow down with the parents' ageing and dispersal of friends. This activity still has a ripple effect, whereas the commitment of the in-group, created by the constant rehearsal of the memory it cherishes, made its members into constant spokesmen for this memory, a powerful voice in the 'chorus of memory', performing, so to speak, in the public sphere.

A telling indicator is how much early Israeli responses in all age-groups to the Intifada (1987–9) tended to pass through the (somewhat distorting) prism of memories of 1948: 'once again insecurity on the roads', 'civilians ambushed', 'our very existence in danger', arguments backed up by references to the first part of the War of Independence (Dec. 1947 to May 1948). This usage of the 1948 vocabulary is to be attributed not merely to the dramatic stories, told and retold by in-group members, by artefacts (and by fiction), but also to the changes undergone by the 'communities of memory', that is by those groups (in- or out-) for whom a certain memory trace is poignantly meaningful. Much in-group activity, from the 1960s on, was consecrated to the maintenance of artefacts, especially monuments. Yet distance from population centres (as well as ageing and dispersal) made this activity increasingly difficult. The state, which had always been suspicious of what it termed spontaneous commemoration, was loath to take over their maintenance. Frequently neighbouring small new towns (or re-gional councils) stepped in and accepted responsibility for them from the hands of the dwindling troops of relatives, war veterans, and friends. These adopting localities tended to be populated by immigrants of the 1950s for whom this step represented a way of linking up with a major national myth and endowing a new locality with a national genealogy, fostering local patriotism.

These new communities of collective memory, spreading in particular from the mid-1970s on among oriental immigrants, gave the 'memory traces' of 1948 a new lease on life. These communities likewise signified a growing integration of groups hitherto not included in the national military mythology – a reflection of deeper social processes, evidenced, for instance, in the growing rate of inter-communal marriages. Com-memoration as legitimator of the Sabra hegemony was slowly phased out. All the more so as integration of 1950s immigrants (particularly of oriental origin) was having a visible impact on forms and contents of commemoration in civil society. Markedly less secular than the old-timers, who would rarely put a monument in a cemetery, or invoke God in Yizkor books, the oriental immigrants introduced new forms already after the 1967 war, but especially from 1973 on: a Torah scroll written to the memory of the fallen soldier – a traditional Jewish mode of commemoration; a donation to a synagogue (chandelier, Ark's curtain, air conditioner) or the naming of one's child after the fallen; Talmud study or psalm recitation by Yeshiva students on the anniversary of the death, etc. Today these forms follow the booklets in terms of popularity, far preceding the old secular, future-oriented forms (e.g. groves). The greater militancy of the National Religious camp (whether Ashkenazi or Sephardi, old-timer or new immigrant) and its entrance into the power-structure, vying for cultural hegemony, further bolstered the religious content – not just modes – of commemoration (as we shall see below,

p. 202). It is only the ultra-Orthodox (Haredi) who are anti- Zionists, and needless to say, the overwhelming majority of Israeli Arabs, who remain outside this web of 'communities of memory', and whose voices are not heard in this collective chorus.

IV

It would be wrong to view the dynamics of remembrance solely through the metamorphosis of the memory of 1948, even though its heavy imprint is still felt in most aspects of Israeli commemorative culture. The input of other wars has to be reckoned with, if only because the interference of new memory traces diminishes (distorts, reinterprets) the impact of old ones.

None is more powerful than the memory of those intensive, half-defeat half-victory weeks of warfare in October 1973. Individual commemoration of the Yom Kippur War is above all expressed in hundreds of booklets, carrying on writing (sometimes through taped and transcribed conversations) the ongoing debate unleashed within Israeli society about the meaning of this war.

What does this multi-vocal chorus tell us? One encounters the universal gamut of reactions to sudden and violent death (guilt feelings, anger, revenge). One likewise finds typical Israeli themes such as the pre-war anxiety of the parents' generation (many of whom had fought in 1948) whether the sons would stand the test of fire. This parents' generation, one must stress, was much larger than in 1948, for almost all the war dead had at least one surviving parent, while in 1948 most immigrant-soldiers who had come after 1940 had no parent, and few relatives, in Palestine. And as the brunt of the 1973 war was borne by the regular army and young reservists aged 18 to 25, who accounted for 70 per cent of casualties, this fact seemed to convey a reassuring answer to the parental doubts. All the more so as the share of the Israeli-born in the 1973 fallen generation was much higher than in the past, keeping pace with the changing make-up of the younger age-groups: two-thirds of those killed were Sabras.

But the attitude of the 1973 parents' generation combines grief (as in previous wars) with particularly heavy guilt feelings. The lack of sufficient Israeli army preparedness made the parents, above all those who had served in 1948, feel responsible for the debacle of the early days of the war. All the more so as they may have served as role models for their sons, and perhaps even motivated them directly to volunteer for combat service. Worse still, shaken in their confidence that society was worth defending on the battlefield, many parents began to wonder aloud whether there was any justification for death, let alone solace.

The most salient thematic change consists of the sombre reality of war which casts its shadow upon this folk literature. Previous wars left in the Yizkor books matter-of-fact descriptions of the conditions of warfare in a manner which tended to work against militaristic glorification. Consider for instance the soldiers' conversations in *The seventh day*, published in the wake of the Six Day War. The overall share of such descriptions was, however, minimal in Yizkor books of the 1950s and 1960s. The sections dealing with the exact circumstances of their subjects' death tended to be laconic.

The post-1973 literature (including that of the Lebanon War) gives pride of place to descriptions of operations as well as of the circumstances of individual deaths. This is a virtually uniform phenomenon, all the more surprising given the spontaneity of this literature, but which could be accounted for, in part, by a 'demonstration effect'.

The 'operational' sections are fully documented. There are oral testimonies culled from comrades and commanders, later visits of the parents to the particular sector of the front (at their initiative or with the army's help). The text is illustrated with sketches, operational maps are peppered with code names. It is documented often with the help of reports of military commissions of inquiry appointed at the pressing and much publicized demand of parents to throw light upon controversial cases (e.g. the way the injured were evacuated from a certain battle).[15] Such reports never appear in the commemoration literature of the 1950s, because parents' protests, in this more conformist age, were channelled through correspondence with officials (including Ben-Gurion), and their none-too-frequent demands for inquiry were rarely satisfied. The blow the Yom Kippur surprise dealt to the credibility of the army high command – till then basking in the glow of 1967 – and their political superiors, is evident in the very multiplicity of such official reports after 1973. Moreover, such reports were now made public. Guilt feelings in high places combined here with the vociferous, no longer respectful and restrained, anguish of bereaved parents, backed up by the battle-bruised comrades who were so active in postwar protest movements.

Other documents which appear in the mid-1970s booklets concern men missing in action (MIA) and presumed dead. The MIA phenomenon was much broader than in any previous Israeli war, and adds a wrenching twist to bereavement, depriving it of the modest succour of

---

[15] *Yizkor – Ya'acov-ze'ev Blitz* (Tel Aviv: privately printed, 1974).

the grave site. The dry language of such official reports barely covers the horror:

Tank Number xxx was the nearest to the Suez Canal. In it were found the bodies of two soldiers directly hit by Egyptian anti-tank missiles. The two other occupants, one of whom being your son . . . might have been thrown out of it or left it after it had been hit and might have been killed by enemy infantry.[16]

This increased exposure of the brutality of war and its devastating effects is attributable in part, to a greater degree of military profession-alism: most parents of the 1973 generation had long military service (regular and reserve) behind them, as did friends and comrades. Yet it reflects above all the shock undergone by a society which led it now to break a tacit agreement honoured previously: if the horrors of war are to be referred to, this was not to be done in direct reference to the circumstances of death of the person(s) commemorated. Self-censorship by fellow soldiers, wishing not to rub salt into the family's wounds, must have persisted to some extent, but the very bluntness one finds in the post-1973 descriptions denotes a battered and at the same time more open society.

A striking note of finality is struck in the appendices of the booklets: technical ones such as the army official form 'List of Personal Objects and Documents Related to an Injured Soldier': watch, key ring, purse, bus schedule, small coins. This is it, says the document. He is no more. Other appendices comprise letters written by parents to the son during the war in the days after his demise or disappearance and returned to them by the military mail. All such letters have but one refrain: 'please give a sign of life'.

This exposure of the horrors of war as well as that of the anguish of parents, wives, and friends makes these booklets gloomier than those produced after previous wars. It could be argued that they render society even less likely to be infatuated by war. The anguish is illustrated by a multiplicity of details related to the long wait for publication of lists of the dead (or MIAs or POWs); unpleasant contacts with an obtuse army bureaucracy; the emotional ups and downs undergone by family and friends. All this is reported in a variety of styles: from the barely literate to the highly articulate. Even the tendency to add a heroic tinge to the dead is obliterated. He may be described warts and all, even in war. One mother recounts how her son reacted to the radio announce-ment on Yom Kippur 1973, at midday, that a war had broken out. 'You did not believe it. You said: "It's impossible; it's an electoral ploy." You lay down and fell asleep. You wanted to forget it all. I waked you up,

[16] *Yizkor – Ya'acov Kramersky* (Kibbutz Mesilot: privately printed, 1974).

confounded and depressed.' A tank commander named Jacob tells in a booklet commemorating his friend Danny, how they last met, a day before the latter would be killed:

On Sunday, 7 October, we came back to the Tassa camp [in Sinai] at seven. We ate breakfast and went through with tank maintenance. One of the guys told me: 'There was somebody here, with glasses, looking for you . . . He didn't say his name, must have gone to chow.' I rushed to the mess and here I see Danny, in unbuttoned overall, black undershirt, unshaved, Uzi slung on his shoulder, looked terrible. I said: 'Danny, how are you?'

Danny: Look, Jacob, it's horrible. We got wiped out yesterday. All my guys are gone.

Jacob: Danny, do me a favour, don't tell me anything. Let's talk about now. We are alive. Let's get on with it.

Danny: Jacob, you can't imagine what happened to me yesterday.

And then he tells me how their tank got stuck last night. Nobody came to pull them out. They were told to fend for themselves. They fought out and joined our forces.

Jacob: Danny, listen, get a hold of yourself.

Danny: If I go, I will not come back.

Jacob: Danny, enough is enough.

I still tried to boost his morale, but in vain. We embraced . . . I accompanied him to his tank, he heaved himself into the turret . . . We waved to each other . . . I bit my fingernails. How did Danny get to such a state, I thought. He never was a coward. I was desperate.[17]

Indeed, the commemoration literature changes its tropes: more of the realistic, less of the heroic. And as we shall see below (pp. 203–4) a third trope, the ironic, would creep in.

What makes the description of war horrors and those of its aftermath so traumatic is not just their exposure, but the wrath and outrage with which it is suffused. The commemoration literature of the 1950s was elegiac; the sense of loss somewhat mitigated by what was taken to be a worthy achievement, the state's birth and survival. The 1967 literature was immersed in a narcissistic, complacent, and self-congratulatory tone: yes, war is horrible, but on the whole we kept our moral fibre and won – a tone which the 1973 generation would dub derisively: 'shooting and crying'. The 1973 literature, on the other hand, is characterized by probing, merciless self-criticism, doubts as to the very justification for the slaughter. True, these were the dominant themes in the mid-1970s public sphere, expressed in the media and in protest movements. A 'feedback loop' operated here, manifest above all in the parents' and friends' conversations out of which the commemoration literature emerged. Yet the very fact that these themes were now expressed

---

[17] *Ner Zikaron Le-danny* (Jerusalem: privately printed, 1974).

through a genre the aim of which had been to cope with loss shows how profound was the 'October Earthquake', privately and collectively. It was difficult even to look for some solace, whereas the failures, especially in the early part of the war, were too glaring to be eclipsed, in the eyes of the bereaved (as well as of most Israelis) by the victories of the later phase.

Criticism of the way operations were conducted was levelled by parents and comrades even in 1948, but not in public.[18] Complaints were sent to the authorities, often to Ben-Gurion in person, through the proper channels. The tone was bitter but on the whole respectful; only in rare cases were medals sent back in protest or a commission of inquiry demanded (in vain). In 1973 the criticism is in the open – an indicator of a more transparent, less conformist society. That this criticism is to be found even in the Yizkor booklets gives it a particular weight.

Here is an account of a reconnaissance unit going into battle in the Golan Heights:

When I arrived at the base camp in the night following Yom Kippur it was three A.M. We found that our unit had less jeeps at its disposal than it was supposed to have by regulation. Some jeeps lacked machine guns. We had to 'steal' them from semi-armed vehicles in storage. No jeep was equipped with the regulation binoculars. We had to scrounge them. All this wasted a lot of time. Worst of all – we didn't find enough maps, and we were about to go into an area we didn't know at all . . . Driving up toward the southern part of the Golan Heights we met a horribly battered group of dozens of our soldiers going down by foot, like refugees, in torn clothes, most without arms. Some had fled from army positions, others had abandoned their tanks. They told us terrible stories.[19]

Another fellow soldier writes:

For seven years we have lived the illusion of omnipotence. This led some of the IDF top command to recklessness, perhaps to corruption. We have been self-satisfied while the Arabs have drawn lessons from their debacle. How strange it was that they became the heroes of night warfare. We were frightened at night for they had night-vision instruments and we didn't.[20]

A scathing barrage of criticism targets the war strategy, for instance the wasteful tank battles of attrition. This sort of criticism was elicited in the past only by one botched battle, the Latrun battle of 1948. This is what one reserve soldier says of a tank battle he had closely studied, in which his brother had been killed:

What enrages me in particular is that his tank stopped dead twice during the

---

[18] IDF archives, files 1512 – 702/60; 1189 – 782/65; 592 – 852/51; 377 – 580/56; 1006 – 220/70.
[19] *Havrei Ha-goshrim* (Kibbutz ha-Goshrim, privately printed, 1975), pp. 11, 16.
[20] Ibid. p. 17.

operation. Is that what you call maintenance? The very fact that General Gorodish dispatched them against an iron wall of Egyptian tanks and infantry, not knowing really how effective the enemy missiles were, is infuriating. There were intelligence reports of these [shoulder-held] anti-tank rockets, but had they never caught his attention?[21]

This reservist goes on to lash out at the political leadership (for short-sightedness, avoiding a peace initiative before the war), yet he doesn't shun self-criticism and even finds some fault with his dead brother: 'One cannot lay all the blame upon the powers that be. They are an integral part of the people and each influences each other.' He points out that this very air of self-satisfaction can be found in his brother's letters, suffused with derogatory references to the Arabs and their culture. These twin factors greatly contributed to what happened in October 1973. Indeed in one of the letters included in the Yizkor booklet, dating from 1969, the brother, then a teenager, reacts enthusiastically to an arrogant militaristic speech delivered at his high school by General Ariel Sharon.

Exposure, openness, and self-criticism are pushed even further in Yizkor booklets published by kibbutzim, which had produced the more conformist specimens of the genre. Their publications now comprise letters of fallen soldiers complaining of the 'conservatism', 'mediocrity', and 'rot' of kibbutz society. Mutual support is found to be lacking, envy to reign supreme.

Enveloped in such an air of crisis, it is hardly surprising that there is questioning of the justification for death in battle. This is certainly true of the secularist booklets which constitute the majority of the genre, though a somewhat smaller majority than in the previous two decades. For most parents and friends, even when facing such a terrible loss, invocation of the transcendental still has no place; sacred agencies are not their recourse, the profane dominates. God is absent from their (tape-recorded) conversations.

The secularist majority still accepted in the mid-1970s the basic justification for war as action taken in defence of the collective. The Egyptian–Syrian joint attack on Yom Kippur in 1973 helped most Israelis stick to this article of faith, which would be really shaken merely by the Lebanon War (1982–3). A tiny minority of the 1970s Yizkor books puts the blame upon Israeli leadership for not offering political compromise in order to reduce Arab motivation to go to war. Many parents and friends said openly, however, that their own particular son/husband/comrade died in vain, in the Yom Kippur war, because of bad strategy/tactics, or sloppy training and maintenance. In the past it was

---

[21] *Ne'edar – Sihot Le-toch Ha-layla* (Tel Aviv: Eked, 1976), pp. 19, 31, 43, 70.

unheard of to speak in this vein in the house of the bereaved or in such an intimate artefact as a Yizkor book. And what's more, to do so before the end of the year of mourning. Many booklets used to end on a partly affirmative note: 'Our loss has meaning but there's no solace.' Now meaning was in doubt, solace virtually impossible.

None of the above applies, however, to booklets originating in the national-religious sector, which represent (from 1967 on) a sizeable part of this folk literature, and a part much more committed to a collectivist ethos than the increasingly individualistic, secularist booklets. The very form of the national-religious booklets is different. It has two parts: the first, the traditional mode of Jewish written homage to the dead – exegesis of canonical texts not necessarily related to the fallen soldier's life or circumstances of death, yet dedicated to 'the elevation of his memory'; the second is modelled on the secularist booklets. Obviously there is a difference in content as well: justification for death in battle was always endowed here with both transcendental and nationalist qualities. And this sense of *zidduk ha-Din* (accepting God's just verdict) is maintained intact in the wake of the 1973 war. The Sacrifice of Isaac and Abraham metaphor would come to be used in the secularist Yizkor in a somewhat sceptical way (does the father have the right to send his son into battle for a blemished society?). It would even be extended in ironic ways, as we shall see below. No echo of all this can be detected in the national-religious Yizkor books. There the metaphor is used reverently, an example of a pure act of faith. 'Ours is not to reason why this soldier died. God has so decreed. We lower our heads, accomplish the *mitzva* (precept) of dying for the sanctification of His name, or dispatching our sons and students to do so. He, in his infinite wisdom, resolved that this sacrifice should be made for His name and for the Jewish people', writes one rabbi in the book dedicated to graduates of his Yeshiva fallen in battle.[22] All this reflects the growing chasm between the secularist and the religious sectors of Israeli society. This chasm accounts, in part, for the rise in 1974 of the Gush Emunim ultra-nationalist fundamentalist movement, as a response to the 'failure of nerve' of secular society in coping with human loss and the prolonged Middle Eastern conflict.

What the national-religious termed 'failure of nerve', the secularist majority after 1973 called 'auto-critique' and 'demystification'. In 1970 during the War of Attrition on the Suez Canal, only a young playwright, Hanoch Levin, dared to mock the bereavement myth. Indeed the War of Attrition was the moment when the first cracks were visible in the Israeli

[22] Rabbi Y. Ba-Gad, in *Yizkor* (Nehalim: Nehalim Yeshiva, 1974).

'security consensus'. Was this war necessary, some (regular and reserve) soldiers, as well as teenagers, asked in 'open letters' to the Prime Minister, which were later published in the press. Hanoch Levin gave a particularly poignant voice to these questions and doubts in an acerbic cabaret play, *Queen of the bathtub* (the said queen being the then Prime Minister, Golda Meir). The Tel Aviv theatre where it was staged was the object of angry and violent protests, led quite often by bereaved relatives who denounced it as sacrilegious. The show had to be taken off after two months. The cabaret number which enraged them most was a song where a fallen soldier talks to his father from his grave:

> Dear Dad, when you stand at my grave,
> Old, weary, and very much childless,
> And you'll see how they put my body into the earth
> And you stand above me, Dad
>
> Don't stand so proud
> Don't raise your head, Dad
> We remained flesh against flesh
> And it's time to cry Dad
>
> So let your eyes cry over my eyes
> Don't keep silent out of respect for me,
> For something more important than Honour
> Lies down at your feet, Dad.
>
> And don't say you made such a sacrifice
> For he who sacrificed was I,
> And don't use high words anymore
> For I already lie very low, Dad.
>
> Dear Dad, when you stand at my grave,
> Old, weary, and very much childless,
> And you see how they put my body under the ground
> – Ask for my forgiveness, Dad.[23]

The metaphor of the dramatic test of Abraham and Isaac was turned on its head. In the early 1970s such a denunciation of the Bereaved Parent myth, pointing out that parents gained in social status and moral authority while sons rotted, was accepted only by a young, mostly dissident audience. After 1973, one finds Yizkor books, notably in kibbutzim, where this sarcastic song had pride of place alongside the 'canonical' modern Hebrew poems on death and mourning. A hitherto marginal argument has moved into the very centre of public discourse, and into that of its major audiences, the 'Family of Bereavement' – that none-too-inaccurate Israeli term, denoting the nebulous web of kin and

---

[23] H. Levin, *Ma Ichpat La-tsipor* (Tel Aviv: Zemora-Bitan, 1987), p. 92.

adoptive kin (friends, comrades) which carries on the remembrance effort.

An even more telling indicator is the most commercially successful of the memorial books, which has become something of a cult object. The book consists of translations of anti-war poetry (by Bertolt Brecht, Jacques Prévert, Bob Dylan etc.) made by a 23-year-old kibbutznik who died in the Yom Kippur war.[24] The tone is irreverent, sardonic, angry.

To the heroic and realistic tropes, an ironic one was added. Nor were Hanoch Levin and that poet-kibbutznik its only voices. Four young satirists, all reservists who had served in the Yom Kippur War, published in 1975 a pastiche of the Yizkor booklet, *Comrades talking about Sahbak*. It sends up a popular sub-genre, which records a conversation 'around the camp fire' about the Fallen (above, p. 181), a genre which had produced a few best-sellers. The 1975 booklet combines tall stories, clichés, and patriotic pieties, about Our Friend (*Sahbak*, a jocular term in soldiers' slang, borrowed from Arabic), a good-for-nothing boy, very conformist, but much liked by everybody, who dies a senseless death in action.

Dr Joseph Burg, a crusty old politician, said that 'before the [Yom Kippur] war everything was better, even the future was better'. In any case, after the war, all would be different; bereavement and remembrance would be starkly different.

In subsequent wars one would find the bereaved, first spearheading the opposition to the war, drawing upon their moral status in the Lebanon War (1982–3); then, during the Intifada, acting in the name of mourning and 'sacred memory', in both political camps, one criticizing the repression and the other supporting it. As society split asunder along a Right/Left axis, and as, moreover, it tended to become more individualistic and hedonistic, the collective memory of war, perhaps even grief itself, became increasingly politicized and controversial.

---

[24] G. Rosental, *Oh Barbara, what a dastardly business is war* (Tel Aviv: Sifriyat Poalim, 1975). The book was edited by his brother. The title poem is by Prévert.

Samuel Hynes

> Writing about memories is less a way of finding out what actually
> occurred than what, in the fullness of time, one is capable of making of
> what may have done so.
>
>   Frank Kermode[1]

A personal narrative is what can be made of what may have happened; a
personal narrative of war, then, is what can be made of remembered
war. Men who write such narratives are *makers*, like poets (who are
etymologically makers), and novelists, and all other constructers of
words. But what exactly do they make? Are such narratives memorial
gestures that fix and communicate public meaning, like war-monuments
– the Cenotaph or the Marine Corps Memorial or the Menin Gate? Or
are they a different kind of gesture, a different act of making?

If we follow James Young, and take *memorial* to be the general term
for a class of collective gestures of public commemoration, including
material objects (monuments), fixed days (Memorial Day), assigned
spaces (Valley Forge Cemetery), and even unique occasions (meetings,
conferences), then we must surely say that the written recollections of
the men who performed the acts that taken together constitute a war
must also be memorials.

But there are problems in the terms of that definition. In what sense
are personal narratives *collective*? Are they generated by some common
impulse beyond the personal? Are they conditioned by states of mind
outside themselves? Do they individually belong to the art of public
memory? Of national memory? Or are they a set of essentially private
transactions between a man who was there and the things that happened
where he was? Is it accurate to say that one man's remembered war can
expand to embrace some larger category of his fellows – his regiment,
his army, all the fighting men in his war? Or does it speak only for a class
of one – himself?

We may find some answers to those questions by looking at the

---

[1] *The Observer*, 23 June 1996, p. 14.

differences between personal narratives and other acts of remembrance. The most obvious is that only personal narratives are *stories*: among memorial gestures only narratives happen along a line of time, in which meaning is not fixed but emergent. Stories deal with causality and change, and war-stories tell us processes of war: what happened to the teller, and with what consequences. Meaning in narrative is that process in time, and not a frozen gesture; and because that is so, the relation between the artefact and the person who experiences it is different from other cases. You participate vicariously in Robert Graves's war when you read *Goodbye to all that*; you don't experience a cemetery that way.

Personal narratives also have voices, and that is another difference. Voice in narrative asserts the individuality of the experience, and imposes private feelings and responses upon events. Look at Lutyens's war-memorial at Thiepval, and then read Edward Liveing's memoir of the first day of the Somme offensive. Are they both memorials? What do they have in common, beyond geographical location? Which one expresses the meaning of what happened on that ground on that day? Which is 'collective memory'? I'd say neither, but for different reasons: not Lutyens, because no pile of bricks and stones can cause us to remember what we have not seen – the deaths of many men; not Liveing, because one man's 1 July 1916 is not everyman's and is not ours, and even the most vivid words will not change that fact.

The problem is in the word *memory* itself. It is common for historians who write about memorials to say that memorials as a class embody and communicate memory; but I find it hard to see how this can possibly be true, unless, like Humpty Dumpty, we make words mean what we *say* they mean. Memory is the mental faculty by which we preserve or recover our pasts, and also the events recovered. Without that link – *now* reaching back to *then* – you may have an image of the past in your mind, but it isn't memory but something else, a social construction, history.

What does it mean, for example, to say that what one experiences at the Vietnam Veterans' Memorial is memory? For actual veterans of that war the names on the stone will call up persons and events in their own personal pasts; but for the rest of us? What we hold in our minds as we stand before the Wall will be the carved names themselves, and the sad army of the dead that they stand for. There is no element of remembering here. Or think of the First World War. I have a clear and quite detailed set of images of that war in my head, and so does every other literate person; but I don't *remember* it as I remember my own war, and no amount of monuments, Armistice Days, and conferences can turn my images into *memory*. For the images and stories in our heads that constitute our versions of other men's wars we must find some other term.

And there is a perfectly good one at hand: what we do, when we summon up our common notions of what the First World War was like, is to call upon a collective, *vicarious* memory: we evoke our shared myth of the war. Myth here, it scarcely needs saying, is not a synonym for falsehood; rather, it is a term to identify the simplified, dramatized story that has evolved in our society to contain the meanings of the war that we can tolerate, and so make sense of its incoherences and contradictions.

In the construction of a myth of war, memorials play a very small role, and personal narratives a very large one. Not any single narrative alone, but narratives collectively, for what war-stories construct is a combining story that is not told in any individual narrative, but takes its substance from the sum of many stories. Over time a process of selection takes place, one anecdote is preserved and another rejected and forgotten. Sometimes (as in the case of the First World War) an ironic tone is adopted as the appropriate mode of telling, and words like *disenchantment* and *disillusionment* come to be used as though they were objective and neutral terms for the soldiers' attitude toward the war's events, and even of *all* wars. Story and way of telling converge, tone determining the selection of events and events determining tone, until a complete, coherent story emerges. We might call that emergent story 'collective remembrance', if we insert the necessary qualifier *vicarious*; but myth is a better, clearer term.

In this process of myth-making, personal narratives both share in the creation and preserve it. Not all of them, to be sure: most narratives, of any war, sit dustily on library shelves, unread partly because they are ill-written and dull, no doubt, but partly because they tell the wrong story, because they don't conform to the myth. Those that *are* read tend to confirm each other – Sassoon supports Graves supports Blunden supports Frederic Manning supports Guy Chapman; Caputo supports O'Brien supports William Merritt supports Tobias Wolff.

We must believe that war narratives also confirm the memories of men who fought but did not write about their wars. Confirm, but also perhaps construct; for the order and meaning that written versions give to the incoherence of war must operate on other memories, making sense of the muddle of images that most men bring back from their wars. So the stories that Sassoon and Graves tell shape and colour the recollections of Private Smith, who never wrote a word about them. In this sense, and only in this sense, personal narratives do create a kind of collective memory in the minds of men who shared a common war. But in other minds, in other generations, they have a different existence, as a complex shared myth of great imaginative power. You can see the power of the First World War myth in the tone and particulars of novels and plays written by authors who have no personal war-memories, but are energized by other men's stories – novels like Pat Barker's *Regeneration* trilogy and Sebastian Faulks's *Birdsong*, and plays like Frank McGuinness's *Observe the sons of Ulster marching towards the Somme*. These are excellent, moving works, and convincing ones; but they are not memory, and they don't draw on memory, except indirectly through the myth of the war that they share.

I have been using 'personal narrative' here as the name of the general category of war-stories written by men who were there, and experienced directly what they wrote about. Within this category there are sub-sets, and we ought to keep them distinct in our minds. Two principal distinguishing elements occur in war-narratives, which vary inversely with each other: call them *immediacy* and *reflection*. The nearer the act of recording is to the events recorded, the greater the element of immediacy – the pure happening of sensory particularity. The further the narrative is from its events, the less pure the happenings will be, and the greater the element of reflection, which shifts the focus inwards, to meaning and subject-response: no longer simply what happened, but what did it mean? How did it affect me? How was I changed by it?

The most immediate of personal narratives are of course the letters that men at war write. Their letters give us the purest, most unmediated version of war, the least shaped, the least reflective. Days are recorded as they come, in all their dailiness, the boredom along with the excitement, the trivial with the historic. Letters generally are unweighted by judgment or retrospection; they simply report.

Diaries and journals are similar in their dailiness and particularity, or almost so, but they differ from letters in one important aspect: in the nature of their audience. The letter-writer speaks to someone else, elsewhere, and shapes his record to that otherness; the diarist speaks to himself. Self addresses self, writer and reader share the same knowledge and the same feelings, and so the telling inevitably turns inwards and becomes reflective.

The least immediate and most reflective personal narratives are those for which I would reserve the term *war-memoir* – thus noting the roles of time and memory in their making. These are the war-books that most of us know, and the ones that collectively provide the fabric of our war-myths. They are distanced from their events by a decade or more, sufficient distance for the narrator looking back on his soldiering self to see almost another person, the young man who came out of innocence into war and was changed by it, as seen and reflected on by the later self, the man after the change.

All these kinds of war-narratives – the letters, the diaries, the memories – are acts of commemoration, but the differences among them of immediacy and reflection make them different acts of mind, with different objects, as we can see by considering a few examples.

Take first, as typical, the *Letters of an American airman*, written by Captain Hamilton Coolidge during the First World War. Coolidge was a 21-year-old Harvard undergraduate when he enlisted in 1917. He trained as a pilot and was sent to France in July 1917, though he didn't fly in combat until a year later. In the last few months of the war he shot down five German planes. Two weeks short of the Armistice his plane was hit by anti-aircraft fire and he was killed.

Coolidge seems, from his letters, an ordinary sort of young man, bright and observant, and excited by his war. His letters are made of observed immediate events in his life – the weather, a new plane, a funny anecdote about prisoners, a trip to Paris – mixed up, in a dissonant way, with descriptions of air fighting, like this passage in which he tells how, with the help of another pilot, he scored his first victory:

We both shot at the Boche and a second later great hot, red flames burst out from beneath his fuselage. I shall never forget the sensation of seeing a stream of flaming tracer bullets from my guns sink into its body and almost instantly flames bursting out as we dove at great speed through the air.[2]

That's what I mean by pure happening. War-letters give you that, but dissonantly, mixed up with details of soldiers' ordinary lives that seem to have nothing to do with the drama of actual killing. So, for example, Frederick Keeling, an infantry sergeant on the Somme in 1916, describes how the troops, removed from the front line for a day, put on a show for themselves, with comic turns and a clog-dancer, and adds: 'I never laughed so much in all my life.'[3] Such disharmonious particulars, trenches and comic turns, bring us as close to the actual experience of that war in that place as a latter-day reader can get. I'm touched and surprised by that clog-dancer, a mile or so from death; but war *is* touching and surprising.

Because war-letters were commonly published posthumously (as both Coolidge's and Keeling's were) they are the most immediate and the most fixed of literary acts of commemoration. In a sense they are monuments, constructed by bereaved friends and relatives to memorial-

---

[2] *Letters of an American airman: being the war record of Capt. Hamilton Coolidge, U.S.A.* (Boston: privately printed, 1919), pp. 153–4.

[3] *Keeling letters & recollections*, edited by E.T., with an introduction by H. G. Wells (London: G. Allen & Unwin, 1918), p. 300.

ize the man who died. Because each man's life ended where the book ends, there could be no retrospection in his telling, no later ironic revision of his thoughts and acts, no disenchantment; his image stands as unchanging as a tombstone. Yet each is a narrative of continuous change, the flow of immediate particulars of war-experience in all their dailiness. War-letters commemorate those two realities: the man who died, and the changing stream of his experience of war. They do so unreflectively, particular by particular.

I said that diaries and journals are like letters in their immediacy, but different in their audience of self. This doesn't mean that all diaries and journals are introspective and reflective (though in some cases they are); but it does mean that the writer is free to record his feelings and responses, unmodified to suit another auditor. Fear can be frankly confessed, and exhilaration too; but I think the element that comes out most clearly in these self-to-self narratives is the way in which war, seen as it happens, mixes the ordinary and the strange, what is familiar with what is unimaginable, and makes war-existence both like a man's previous life, and altogether unlike any life he can imagine.

Here is a brief example from the First World War – from *The war diary of the Master of Belhaven*, by Lt. Colonel the Hon. Ralph G. A. Hamilton. Hamilton was one of the old breed of army officer, a Regular and an Honourable; he was commanding an artillery brigade on the Somme in the summer of 1916 when he recorded this visit to a front-line trench:

The heat was terrific and the smells simply too awful for words. The only thing I can at all compare it to was the rhino that G. and I shot before leaving East Africa, and that was mild in comparison to this ... In many places the men who had been killed a week or ten days ago were lying in the bottom of the trench, and one had to walk and crawl over them. Many had been buried by the shells, and only their faces or hands or feet could be seen. They had been trampled into the soft earth by the many reliefs who had passed along the trench since they were killed. Many of the bodies were not complete; in one place a pair of legs were lying on a path and no signs of the rest.[4]

Here are the war's ordinary dead – dismembered, buried, trampled by their fellows, in a grotesque scene that reminds Hamilton of nothing except a grotesque comparison, the dead rhino. Nothing in his Regular Army experience could prepare him for the trench, or provide him with comparisons.

Another example, this time from a classic diary of the Second World War, James J. Fahey's *Pacific War diary*. Fahey was an ordinary enlisted

---

[4] Lt. Col. the Hon. Ralph G. A. Hamilton, *The war diary of the Master of Belhaven* (London: John Murray, 1924), pp. 226–7.

man of that war: working class (he had been a garbageman in Massachusetts), not very educated, not a man who thought much about the war he was in. He joined the Navy in 1942 and served as a seaman on the cruiser *Montpelier* in engagements at Guadalcanal, the Marianas, the Philippines, and Okinawa.

Fahey's great virtue is that he put down everything that happened indiscriminately: what he had for breakfast, the latest rumour, what a kamikaze attack is like to a man on the deck. He does so without any evident sense that one event is more important than another, or that he is creating himself as he writes: everything is seen with a sharp but innocent eye, everything is equally real and possible, because he sees it happening. And so we get from him an essential truth of war – the ordinariness of its extraordinary strangeness. Here is Fahey's entry for 9 July 1944. The *Montpelier* is cruising near Saipan, where the fighting for the island is almost over:

After chow I took a shower and sat in the sun and got some tan. There is not much doing so they let us get some rest. A body floated by on a stretcher, it was all blown up and some kind of a cloth was over its head. You could see blond hair sticking out. It was one of our Marines that was killed on Saipan. The Doctor got in a whaleboat and took a look at it ... It is about 3 p.m. and I sit in the sun with just my pants on, getting some tan. Some of the officers are doing the same. I can see smoke coming from the northern tip of Saipan. You can see the Japs jumping off the high cliffs to their death.[5]

A sailor sits on deck getting a tan, and in the distance people commit suicide; it's the juxtaposition of such discordant details that give diary-wars like Fahey's their most distinctive quality, the *strangeness* of war-experience.

Diaries and journals get that strangeness best because experience there is not filtered and mediated by time, or by an audience beyond the self. You might say that that strangeness is what these documents commemorate; they exist to subvert the notion that war can be both familiar and imaginable to persons who were not there.

Letters and diaries of soldiers record what is memorable as it happens. The third kind of narrative – the memoir – records the remembered war that persists in the mind through a lifetime. Shakespeare imagined such a memory in a veteran of Agincourt:

> Old men forget; yet all shall be forgot,
> But he'll remember with advantages
> What feats he did that day.

[5] James J. Fahey, *Pacific War diary 1942–1945* (Boston: Houghton Mifflin, 1963), p. 187.

That was no doubt true of Agincourt, and it has been true of battle memories ever since. Elisha Stockwell was fifteen when he joined the Wisconsin Volunteers in 1861, and eighty-one when he wrote his recollections; John Harris fought in the Peninsula with Wellington in 1805, but didn't tell his story until forty years later; Alvin Kernan served in the American Navy in the Second World War, and published his book about his war in 1995.

Not all memoirs have waited so long to get written, but the best have appeared well after the events they narrate. The First World War memoirs that we still read came in a wave at the end of the 1920s, and the best personal narratives of the Second World War have been even longer in gestation, and are still being published. In these remembered wars the time that separates events from writing about them is clearly an important shaping factor. The experiences are those of a young self. Young men at war feel life and death with an intensity that is beyond their peacetime emotions; they know comradeship, a closeness to other men that ordinary life doesn't often provide; they see friends die, and they feel grief that is different from what they have known before, back home where folks die naturally and mostly old; and they feel fear, and the exhilaration of fear overcome. And by all these new experiences and feelings they are changed.

It is their older selves, the selves on the other side of those deep changes, who write the memoirs. They look back on themselves when young as on another life, and the questions they ask of memory are different from those a young man asks. The usual narrative questions are posed: what happened there? What happened then? But behind them are deeper questions: who was I then? What changed me? What did I become? Courage is no longer the challenge – that question has been answered; truth of being is what matters now. So William Manchester, after thirty years of not remembering his life as a young marine in the Pacific War, returned to the islands where he had fought to rediscover it, and wrote *Goodbye, darkness*. 'This, then', he writes at the end of his narrative, 'was the life I knew, where death sought me, during which I was transformed from a cheeky youth to a troubled man who, for over thirty years, repressed what he could not bear to remember.'[6] By then he *had* remembered, and had come to terms with his memories.

To perceive the changes that war has made in a man requires the passage of time and the establishment of distance from the remembered self, and it is not surprising that most war memoirs come late, that

[6] William Manchester, *Goodbye, darkness* (Boston: Little, Brown, 1980), p. 398.

memory dawdles and delays. For most men, understanding comes slowly; and imagination must wait upon memory to reveal itself. When it does, it picks its favourites, who are usually not war's favourites. Heroes are by and large no good for war memoirs; they stand too close to the centre of the war's values, and whether they mean to or not they act out the mottoes on the flags and the slogans on the posters. What suits memory best, it seems, is a war life lived close to the action, but at some distance from the values, lived by a man who is by nature or circumstances an outsider, who can be a witness as well as a soldier. Robert Graves was an untidy, undisciplined officer, Manchester went into battle against orders, Tim O'Brien tried to go AWOL, Keith Douglas left his behind-the-lines unit without permission in order to get into the fighting (soldiers don't usually run away in that direction).

Memory also likes the man without medals: Graves had none, and neither did Douglas, and they wrote two of the best modern war memoirs. Sassoon seems an exception to this rule; he won a Military Cross. Yes, but he threw it into the Mersey, and one might argue that by the act he freed himself to write one of the great war memoirs.

Among memoirs, Sassoon's is something of an anomaly; it's the only one I know of that appeared in three volumes, published under different titles and at different dates: *The memoirs of a fox-hunting man* (1928), *Memoirs of an infantry officer* (1930), and *Sherston's progress* (1936). The three were later collected in one volume as *The complete memoirs of George Sherston* (1937), but it is important to keep in mind their initial separateness; for though the three together contain a single complete narrative of one man's war, each volume is its own distinct act of commemoration.

The memoirs of a fox-hunting man has nothing to do with war for three-quarters of its length; it is simply a narrative of life in an idealized English countryside, all fox-hunting and cricket and landscape. Why begin a war-memoir with these pastoral pages? Because the book is about more than Sassoon's youth; it is about a world that the war ended, a vision of a dream-England before the war. That vision is an important part of the English myth of the war: this England is what men fought for – not their city slums or their suburban semi-attached houses, but rural England, bucolic and unchanged, the England you get in this passage from the book, in which young Sherston/Sassoon rides through the countryside to a cricket match:

The air was Elysian with early summer and the shadows of steep white clouds were chasing over the orchards and meadows; sunlight sparkled on green hedgerows that had been drenched by early morning showers. As I was carried past it all I was lazily aware through my dreaming and unobservant eyes that this was the sort of world I wanted. For it was my own countryside, and I loved it with an intimate feeling, though all its associations were crude and incoherent. I cannot think of it now without a sense of heartache.[7]

What Sassoon did, in the first three-quarters of his *Fox-hunting man*, was to fix the relationship between this dream Edwardian country landscape and the war; he created a basic model for the nostalgia for pre-war England that is so powerful an element in English war-memoirs. That's one reason for the decade-long delay between Sassoon's experience and the writing of it: nostalgia is the product of time.

But it isn't only that dream-England that Sassoon says goodbye to in *Fox-hunting man*; there is also the traditional figure of a soldier that is created slowly through the peacetime pages of the book, only to be obliterated at the end, when real, modern war enters. This soldier-figure is implied in Sassoon's title: fox-hunting men like him, well-born and country-bred, with private incomes, good at field sports, and not too brainy, were the pool from which the fashionable cavalry regiments had always drawn their junior officers. When war was declared, young men of this county class rushed to enlist, as Sassoon did, and rode off to war, usually on their own horses. By the end of the first year of war most of them were dead, and those who survived had been dismounted, to serve as infantrymen, as Sassoon did. So there is this other goodbye in Sassoon's first volume: goodbye to romantic war, goodbye to cavalry charges and lances and sabres and plumes waving, goodbye to the old officer caste of country gentlemen at arms.

Fox-hunting man is primarily a book of nostalgia, a long look back across the chasm of the war years to an earlier England that at that distance seemed simpler, happier, and more stable than the troubled England of the postwar years. If it is an act of commemoration, it is that lost Edwardian world that it commemorates and not the war. War enters in the last pages, in which Sassoon becomes an infantry officer and reaches the western front, but it functions less as a war-narrative than as a manifestation of how history burst upon a dream of England and swept it away forever.

Sassoon's second volume, *Memoirs of an infantry officer*, is probably the most famous English narrative of the war, the one that has most influenced the shaping of the myth of the war that we all share. Yet the story it tells is not really representative of what that war was like for most ordinary fighting men who were there.

Consider this point: *Infantry officer* is set on the western front during Sassoon's first two tours of duty there, and in England during the

[7] Siegfried Sassoon, *Memoirs of a fox-hunting Man* (London: Faber & Gwyer, 1928), pp. 94–5.

months following the second tour: that is, from April 1916 to July 1917. Yet it is not shaped around the battles fought then (which included the Somme offensive), but around three individual acts of remarkable courage that might have occurred anywhere.

Look at the first two actions for a moment. The occasion of the first, in May 1916, was an order that troops of Sassoon's regiment were to attack the German trenches opposite them. Sassoon was not in the party, but when the raid failed and the survivors returned, Sassoon went out into no man's land on his own to find a wounded man. He did find him, and brought him back, but by the time they reached their own trench he was dead. For this act Sassoon got his Military Cross.

The second action was another raid, this time on the fourth night of the Somme battle. Sassoon was sent forward with a few men to occupy a captured trench and to attack the retreating enemy with grenades. When the second part of the order, the bombing attack, was rescinded, he sent his men back but went forward alone, into the next German trench, in time to see the German troops fleeing. Then he returned to his own unit. For this act he was severely reprimanded by his colonel.

Anyone would call these two acts courageous, and in one case the army officially agreed. But think what is implied by the two episodes. Both were done in direct disobedience of orders, and neither accomplished anything. Furthermore, neither was a part of any collective military action; there is no visible British army in either story, and no opposing enemy. Nobody kills anybody, or captures any enemy position, and the war-situation is not altered in any way.

This point becomes clearer and more emphatic if you set Sassoon's personal narratives of his raids against his battalion's official war-diary, the day-to-day reports of the battalion's activities. Here is the diary for 25 May 1916:

Battalion in the line. Raid on KIEL TRENCH by 25 men under Lieut. N. Stansfield; detailed account in Appendix 'A' (Battalion Orders 29/5/16).[8]

If you consult the Battalion Orders referred to, you find a report that more or less confirms Sassoon's version up to the point at which he crawled out to search for the wounded man; that incident is simply not mentioned, and Sassoon's name nowhere appears. Yet this is the act for which he won his Military Cross.

The war-diary for the 5 July raid is similar, though more detailed:

Reserve Bombers and C Company [Sassoon's] ordered to take the right half of QUADRANGLE TRENCH. Bombers to force their way down the saps

[8] War diary, 1st Battalion, Royal Welsh Fusiliers: Public Record Office, Kew (WO 95/1665).

running to QUADRANGLE SUPPORT, to seize the junction of these saps and to establish a bombing post there.

And 'Later':

Order for C Company to move forward cancelled. Royal Irish report having failed to gain WOOD TRENCH. Orders issued to try and bomb along towards WOOD TRENCH and assist R. I. ... It was however found that between QUADRANGLE TRENCH & WOOD TRENCH a gap of 60 or 70 yards existed across the Railway, which was swept by M.G. fire. A patrol did get across but daylight was now coming on and the Royal Irish withdrew.[9]

Sassoon must have been that 'patrol'; but he is not named.

The battalion war diaries are the army's war-stories: battalions receive orders, companies send out patrols, men act in groups and succeed or fail in groups. By comparison, Sassoon's stories aren't acts of war at all: they are simply adventures, which the army rightly ignores, because they had no military consequences. Yet these acts are central episodes in a narrative that is a classic act of commemoration. We must ask, then, what exactly they commemorate. It seems clear that they commemorate the traditional romantic idea of personal military courage, an idea that is embodied in a long literature of war-stories from Homer to Henty. It commemorates the brave individual rush into danger, in which the solitary soldier is an agent in his own war, and it does so *because* the modern mass-war that Sassoon fought in had made that kind of individual gesture obsolete and irrelevant, as dead as Horatius at the bridge. Sassoon's adventures are heroic and pointless; they belong to a lost, idealized past, like the dream of England. That's the point.

In making his war personal and heroic, Sassoon made it recognizable to readers who knew war only in its literary forms. Other personal narratives of modern war would defamiliarize it; Sassoon made it familiar. A reader could imagine himself acting as Sassoon acted, being romantic out there in no man's land, as he could imagine acting like other heroes in books. Sassoon, you might say, had turned the western front into literature.

The third of Sassoon's centred gestures seems at first to have nothing to do with courage, to be in fact the opposite. In 1917 Sassoon, home on sick leave, wrote a letter to his commanding offer in which he resigned from the war. The letter begins like this:

I am making this statement as an act of wilful defiance of military authority, because I believe that the War is being deliberately prolonged by those who have the power to end it. I am a soldier, convinced that I am acting on behalf of soldiers. I believe that this War, upon which I entered as a war of defence and liberation, has now become a war of aggression and conquest ... I have seen and

[9] War diary, same references.

endured the sufferings of the troops, and I can no longer be a party to prolong these sufferings for ends which I believe to be evil and unjust.[10]

He was quitting the war: not deserting – soldiers have always done that – but declining to participate in it any further, because it had gone wrong. And to make his defiance even more wilful he sent copies of his letter to the newspapers, where it was widely publicized.

In his letter Sassoon claimed for himself the name of soldier; but that is obviously not the case. A soldier doesn't walk out on a war, or act in wilful defiance of authority, nor does he have a private conscience to tell him when to obey orders. No, Sassoon was being what he had always been, a foolhardy, self-dramatizing individual, like the fox-hunter who rushes at the tallest hedges to see if he can jump them. Such acts require courage of a sort, but not a soldier's sort. That letter of protest and resignation, written in war-time and chancing a court-martial and even a firing squad, was as much an example of that fox-hunter's courage as the two night raids: as courageous, as personal, and as pointless. For readers who were appalled by the idea of modern war, it was another familiar-izing gesture, something they might do (with a bit more courage).

What does the letter commemorate, exactly? Not a new-found oppo-sition to war in general; Sassoon didn't become a pacifist in 1917 (he eventually returned to the western front and was wounded once more before his personal war ended). I think, rather, that it commemorates the spirit in which Englishmen went to war in 1914, a spirit that has connections with the dream-England of *Fox-hunting man*. That spirit was gone, destroyed by the realities of trench warfare and soldiers' disillusionment with their leaders at home, and Sassoon's letter is a sort of elegy for it. Like the stories of the two raids, the letter episode is a monument to a lost ideal of war, as *Fox-hunting man* is a monument to a lost ideal of England. In both books the primary mood is nostalgia – for the lost Good Place, the lost Good War.

Sherston's progress, the last book in Sassoon's trilogy, is the shortest, the least interesting, and the least shaped – less like a literary man's memoir than like a diary, which in fact it mostly is, transcribed directly from the war-diary that Sassoon kept. It does, however, have one interesting passage, the coda-like final chapter. At this point, though the war is still going on, Sassoon's personal war is over; he has been wounded in the head (by one of his own men), and is back in England convalescing. In the book's last pages he lies in a hospital bed and thinks about the exactions that the war machine has inflicted on him, what he achieved in it, and what is left. 'My war had stopped', he writes,

---

[10] Siegfried Sassoon, *Memoirs of an infantry officer* (London: Faber & Faber, 1930), p. 308.

but its after effects were still with me ... I saw myself as one who had achieved nothing except an idiotic anti-climax, and my mind worked itself into a tantrum of self-disparagement. Why hadn't I stayed in France where I could at least escape from the war by being in it? Out there I had never despised my existence as I did now.[11]

We must see this passage as a conclusion to the entire trilogy, I think, the last of the book's annihilations of self. The war annihilated the fox-hunting man, the turn that the war took away from idealism annihilated the believing infantry officer, and now the end of personal war has annihilated whatever was left. Removed from the war that he no longer believed in, Sassoon is nothing, an emptiness where a self should be. To live, he will have to create a new self and a new life; but how is he to do that when war has left him with no conviction about anything 'except that the war was a dirty trick which had been played on me and my generation'?[12]

The tone of that coda, with its sense of disillusionment and loss of self, is specific to the First World War, but the more general point is not: war annihilates the past selves of young men, changes them so utterly from youths into soldiers that a return to a past life is impossible; and then, at the end, it dumps them into the strange new disorder that is peace, to construct new lives. If *Sherston's progress* is an act of commemoration, what it commemorates is not the end of the war, but the power war has to empty and transform the lives of the men who endure it and survive.

The complete memoirs of George Sherston is the most comprehensive of First World War memoirs – the most inclusive in its themes, the most self-aware, the most consciously constructed. But its principal elements are visible in many other memoirs: the nostalgia for the lost past, the will to be an agent in one's own personal war, the sense of irreversible change in self and the self's world. You'll find those elements in the narratives of many of the major memoirists, in Graves and Chapman and T. E. Lawrence in the First World War, in Manchester and Eric Lomax and Farley Mowat in the Second, in Caputo and O'Brien in Vietnam. They are present in those memoirs, as they are not in letters and diaries, because memory delays; these are the elements of retrospection and reflection, of war remembered as another time.

If we consider personal narratives of war as a general category, taking all together the letters, the diaries and journals and the memoirs, what conclusions can we justifiably reach about their common characteristics? We can say that each example tells the story of one man in actions

[11] Siegfried Sassoon, *Sherston's progress* (London: Faber & Faber, 1936), p. 277.
[12] Ibid. p. 278.

involving many, and that each speaks in its own individual voice, which is not the voice of history, nor of collective memory. We might add that the span of time in a narrative is not historical either, but personal, that few personal narratives begin when a war begins and end when it ends, but tell only that part of the whole story that is a man's personal war, and show no interest in the military idea of closure in victory or defeat. Indeed, in personal narrative The War, as a global historical reality, scarcely exists; only men exist, and act, and sometimes die, and when they do, they do so *personally.*

It is important that in our defining of the term we also give attention to what personal narratives are not. They are not usually narratives of trauma experienced and healed (or not healed). The element of war-trauma varies greatly from war to war; some narratives of the First World War contain it (Graves's *Goodbye to all that* is an obvious example), and Vietnam War narratives even more commonly (see Ron Kovic's *Born on the fourth of July,* and Lewis B. Puller's *Fortunate son*). But Second World War narratives are almost entirely free of it, except for some prisoner-of-war narratives, and then only when the captors are Japanese.

Personal narratives are not victims' stories either; no man with a weapon in his hand can be entirely a victim, and the narratives show that men did not think of themselves as such. Every narrator believes himself to have been to some degree an agent in his personal war, and agents aren't victims. The victim-view is a later reaction to wars by persons who weren't there; understandable and humane, but wrong. Nor are personal narratives horror stories. Narratives will often contain episodes that to the chair-borne reader sound horrible, but the man on the scene is likely to respond to the unimaginable violence and death he sees not with horror, but with astonishment.

Most important, personal narratives are almost never polemically anti-war. Readers, being themselves against war, would like the narratives they read to support their convictions. But they don't, as a whole. Both Sassoon and Graves specifically deny that their writing is directed against war as an institution. And so do others. Indeed, many narratives testify to the satisfactions of military life during war – the comradeship, the excitement, the satisfactions in complex physical skills, the pride men feel in hardships shared and endured. Memoir after memoir ends: 'I wouldn't have missed it.' Even when a man expresses disillusionment with his own war, as Sassoon did at the end of *Shertson's progress*, he doesn't generalize to all wars. We must accept as fact that men on the whole are glad they went to war; their narratives tell us that.

What, then, do personal narratives commemorate, that they should be included in a book on war and remembrance? The best way to put it, I think, is to say that each narrative among the thousands that exist of modern wars, commemorates *one* life lived in the mass action of a modern war, that each is a monument of a kind to that one soldier, or sailor, or pilot, and to no one else, and that by existing they refute and subvert the collective story of war that is military history. Not one of these men was necessary to the war he fought, not one affected the winning or losing; individually they were irrelevant. But they were there; they bear witness to their human particularity, and to their particular visions.

Collectively these narratives contribute, by a sifting process that is gradual and probably not conscious, to the emerging, evolving story of their wars, a story that is neither history nor memory, but myth – a compound war-story that gives meaning and coherence to the incoherences of war-in-its-details, which is what each narrative separately tells.

Are they necessary, these personal narratives? To *us*, probably not: I can see no social or psychological necessity for individuals or societies to possess either myths of their past wars or the particular accounts from which such myths are made. Those myths, however bloody and horrible, have no apparent restraining power over nations or peoples when the next war comes; young men will go to war, regardless. Are they necessary to *them*, the veterans of past wars? Perhaps yes: for them these narratives will re-constitute memory, and stand as monuments to shared experience, bringing their wars back down out of generalization of collective action into the narrow realm of human acts, where individuals live and die. Perhaps they constitute a kind of dialogue among the only readers who can connect narratives to actual memory, and so understand what personal narratives really mean – that is, the men who were there, The rest of us will read them, for our various reasons: because war interests us, because we are curious about extreme experiences, because we *weren't* there. And if we do, we will no doubt construct in our minds images that will be in a sense our memorials to those wars we didn't fight. But they won't be memory; we can't construct that.

11 Against consolation: Walter Benjamin and the refusal to mourn

Martin Jay

No student of the mysteries of collective memory can fail to acknowledge that those who do the remembering stubbornly remain individuals whose minds resist inclusion in a homogenous group consciousness. The dialectic of exterior, public commemoration of the past and its interior, private traces refuses easy reconciliation. It is thus fitting that a book on the ways in which cultures struggle to remember and memorialize concludes with a chapter focusing on a single figure, whose life and work was devoted in large measure to an exploration of the ways in which the past haunted the present, as well as offered a possible resource for the future.

What makes the choice of this specific individual especially appropriate is that his thoughts on the modalities of memory were stimulated by the violent trauma of the First World War, the cataclysmic event whose rupturing of the continuity with the world that preceded it brought to a head the 'memory crisis' that began in the nineteenth century.[1] Moreover, while a fiercely idiosyncratic thinker, '*à l'écart de tous les courants*', as his friend Theodor W. Adorno called him,[2] Walter Benjamin arrived at insights into the dialectic of memory and trauma that gradually found a receptive audience. They have, in fact, come to be extraordinarily influential on many current considerations of these highly vexed themes. Our collective memory of the modern era, it can be said with only slight exaggeration, has increasingly been shaped by the unique ruminations of this isolated intellectual.

In August, 1914, Walter Benjamin, along with many other 22-year-old German men, volunteered for the Kaiser's army. He acted, however, according to his friend Gershom Scholem, 'not out of enthusiasm for the war but to anticipate the ineluctable conscription in a way that would have permitted him to remain among friends and like-minded

---

[1] Richard Terdiman, *Present past: modernity and the memory crisis* (Ithaca, N.Y.: Cornell University Press, 1993).
[2] Theodor W. Adorno, *Über Walter Benjamin* (Frankfurt: Suhrkamp, 1970), p. 96.

221

people'.[3] Benjamin was, as it happened, refused, and when it came the turn of his age-group to be drafted that fall, he faked palsy and was able to postpone induction until another order arrived to report in January 1917. Again he was able to avoid conscription by trickery, undergoing hypnosis to simulate the symptoms of sciatica.[4] Shortly thereafter, Benjamin left Germany for Berne, Switzerland with the hypnotist, who was also his new wife, Dora Kellner. This was Benjamin's first emigration from his native country in a period of crisis, but not his last. After the Armistice, following a short stay in Austria, the Benjamins returned to Berlin in March 1919, where he spent the turbulent years of the Weimar Republic until forced to flee to Paris in 1933.

Walter Benjamin was thus spared the glory and misery of the *Fronterlebnis*, the community of the trenches that so powerfully marked his generation for the rest of their lives, if they were lucky enough, that is, to survive it. But he did not, in fact, escape the violence caused by the war. Indeed, it might be said to have sought him out immediately after the hostilities were declared. On 8 August 1914, two of his friends, the 19-year-old poet Friedrich (Fritz) Heinle, to whom he was passionately devoted, and Heinle's lover, Frederika (Rika) Seligson, the sister of one of Benjamin's closest comrades in the Youth Movement, Carla Seligson, committed suicide together in Berlin. Their act, carried out by turning on the gas, was designed as a dramatic protest against the war, a war in which lethal gas was, as we know, to take many more victims. Benjamin learned of the news when he was awakened by an express letter from Heinle with the grim message 'You will find us lying in the Meeting House.'[5] The place of their deaths was not chosen accidentally; 'the Meeting House' (*Sprechsaal*) was the apartment Benjamin had rented as a 'debating chamber' for his faction of the Movement.

All accounts concur that Benjamin was inconsolable for months, and indeed seems never to have fully recovered from the loss of Heinle, to whom he could only bear to refer in later years as 'my friend'.[6]

---

[3] Gershom Scholem, *Walter Benjamin: The story of a friendship*, trans. Harry Zohn (New York: Schocken, 1981), p. 12. Benjamin himself later wrote that he joined 'without a spark of war fever in my heart'. *Gesammelte Schriften*, 12 vols. (Frankfurt am Main, 1980), VI, p. 481.

[4] Ibid. p. 35.

[5] Walter Benjamin, 'A Berlin chronicle', *Reflections: essays, aphorisms, autobiographical writings*, trans. Edmund Jephcott (New York: Harcourt, 1978), p. 18.

[6] Scholem, *Walter Benjamin*, p. 11. For accounts of the impact of his death, see John McCole, *Walter Benjamin and the antinomies of tradition* (Ithaca N.Y.: Cornell University Press, 1993), p. 54, and Hans Puttnies and Gary Smith, *Benjaminia* (Giessen: Anabas, 1991), p. 18. The fullest account of their friendship can be found in Rolf Tiedmann's *Nachwort* to Benjamin, *Sonette* (Frankfurt: Suhrkamp, 1986). They had, in fact, only met in the spring of 1913 and had gone through a period of some estrangement the following winter, but clearly the tie was strong.

According to Pierre Missac, who came to know Benjamin in 1937, he was able to overcome his shame at surviving only by 'mythologizing the lost friendship'.[7] In the quarter-century that followed the initial trauma, ended only by his own suicide in 1940, Benjamin composed seventy-three unpublished sonnets, discovered in the Bibliothèque nationale in 1981. Some fifty-two of these he arranged in a cycle dedicated to Heinle, prefaced by a motto from Hölderlin's *Patmos*, which began: 'Wenn aber abstirbt alsdenn/ An dem am meisten/ Die Schönheit hing.'[8] His will, which was discovered in 1966, revealed that 'my entire estate contains in addition to my own writings primarily the works of the brothers Fritz and Wolf Heinle', the latter having also been a poet and friend, who died prematurely in 1923 at the age of twenty-four.[9] Until the end, Benjamin had hoped to get his friend's own poetry published, a desire that was to remain unfulfilled until many years later.[10]

Although several commentators have shown that Benjamin's disillusionment with the Youth Movement began well before the war, the suicides intensified and brought to a climax his disgust for the devil's pact he saw between the Movement's alleged idealism, its celebration of pure *Geist*, and its patriotic defence of the state.[11] With the death of the adolescent Heinle came the end of Benjamin's faith in the redemptive mission of youth itself, although he remained stubbornly wedded to its ideals. In March 1915 he abruptly broke with his mentor in the Youth Movement, Gustav Wyneken, in a harsh letter that detailed his feelings of betrayal.[12] During the rest of the war, Benjamin distanced himself from others who defended it, such as Martin Buber, and brutally dropped old friends from the Youth Movement, such as Herbert Belmore.[13] Instead, he gravitated towards like-minded critics of the

[7] Pierre Missac, *Walter Benjamin's passages*, trans. Shierry Weber Nicholsen (Cambridge, Mass.: MIT Press, 1995), p. 4.

[8] Benjamin, *Sonette*, p. 6.

[9] The will is cited in Scholem, *Walter Benjamin*, p. 187.

[10] Werner Kraft saw them into print in *Akzente*, 31 (1984). See his accompanying essay, 'Friedrich C. Heinle', as well as his earlier piece, 'Über einen verschollenen Dichter', in *Neue Rundschau*, 78 (1967).

[11] Tiedemann writes, 'Not only in his life but in his work was the war a caesura, but an even stronger one was the suicide of Heinle caused by it' (p. 117). For accounts, see Richard Wolin, *Walter Benjamin: an aesthetic of redemption* (Berkeley: University of California Press, 1994), chapter 1; McCole, *Walter Benjamin and the antinomies of tradition*, chapter 1. Before the war Benjamin had defended Heinle to Wyneken against the claim of Georges Barbizon that he was conspiring to take over the Youth Movement journal *Der Anfang*. See the letter of 4 April 1914 to Wyneken in Benjamin, *Gesammelte Briefe*, vol. I, *1910–1918*, ed. Christoph Gödde and Henri Lonitz (Frankfurt: Suhrkamp, 1995), p. 203.

[12] Benjamin to Gustav Wyneken, 9 March 1915, in Benjamin, *Briefe*, 2 vols., ed. Gershom Scholem and Theodor W. Adorno (Frankfurt: Suhrkamp, 1966), vol. I, pp. 120–1.

[13] Herbert W. Belmore, 'Walter Benjamin', *German Life and Letters*, 15 (1962).

conflict, although never himself actively engaging in anti-war agitation, and wrote increasingly apocalyptic treatises on the crisis of Western culture. His estrangement from the German university community, which reached its climax with the now notorious rejection of his *Habilitationsschrift* at the University of Frankfurt in 1925, began with his disgust at the spectacle of so many distinguished professors enthusiastically supporting the so-called 'ideas of 1914'.[14] The empty bombast of their chauvinist rhetoric hastened his abandonment of traditional notions of linguistic communication, as well as whatever faith he may have had left in the German Jewish fetish of *Kultur* and *Bildung*.[15]

It has long been recognized in the extensive scholarship on Benjamin that the war had a decisive effect on all his later work. As one commentator typically put it, 'it is the First World War which provides the traumatic background to Benjamin's culture theory, Fascism its ultimate context'.[16] In particular, it has been acknowledged as a powerful stimulus to his remarkable thoughts on the themes of experience and remembrance, which were to be so crucial a part of his idiosyncratic legacy. One of the most frequently cited passages in his work, from his 1936 essay 'The storyteller', is often cited to show its relevance. It reads:

With the [First] World War a process began to become apparent which has not halted since then. Was it not noticeable at the end of the war that men returned from the battlefield grown silent – not richer, but poorer in communicable experience? What ten years later was poured out in the flood of war books was anything but experience that goes from mouth to mouth. And there was nothing remarkable about that. For never has experience been contradicted more thoroughly than strategic experience by tactical warfare, economic experience by inflation, bodily experience by mechanical warfare, moral experience by those in power. A generation that had gone to school on a horse-drawn streetcar now stood under the open sky in a countryside in which nothing remained unchanged but the clouds, and beneath those clouds, in a field of force of destructive torrents and explosions, was the tiny, fragile human body.[17]

---

[14] For a discussion, see Julian Roberts, *Walter Benjamin* (London: Macmillan, 1983), p. 38.

[15] For a discussion of the impact of the war on Benjamin's theory of language, see Anson Rabinbach, 'Between Enlightenment and Apocalypse: Benjamin, Bloch and modern German Jewish Messianism', *New German Critique*, 34 (Winter 1985). He argues that 'On language as such and on the language of man', of 1916 'must be read between the lines as an esoteric response to Buber's pro-war and pro-German position' (p. 105). For a discussion of Benjamin in the context of a generational revolt against the German Jewish fetish of *Kultur*, see Steven E. Aschheim, 'German Jews beyond *Bildung* and liberalism: the radical Jewish revival in the Weimar Republic', in his *Culture and Catastrophe* (New York: New York University Press, 1996).

[16] Peter Osborne, *The politics of time: modernity and the avant-garde* (London: Verso, 1995), p. 227.

[17] Walter Benjamin, 'The storyteller: reflections on the work of Nikolai Leskov',

The modern crisis of experience, or more precisely of the integrated, narratively meaningful variety known as *Erfahrung* as opposed to mere discontinuous, lived experience or *Erlebnis*, was thus brought to a head, Benjamin tells us, by the war and its aftermath. Despite the efforts by celebrants of the *Fronterlebnis* such as Ernst Jünger to recapture its alleged communal solidarity, Benjamin knew that the technologically manufactured slaughter of the Western Front was anything but an 'inner experience' worth re-enacting in peacetime. In his trenchant 1930 review of the collection edited by Jünger entitled *War and warrior*, he ferociously denounced the aestheticization of violence and glorification of the 'fascist class warrior' he saw lurking behind this new cult of 'eternal' war.[18] There could be nothing 'beautiful' about such carnage.

These aspects of Benjamin's response to the war are well known. What is perhaps less widely appreciated and will thus be the focus of what follows is the fact that Benjamin, never a straightforward pacifist hostile to all violence,[19] also steadfastly defied all attempts to heal the wounds caused by the war. However much he may have lamented, at least in certain of his moods, the lost experience underlying the story-teller's craft, Benjamin resisted short-circuiting the process of recovering the conditions that allowed it to occur – or more precisely, creating the new ones that might allow it to reappear. He refused, that is, to seek some sort of new symbolic equilibrium through a process of collective mourning that would successfully 'work through' the grief. Scornfully rejecting the ways in which culture can function to cushion the blows of trauma,[20] he wanted to compel his readers to face squarely what had happened and confront its deepest sources rather than let the wounds

---

Illuminations, ed. Hannah Arendt, trans. Harry Zohn (New York: Harcourt, Brace and World, 1968), p. 84.

[18] Walter Benjamin, 'Theories of German Fascism: on the collection of essays *War and warrior*, edited by Ernst Jünger', *New German Critique*, 17 (Spring 1979), pp. 120–8.

[19] See in particular, his controversial essay 'Critique of violence', in *Reflections*. According to Irving Wohlfahrt, 'Benjamin saw in pacifism no alternative to the cult of war but only its mirror image'. 'No-man's-land. On Walter Benjamin's "destructive character"', *Diacritics*, 8 (June 1978), p. 55.

[20] According to Kai Erikson, 'Traumatized people often come to feel that they have lost an important measure of control over the circumstances of their own lives and are thus very vulnerable. That is easy to understand. But they also come to feel that they have lost a natural immunity to misfortune and that something awful is almost *bound* to happen. One of the crucial tasks of culture, let's say, is to help people camouflage the actual risks of the world around them – to help them edit reality in such a way that it seems manageable, to help them edit it in such a way that the dangers pressing in on them from all sides are screened out of their line of vision as they go about their everyday rounds.' 'Notes on trauma and community', in *Trauma: explorations in memory*, ed. Cathy Caruth (Baltimore: Johns Hopkins University Press, 1995), p. 194. Benjamin's disdain for culture as a means of camouflage was apparent in all of his subsequent work.

scar over. Rather than rebuilding the psychological 'protective shield' (*Reizschutz*) that Freud saw as penetrated by trauma, he laboured to keep it lowered so that the pain would not be numbed. For the ultimate source of the pain was not merely the war itself. As Kevin Newmark has noted,

Benjamin seems, ultimately, to generalize Freud's hypothesis – produced in response to the traumas of World War I – about the destabilizing and repetitive memory-traces left in accident victims into a global economy of modern life. And in so doing, he gives himself the means of repeatedly bemoaning the traumatic loss of 'experience' entailed for the subject when the mode of all possible experience is recognized as a recurrent strategy of defense against the 'inhospitable, blinding age of large-scale industrialism.'[21]

This generalization was evident, *inter alia*, in his influential discussion of Baudelaire's response to the shocks of modern life. The poet's lyric parrying of distressful stimuli, he argued, was in the service of preventing them from becoming truly traumatic, keeping them, that is, at the level of unreflected episodes with no long-term effect on the mind, which failed to register them beyond the moment of impact.[22] Although he understood the reasons for doing so, Benjamin warned explicitly against such defensiveness, which was of a piece with other techniques of anaesthesia developed in the nineteenth century to dull the pain of modern life.[23] Shock-parrying purchases its fragile peace, he claimed, at the cost of a deeper understanding of the sources of the shocks, which might ultimately lead to changing them.[24] Shocks, in short, must be allowed to develop into fully-fledged traumas, for reasons that will be clarified later.

In so arguing, Benjamin was profoundly at odds not only with the nineteenth-century culture of anaesthesia, but also with the postwar, international 'culture of commemoration' that, as George Mosse, Annette Becker, and Jay Winter have recently shown, desperately drew on all the resources of tradition and the sacred it could muster to

[21] Kevin Newmark, 'Traumatic poetry: Charles Baudelaire and the shock of laughter', in Caruth (ed.), *Trauma*, pp. 238–9.

[22] Benjamin, 'On some motifs in Baudelaire', in *Illuminations*, p. 162f.

[23] On the issue of anaesthesia and Benjamin, see Susan Buck-Morss, 'Aesthetics and anaesthetics: Walter Benjamin's artwork essay', *October*, 62 (Fall 1992).

[24] For a suggestive discussion of the distinction between shock and trauma, see Hal Foster, 'What is neo about the neo-avant-garde?', *October*, 70 (Fall 1994). He stresses the delayed temporality in the trauma, which is 'a complex relay of reconstructed past and anticipated future – in short, a deferred action that throws over any simple scheme of before and after, cause and effect, origin and repetition'. The avant-garde, he goes on, was traumatic precisely in this sense: 'a hole in the symbolic order of its time that is not prepared for it, that cannot receive it, at least not immediately, at least not without structural change' (p. 30). Benjamin seems to have been anxious to resist symbolic recuperation of trauma for the same reason.

provide meaning and consolation for the survivors.[25] Rejecting, for
example, the cult of nature that led to the construction of *Heldenhaine*
(heroes groves) of oaks and boulders in the German forests, Benjamin
wrote:

It should be said as bitterly as possible: in the face of this 'landscape of total
mobilization' the German feeling for nature has had an undreamed-of upsurge
. . . Etching the landscape with flaming banners and trenches, technology
wanted to recreate the heroic features of German Idealism. It went astray. What
is considered heroic were the features of Hippocrates, the features of death.
Deeply imbued with its own depravity, technology gave shape to the apocalyptic
face of nature and reduced nature to silence – even though this technology had
the power to give nature its voice.[26]

No pseudo-romantic simulation of pastoral tranquillity in cemeteries
that were disguised as bucolic landscapes could undo the damage. No
ceremonies of reintegration into a community that was already deeply
divided before the war could suture the wounds.

The same impulse informed Benjamin's celebrated defence of allegory
in *Origin of German tragic drama*, which has been recognized by Susan
Buck-Morss as 'a response to the horrifying destructiveness of World
War I'.[27] Understood as a dialectic of unmediated extremes, opposed to
the mediating power of symbolism, allegory refused to sublimate and
transfigure a blasted landscape like that of the war into a locus of beauty,
a forest of symbolic correspondences.[28] 'Whereas in the symbol destruction is idealized and the transfigured face of nature is fleetingly revealed
in the light of redemption', Benjamin argued, 'in allegory the observer is
confronted with the *facies hippocratica* [death's head] of history as a

---

[25] George L. Mosse, *Fallen soldiers: reshaping the memory of the world wars* (New York:
Oxford University Press, 1990); Annette Becker, *La guerre et la foi: De la mort à la
mémoire, 1914–1930* (Paris: A. Cohn, 1994), and Jay Winter, *Sites of memory, sites of
mourning: The Great War in European cultural history* (Cambridge: Cambridge University
Press, 1995). He was not, to be sure, the only critic of this culture of commemoration.
See, for example, the chapter on 'Anti-monuments', in Samuel Hynes, *A war imagined:
the First World War and English culture* (New York: Atheneum, 1990), which discusses
figures like the journalists C. E. Montague and Philip Gibbs and the painter Paul Nash.

[26] Benjamin, 'Theories of German Fascism', p. 126.

[27] Susan Buck-Morss, *The dialectics of seeing* (Cambridge, Mass.: MIT Press, 1989),
p. 178. McCole notes that 'behind the study of allegory, in turn, is the prologue to
"The life of students" written in the first months of the war'. *Walter Benjamin and the
Antinomies of tradition*, p. 265. He discusses this apocalyptic and decisionist text on
pp. 63f.

[28] According to McCole, 'The desire to unmask the official monuments to progress, the
stabilized totalities and transfigured appearances of the dominant culture, by casting
them in the light of the petrified, primordial landscape created on the battlefields of the
war – that gave Benjamin his eye for the coherence of the allegorical way of seeing'
(*Walter Benjamin and the antinomies of tradition*, p. 139). I would emend this claim only
slightly to include the monuments to the war dead produced by the dominant culture
after 1918.

petrified, primordial landscape. Everything about history that, from the
very beginning, has been untimely, sorrowful, unsuccessful, is expressed
in a face – or rather in a death's head.'[29]

Benjamin's saturnine attraction to *Trauerspiel*, the endless, repetitive
'play' of mourning (or more precisely, melancholy), as opposed to
Trauerarbeit, the allegedly 'healthy' 'working through' of grief, was,
however, more than a response to the war experience in general. It was,
I want to argue, specifically linked to his reluctance to close the books
on his friends' anti-war suicides.[30] As he argued in the case of another
suicide, that of the innocent Ottilie in Goethe's *Elective affinities*, the
work to which Benjamin devoted a remarkable study in 1922,[31] making
sense of such acts in terms of sacrifice, atonement, and reconciliation
could only reinforce the evil power of mythic fatalism (and the myth-like
social compulsions of bourgeois society).

To understand Benjamin's uncompromising resistance to both the
cult of the *Fronterlebnis* and the culture of commemoration, including its
pseudo-pastoral naturalism, it is thus necessary to recall the precise
nature of the trauma that he personally suffered in the war. For the
suicides of two teenagers vainly protesting the outbreak of hostilities
cannot have had the same meaning as the deaths of the soldiers who
were assumed to have gallantly fought for their country. Although both
could be made intelligible, even ennobled, through a rhetoric of sacrifice, in the case of the former, the cause could be construed as even
more of a failure than in that of the latter. It certainly was one little
honoured in the inter-war era. Benjamin's bitterness is evident in the
autobiographical 'Berlin chronicle' he composed in 1932, in which he
wrote of the obstacles he experienced in attempting to lay Fritz Heinle
and Rika Seligson to rest: 'Even the graveyard demonstrated the bound-

[29] Benjamin, *The origin of baroque tragic drama*, trans. John Osborne (London: Verso, 1977), p. 166.
[30] For a discussion of the distinction between *Trauerspiel* and *Trauerarbeit*, see Philippe Lacoue-Labarthe, *Typography: mimesis, philosophy, politics*, ed. Christopher Fynsk, introduction by Jacques Derrida (Cambridge, Mass.: Harvard University Press, 1989), p. 234. The same preference for a kind of play that resisted closure was evident in the scripts for Benjamin's radio plays of the 1930s. 'What is significant', according to Jeffrey Mehlman, 'is the author's insistence on repetition (*Wiederholung*) in opposition to imitation (*Nachahmung*) as the grounding virtue of play. For imitation (of parents) is the stuff of narcissism, the subjectivist psychologizing that Benjamin seems intent on keeping at bay. Whereas repetition, however oriented toward mastery, retains its traumatic or catastrophic valence to the end.' *Walter Benjamin for children: an essay on his radio years* (Chicago: University of Chicago Press, 1993), p. 5.
[31] Benjamin, 'Goethes Wahlverwandschaften', *Gesammelte Schriften*, vol. I, eds. Rolf Tiedemann and Hermann Schweppenhäuser (Frankfurt: Suhrkamp, 1974). At times, to be sure, Benjamin had a more nuanced attitude towards myth, as a stage through which culture must pass before genuine *Erfahrung* could be achieved. See Winfried Menninghaus, 'Walter Benjamin's theory of myth', in Smith, *On Walter Benjamin*.

aries set by the city to all that filled our hearts: it was impossible to procure for the pair who had died together graves in one and the same cemetery.'[32]

But rather than remaining a prisoner of his resentment, Benjamin ultimately made a virtue out of that failure, or at least turned it into a warning against the premature, purely aesthetic smoothing over of real contradictions. It was this intransigence that saved him, however close he may seem to have come, from wallowing in the self-pitying 'left-wing melancholy' of the homeless Weimar intellectuals, as well as from the seductive nostrums offered by those on the right.[33] Unlike the commemorative lyrics filled with the traditional healing rhetoric that has allowed Jay Winter to claim that 'a complex process of re-sacralization marks the poetry of the war',[34] Benjamin's sonnets to his war dead – or rather anti-war dead – enacted a ritual of unreconciled duality. Here eternal salvation and no less eternal sorrow remained in uneasy juxtaposition, as antinomies that resist mediation. As Bernhild Boie has noted, whereas the nationalist mobilization of religious rhetoric, in the work of, say, Friedrich Gundolf, sacrificed individual souls for the collective good, Benjamin's poems refused to do so: 'Because Gundolf pompously sacralized the profane horror of the hour, he robbed conscience of its responsibility. Benjamin had conceptualized his sonnet cycle as the radical antithesis of such violence.'[35] Only by a ritualized repetition – the value of ritual, according to Adorno, having been taught to Benjamin by the poetry of Stefan George[36] – could the violence of amnesia be forestalled. Only by refusing false symbolic closure in the present might there still be a chance in the future for the true paradise sought by the idealist self-destroyers buried in their separate and separated graves.

The trope of troubled burial is, in fact, one to which Benjamin

---

[32] Benjamin, 'A Berlin chronicle', *Reflections*, p. 20.

[33] Benjamin, 'Linke Melancholie. Zu Erich Kästners neuem Gedichtbuch', *Die Gesellschaft*, 8, 1 (1931), pp. 181-4.

[34] Winter, *Sites of memory, sites of mourning*, p. 221.

[35] Bernhild Boie, 'Dichtung als Ritual der Erlösung. Zu den wiedergefundenen Sonetten von Walter Benjamin', *Akzente*, 32 (1984), pp. 30–1.

[36] Theodor W. Adorno, 'Benjamin the letter writer', in *On Walter Benjamin: critical essays and recollections*, ed. Gary Smith (Cambridge, Mass.: MIT Press, 1991), p. 330–1. Benjamin, to be sure, rejected the aestheticizing elitism and myth-mongering of the George Circle, as shown in his frequent criticism of Friedrich Gundolf. Tiedemann, in fact, argues that the sonnets to Heinle show an explicit rejection of the striving for redemptive form in George. See his *Nachwort*, pp. 88–9. The link between ritual and other aspects of Benjamin's work is stressed by Andrew Benjamin, who argues that 'it will be in relation to ritual that a conception of experience that involves allegory will emerge. Events are particularized and cannot be repeated. The continuity of ritual is the repetition of the storyteller.' 'Tradition and experience: Walter Benjamin's "On some motifs in Baudelaire"', in *The problems of modernity: Adorno and Benjamin*, ed. Andrew Benjamin (London: Routledge, 1989), p. 127.

returned only a few pages after describing the suicides in the 'Berlin Chronicle', where he generalized about the relation between memory, experience and language. 'Language', he wrote,

shows clearly that memory is not the instrument of exploring the past but its theater. It is the medium of past experience, as the ground is the medium in which dead cities lie interred. He who seeks to approach his own buried past must conduct himself like a man digging. This confers the tone and bearing of genuine reminiscences. He must not be afraid to return again and again to the same matter; to scatter it as one scatters earth, to turn it over as one turns over soil.[37]

Benjamin's own method of digging and redigging his personal past in memoirs like 'A Berlin chronicle' or *Berlin childhood around 1900* was, of course, generalized into a tool of cultural rediscovery – or rather redemptive reconstellation – in his never completed *Passagenwerk*. It followed the principle he derived from that restless, obsessive returning to the displaced graves he had experienced in his relation to his dead friends: 'remembrance must not proceed in the manner of a narrative or still less that of a report, but must, in the strictest epic and rhapsodic manner, assay its spade in ever-new places, and in the old ones delve to ever-deeper depths'.[38]

Benjamin's insistence on not letting the dead rest in peace, at least as long as they remained in false graves, was at the heart of his celebrated critique of historicist attitudes towards the past. Whereas historicists assumed a smooth continuity between past and present, based on an Olympian distance from an allegedly objective story, he assumed the guise of the 'destructive character' who wanted to blast open the seemingly progressive continuum of history, reconstellating the debris in patterns that would somehow provide flashes of insight into the redemptive potential hidden behind the official narrative.[39] It is hard not to hear echoes of his personal anguish over the suicides of Heinle and Seligson when he remarked in the *Passagenwerk* that the task of remembrance is 'to save what has miscarried'.[40] The complicated notion of salvation (*Erlösung*) with which he worked, at once theological and political, contained the imperative to rescue what had been forgotten by the victors of history.

As Stéphane Mosès has argued, such an act of total recall – what might be called a benign variant of the malady of memory dubbed

---

[37] Ibid. p. 27.   [38] Ibid. p. 26.

[39] Benjamin, 'The destructive character', *Reflections*. The last line of this piece, first published in 1931, shows what was still on Benjamin's mind: 'The destructive character lives from the feeling, not that life is worth living, but that suicide is not worth the trouble' (p. 303).

[40] Benjamin, *Passagen werk* (Frankfurt am Main: Suhrkamp, 1982), p. 6ll.

'hypermnesia' by the French psychologist Théodule Ribot[41] – was ultimately aimed at an '*un-knotting* of the *aporias* of the present'[42] through the mobilization of the utopian potential of the past for future transformation. Rather than constructing spatial topoi of commemoration, those *lieux de mémoire* or *Kriegerdenkmale* that functioned to solidify national identity in the present and justify the alleged sacrifices made in its name, the explicitly u-topian – in the literal sense of 'no place' – and ritualized remembrance of past miscarriages must intransigently resist current consolation.

It would perhaps be exaggerated to claim that Benjamin, like Georges Bataille, the friend who saved many of Benjamin's texts after the Second World War, consistently wrote 'against architecture', to borrow the title of the English translation of Denis Hollier's study of Bataille.[43] Benjamin's ambivalent fascination with the glass architecture of complete transparency and public openness promoted by the utopian novelist Paul Scheerbart must, after all, be acknowledged, as must his enthusiasm for the work of Sigfried Giedion and Adolf Loos.[44] But Benjamin did vigorously protest nonetheless against the attempt to embody symbolic fullness in visible, opaque, built forms above the earth, such as the tower, the cenotaph or the pyramid. Even before the war, he was suspicious of this cultural practice. In his *Berlin childhood around 1900*, he recalled youthful visits he had made to the triumphal column that had been erected in the capital of a united Germany to commemorate the famous Prussian victory over the French at Sedan. At its base was a gallery of murals, from which he had always averted his gaze out of fear that they would remind him of the illustrations from Dante's *Inferno* he had seen in the house of one of his aunts. 'The heroes whose deeds glimmered there in the hall of the column', he wrote, 'seemed as quietly infamous as the crowds who did penance whipped by whirlwinds, imprisoned in bleeding tree-stumps, or frozen into blocks of ice. So this gallery was the Hell, the counterpart of the circle of grace around the radiant Victoria above.'[45]

[41] Théodule Ribot, *Les Maladies de la mémoire* (Paris: Alcan, 1881).
[42] Stéphane Mosès, 'The theological-political model of history in the thought of Walter Benjamin', *History and Memory*, 1, 2 (Fall/Winter 1989), p. 31.
[43] Denis Hollier, *Against architecture: the writings of Georges Bataille*, trans. Betsy Wing (Cambridge, Mass.: MIT Press, 1989).
[44] On his fascination with Scheerbart, see Missac, *Walter Benjamin's passages*, chapter 6. On Benjamin's general attitude towards modern architecture, including the work of Loos, see Michael Müller, 'Architektur für das schlechte Neue. Zu Walter Benjamins Verarbeitung avantgardistischer Positionen in der Architektur', *Links hatte noch alles sich zu enträtseln . . .' Walter Benjamin im Kontext*, ed. Burkhardt Lindner (Frankfurt: Syndikat, 1978).
[45] Benjamin, *Berliner Kindheit um 1900* (Frankfurt: Suhrkamp, 1989), p. 17. The translation is by Shierry Weber Nicholsen from the forthcoming English version of the book. I thank her for letting me see it before publication.

No amount of ceremonial gilding, in short, would efface the grim fate of the victims of even the most famous victory.

As is well known, both Benjamin and Bataille were hostile to the general Hegelian logic of sublimation and sublation that sought to transfigure horror into something culturally elevating. Both were suspicious of calls for a return to a lost *Gemeinschaft* through symbolic restoration in architectural terms.[46] Indeed, as Irving Wohlfahrt has noted, Benjamin's more general relation to the past 'marks a clear departure from the Hegelian digestive system, an encyclopedic, (anal-) retentive, self-interiorizing memory (*Er-Innerung*) which preserves and negates" (*aufheben*) the entirety of its prehistory'.[47] Such 'digestive' remembering can only be premised on a certain forgetting, the forgetting of everything that resists incorporation into its system, such as the suicides of anti-war protestors, which are then abjected as so much unnecessary waste.[48]

In fact, even the war itself, Benjamin once speculated, might be understood on one level as a comparable kind of misconceived struggle to heal the fissures that rend modern life. It had been, he wrote in *One-way street* of 1928, a 'desperate attempt at a new commingling with the cosmic powers',[49] which would overcome the gap between man and nature that had disastrously widened since the time of antiquity through the application of technical means. 'This immense wooing of the cosmos was enacted for the first time on a planetary scale, that is, in the spirit of technology. But because the lust for profit of the ruling class sought satisfaction through it, technology betrayed man and turned the bridal bed into a bloodbath.'[50] Benjamin may have held out hope for a different version of benign technology not in the service of that lust for profit, and thus did not reject the desire for reconciliation between man and nature out of hand. But he was resolutely against the distorted effort that characterized the war, as well as the aestheticization of

---

[46] For a discussion of Benjamin's thoughts on the metropolis, which highlights his rejection of *Gemeinschaft* as impossible to restore, see Massimo Cacciari, *Architecture and nihilism: on the philosophy of modern architecture*, trans. Stephen Sartarelli (New Haven: Yale University Press, 1993), pp. 92f. It is for this reason that Richard Terdiman's placement of Benjamin in the same camp as those nostalgic theorists influenced by Tönnies's classic distinction between *Gemeinschaft* and *Gesellschaft* is problematic. See Terdiman, *Present past*, p. 206.

[47] Wohlfahrt, 'No-man's-land', p. 63.

[48] On the dialectic of remembering and forgetting in Benjamin, see Timothy Bahti, 'Theories of knowledge: fate and forgetting in the early works of Walter Benjamin', in *Benjamin's ground: new readings of Walter Benjamin*, ed. Rainer Nägele (Detroit: Wayne State University Press, 1988).

[49] Benjamin, 'One-way street', *Reflections*, p. 93.

[50] Ibid.

destructive technology that he saw in the postwar writings of Jünger and other 'reactionary modernists'.[51]

Only a variant of what Lenin had called 'revolutionary defeatism', a willingness to ride the catastrophe until the end rather than stop it prematurely before its full destructive fury could be allowed to do its work, would provide a sober alternative to such aestheticization. The daily catastrophe of even peacetime society had to be understood as such, and this knowledge had to facilitate a more fundamental reckoning with the forces that led to the war in the first place. As he put it at the conclusion of his essay on Jünger's volume on *War and warrior*, referring to 'the habitués of the chthonic forces of terror', they will possess 'a key to happiness' only 'when they use this discovery to transform this war into civil war and thereby perform that Marxist trick which alone is a match for this sinister runic humbug'.[52]

Not surprisingly, Benjamin could not stomach the religious rhetoric of Resurrection employed by certain artists after the war to give meaning to those who died in battle.[53] 'Everything saturnine', Benjamin wrote in *The origin of German tragic drama*, 'points down into the depths of the earth.'[54] Thus, the labyrinth, that subterranean tangle so often evoked in descriptions of the trenches on the Western Front,[55] was preferable to the monument as a spur to the right kind of remembrance.[56] Although originally an archaic topography, it was revived, Benjamin later argued, in the modern city, the locus of the *flâneur* and the prostitute, where the minotaur mythically situated at its centre embodies the image of 'death-dealing forces'.[57]

Accordingly, it is only the dead body acknowledged as nothing but the corpse that it has become, only, that is, a melancholy acceptance of the destruction of the organic, holistic, lived body, that prepares the remains for their allegorical and emblematic purposes. 'The human body', Benjamin grimly wrote, 'could be no exception to the commandment which ordered the destruction of the organic so that the true meaning,

---

[51] For a discussion of this phenomenon, which draws on Benjamin, see Jeffrey Herf, *Reactionary modernism: technology, culture, and politics in Weimar and the Third Reich* (Cambridge: Cambridge University Press, 1984).

[52] Benjamin, 'Theories of German Fascism', p. 128.

[53] See Winter, *Sites of memory, sites of mourning*, chapter 6, for a discussion of the appropriation of the Resurrection by artists like Georges Rouault.

[54] Benjamin, *The origin of German tragic drama*, p. 152.

[55] For a discussion, see Eric J. Leed, *No man's land: combat and identity in World War I* (Cambridge: Cambridge University Press, 1979), chapter 3.

[56] See Hollier, *Against architecture*, pp. 57–73, for the importance of the labyrinth in Bataille. On its role in Benjamin's work, see Mehlman, *Walter Benjamin for children*, pp. 63f. He comments on the parallel with Bataille.

[57] Walter Benjamin, 'Central park', *New German Critique*, 34 (Winter 1985), p. 53.

as it was written and ordained, might be picked up from its fragments
. . . The characters of the *Trauerspiel* die, because it is only thus, as
corpses, that they can enter into the homeland of allegory. It is not for
the sake of immortality that they meet their end, but for the sake of the
corpse.'[58]

Although it is impossible to know for certain that Benjamin's refusal
to seek consolation for the trauma of his friends' suicides found an
expression in his bleak ruminations on unresurrected, fragmented
corpses in his book on baroque tragic drama, the parallel between the
two is striking. In both cases, the proper attitude was one of allegorical
melancholy rather than symbolic mourning. The restless ghosts of
Heinle and Seligson seem to haunt the pages of this book and much else
in Benjamin's *oeuvre*, which one commentator has gone so far as to call a
'love affair with death'.[59]

Benjamin's morbid preoccupations were thus the opposite of those
that fed the widespread revival of spiritualism, which accompanied that
superstitious belief in the uncanny presence of lost comrades prevalent
among soldiers at the front.[60] For whereas the soldiers yearned for the
dead miraculously to return to life and thus end their own grieving,
Benjamin, resolutely hostile to vitalism of any kind, sought to keep the
grief unconsoled by focusing on the de-animization that had produced
the corpse. 'Criticism', he was to argue in *The origin of German tragic
drama*, 'means the mortification of the works . . . not then – as the
romantics have it – awakening of the consciousness in living works, but
the settlement of knowledge in dead ones.'[61] Mortification of the non-
textual world as well, or at least facing the catastrophe that had already
occurred, was preferable to wishing it away. Rather than seek life in
death, the animate in the inanimate, it was better to acknowledge the
ubiquity of *mementi mori* and decry the false consolations offered by
magical thinking.[62] Only in so doing might the utopian hope for an

---

[58] Benjamin, *The origin of German tragic drama*, pp. 216–17.
[59] Rey Chow, 'Walter Benjamin's love affair with death', *New German Critique*, 48 (Fall
1989).
[60] Winter, *Sites of memory, sites of mourning*, pp. 64f.
[61] Benjamin, *The origin of German tragic drama*, p. 182.
[62] Gary Smith has argued that in the early 1920s Benjamin did share a certain rhetoric of
spiritual esotericism with other heterodox Jewish thinkers of his day, including Oskar
Goldberg, Erich Unger, Erich Gutkind, and Gershom Scholem. See Smith, '"Die
Zauberjuden": Walter Benjamin and other Jewish esoterics between the world wars',
The Journal of Jewish Thought and Philosophy, 4 (1995). However, he acknowledges that
Benjamin always found Goldberg distasteful and ultimately came to dissociate himself
explicitly from the other 'Magic Jews'. See Benjamin's letter to Scholem of
24 December 1934, where he uses the term derisorily. *The correspondence of Walter
Benjamin and Gershom Scholem, 1932– 1940*, ed. Gershom Scholem, trans. Gary Smith
and Andre Lefevre (Cambridge, Mass.: Harvard University Press, 1992), p. 148.

ultimate apocatastasis, the redemption of all the fragments of fallen reality, the admission of all souls into heaven, be maintained.[63] Only then might happen a true awakening from the spell of myth and mystification that produced the conditions that led to the war in the first place.

Benjamin's desperate gamble that such an outcome might possibly follow from the rigorous denial of any consolation in the present has aroused considerable discomfort in many of his commentators. The nihilist streak evident in his antinomian evocation of divine violence and refusal to endorse the humanist pieties of conciliation and communi-cation – as if the promise of the Youth Movement's *Sprechsaal* had been smashed forever by the self-destructive violence committed in its halls – seems to some a literal dead end. According to Gillian Rose, 'it is this unequivocal refusal of any dynamic of mutual recognition and struggle which keeps Benjamin's thinking restricted to the stasis of desertion, *aberrated mourning*, and the yearning for invisible, divine violence'.[64] His defence of repetitive, never-worked-through remembrance Rose grounds in the Jewish notion of *Zakhor*, which she claims 'has the consequence of devaluating historiographical discernment in different times and places. It encourages eschatological repetition in the place of political judgment. But for Benjamin, all political judgment is melan-cholic and violent.'[65] What she calls 'inaugurated' as opposed to 'aber-rated mourning' contains the potential for forgiveness that Benjamin, with his furious fixation on the injustice of his friends' anti-war suicides, could never realize. As such, Benjamin's position may seem uncomfor-tably close to what the recent historian of psychoanalysis Peter Homans has called the Nazis' own 'refusal to mourn'.[66] For, to put it in the vocabulary of Judith Lewis Herman, it favours the maintenance of

---

[63] On the idea of apocatastasis in Benjamin, see Irving Wohlfahrt, 'Et Cetera? De l'historien comme chiffonnier', in *Walter Benjamin et Paris*, ed. Heinz Wismann (Paris: Cerf, 1986), pp. 596–609.

[64] Gillian Rose, *Judaism and modernity: philosophical essays* (Oxford: Blackwell, 1993), p. 209.

[65] Ibid. p. 207.

[66] Peter Homans, *The ability to mourn: disillusionment and the social origins of psychoanalysis* (Chicago: University of Chicago Press, 1989). He argues that the Nazis, 'intolerant of chaos[,] . . . sought to reinvent with great rapidity and astonishing creativity a total common culture in which a sacred symbolic structure overcame time, the sense of transience and diachrony . . . For them, the manic defense and persecutory activity successfully energized a new cosmology which abolished the ability to mourn and what I would also call "the capacity to be depressed". It was as if they had said, There has been no loss at all' (p. 338). The larger argument of the book is that psychoanalysis, unlike Nazism, was based on a healthy ability to mourn the loss of cultural meaning produced by secularization.

'traumatic memory', which simply repeats the past, over 'narrative memory', which works it through by telling intelligible stories.[67]

Jeffrey Mehlman, from a vantage point far less Hegelian than Rose's, suggests other dangers. Benjamin's insistence on valorizing catastrophe rather than trying to heal it, on 'plunging into evil, albeit to defeat it from within',[68] echoes the Jewish messianic tradition that Scholem had shown often promoted mystical transgression as a means to redemption. It also recalls the tragic episode of the seventeenth-century false messiah Sabbatai Zvi, in which catastrophe was mingled with fraud, an explosive mixture that Mehlman ingeniously discerns in the scripts of Benjamin's radio plays of the early 1930s. Sabbatianism, he notes, rejected the symbolic reading of the world in the earlier Kabbalah in favour of an allegorical one, in which there was no apparent or natural unity between sign and signified. But this dissolution had its great danger. For now, to be a good Jew and to appear to be one were no longer necessarily the same, which opened the door to the possibility of a false messiah, such as the Sabbatai Zvi.

In the case of what he calls Benjamin's 'neo-Sabbatianism',[69] the same dangerous possibility exists. That is, there could be no guarantee that Benjamin's desperate wager on melancholic intransigence and resistance to commemorative healing would ultimately bring about the genuine redemption for which he so fervently yearned. Especially when he yoked his negative theology to the Marxist dream of a classless society, as he did in the final lines of his essay on Jünger's *War and warrior* when he advocated the transformation of war into a civil war, the potential for catastrophe to produce fraud rather than salvation was increased still further.[70] When one recalls Benjamin's own willingness to use fraudulent means to dodge the draft during the First World War – one of the few links in the chain left unforged by Mehlman's superheated associative imagination – it may well seem as if he were not above

---

[67] Judith Lewis Herman, *Trauma and recovery* (New York: Basic Books, 1992). For a critique of this argument, which comes close to Benjamin's position without drawing on it, see Ruth Leys, 'Traumatic cures: shell shock, Janet, and the question of memory', *Critical Inquiry*, 20, 4 (Summer 1994), pp. 623–62. She shows that for Pierre Janet, fully narrating the past was itself insufficient, as some liquidation of it as well was necessary to 'cure' shell shock.

[68] Mehlman, *Walter Benjamin for children*, p. 80.   [69] Ibid. p. 94.

[70] Mehlman hints at the end of his book that it is not so much the Marxist dream of a classless society that constitutes the fraudulent echo of Sabbatianism, but the Enlightenment dream of assimilation itself. The latter, he claims, leads to the '"silent Holocaust" of Jewish self-denial which is the daily mode of ordinary Jewish life in the West'. *Walter Benjamin for children*, p. 97. In effect, Rose attacks Benjamin for his allegiance to a Jewish notion of repetitive, ahistorical memory, whereas Mehlman criticizes him for fostering the dissolution of Jewish particularity in the universal solvent of the Enlightenment.

exploiting both catastrophe and fraud for his own dubious redemptive fantasies.

A third critique is made by those who claim that by holding on to such fantasies in whatever form Benjamin drew inadvertently near to the very Fascist aestheticization of politics he was ostensibly trying to fight. This is the damning conclusion, for example, of Leo Bersani's *The culture of redemption*.[71] From this perspective, Benjamin's apparent resistance to symbolic mourning, his defiance of the imperative to work through his grief, is understood as still in the service of an ultimate reconciliation, which is impossible to attain. Whereas neo-Hegelians like Gillian Rose fault Benjamin for rejecting a good version of mourning – inaugurated rather than aberrated in her vocabulary – anti-Hegelians like Bersani see a desire for *any* version of mourning as problematically holistic and harmonistic, based on a nostalgia for an origin prior to the fall, a state of bliss that never really existed.[72]

What these critics perhaps fail to register is the critical distinction between a refusal to mourn that knows all too well what its object is – in Benjamin's case, the anti-war suicides of his idealist friends – and is afraid that mourning will close the case prematurely on the cause for which they died, and a refusal to mourn based on a denial that there was anything lost in the first place. Whereas Benjamin defended allegorical melancholy to keep the wound open in the hope of some later utopian redemption, understanding ritual and repetition as a placeholder for a future happiness, the Nazis sought symbolic closure without any delay, hoping to fashion a seamless continuity between the revered war dead and their own martyrs.[73] Rather than melancholic, their refusal to mourn was maniacal, in the clinical sense of a mania that giddily denies the reality of the lost object. Melancholy and mania, as Freud famously argued, may both be sides of the same inability to mourn, but in this case, the differences, it seems to me, outweigh the similarities.

What makes Benjamin's hopes for redemption so hard to grasp is that

---

[71] 'The cultic use value of art that Benjamin claims we have lost is actually an archaic version of the fascist use of art as he dramatically defines it in "The work of art in the age of mechanical reproduction": the aestheticizing of politics.' Leo Bersani, *The culture of redemption* (Cambridge, Mass.: Harvard University Press, 1990), p. 60.

[72] For a consideration of the issue of origin in Benjamin, see John Pizer, *Toward a theory of radical origin: essays on modern German thought* (Lincoln, Nebr.: University of Nebraska Press, 1995). Pizer argues that the concept of *Ursprung* in Benjamin, derived in part from Karl Kraus, must be understood as more than a simple return to plenitudinous grace. But he rejects the deconstructionist reading of Benjamin as being entirely against all notions of origin.

[73] According to Mosse, 'the martyrs of the Nazi movement were identified with the dead of the First World War, and identical symbols were used to honor their memory: steel helmets, holy flames, and monuments which projected the Nazi dead as clones of the soldiers who had earlier fought and died for the fatherland', *Fallen soldiers*, p. 183.

they seem not to have been grounded in a simple desire to undo the trauma of the anti-war suicides and resurrect the dead or even merely to realize the anti-war cause for which they died. Instead, the model of redemption he seems to have favoured, I want to suggest, may paradoxically have been based on the lesson of trauma itself. Was he perhaps talking more of himself than of Baudelaire when he wrote in 'On some motifs in Baudelaire' that 'psychiatry knows traumatophile types'?[74] It will be recalled that Benjamin's critique of Baudelaire's poetic parrying of the shocks of modern life was directed at the anaesthetic refusal to register the pain of the trauma; which meant keeping the protective shield of the psyche up at all costs. Like the aesthetic response of symbolic sublimation, defensive parrying struggled to regain the subject's mastery over a world that seemed out of control. In a certain sense, both aesthetic and anaesthetic responses missed something in their haste to move beyond that pain. Or put differently, both were too hasty in trying to reconcile the unreconcilable. What was unreconcilable about trauma has been noted by Freud, who understood, to cite Cathy Caruth, 'that the impact of the traumatic event lies precisely in its belatedness, in its refusal to be simply located, in its insistent appearance outside the boundaries of any single place or time . . . trauma is not simple or single experience of events but . . . events insofar as they are traumatic, assume their force precisely in their temporal delay'.[75]

Benjamin's redemptive fantasies, such as they were, were thus not for harmonistic closure and plenitudinous presence. They were u-topian, as we have seen, precisely because they denied a positive place that could be the locus of fulfilment. They were also temporally disjunctive, *pace* his frequent evocation of the mystical notion of *Jetztzeit* (Now-time). Favouring instead what might be called the stereoscopic time of the dialectical image, they incorporated that experience of lag time produced by trauma. They were thus based on a notion of memory that differed from a Hegelian *Erinnerung*, in which the past was digested by the present in a heightened moment of totalizing interiorization. Instead, Benjamin's notion of *Gedächtnis* preserved the very dissociation between past and present, the temporal delay of the trauma itself, that made a constellation – and not a collapse – of the two possible. For only if the distinctness of past and present and the heterogeneity of multiple spaces were maintained could a true apocatastasis, a benign hypermnesia without exclusion and incorporation, be achieved. Only if the intractable otherness of the lost object is preserved and not neutralized through a process of incorporation can the possibility of genuine

[74] Benjamin, 'On some motifs in Baudelaire', p. 165.
[75] Cathy Caruth, 'Introduction' to Caruth, *Trauma*, p. 9.

Erfahrung be realized.[76] Thus, in some profoundly paradoxical sense, the catastrophe and the redemption were the same, and the infinite ritual repetition without closure not a means, but an end. The true fraud, *pace* Mehlman, is thus the very belief in the resurrection of the dead, their symbolic recuperation through communal efforts to justify their alleged 'sacrifice' and ignore their unrecuperable pain.

It is for this reason that Benjamin's intransigent resistance to symbolic healing and positive commemoration merits continued respect. For even if one is unable to share his belief in utopian apocatastasis, it must be acknowledged that he gave the lie to the assumption that the victims of the war – or more profoundly, of the society ruled by myth and injustice that could have allowed it to happen – could be best understood as heroic warriors who died for a noble cause. This is a lesson that ironically can be learned as well from the fate Benjamin himself suffered on the eve of the Second World War. For his suicide on the French/ Spanish border also defied symbolic closure. Indeed, his rest proved as peaceless as those of Fritz Heinle and Frederika Seligson in 1914. As Pierre Missac observed in words that can fittingly serve as the final ones of this paper:

His body . . . disappeared after his death. We have nothing but one more death without burial among so many others; no name on a common grave, even for someone who, while alive, provided a name for the nameless; not even the white cross of the military cemeteries sprinkled across Europe and the Pacific. All the more reason why no *tombeau* will evoke Benjamin's memory, only the interminable prose pieces after Babel, among them the present work.[77]

---

[76] According to Angelika Rauch's insightful gloss on Benjamin's position, 'As memory of an experience, commemoration or remembrance must refuse the labor of mourning because such a *Trauerarbeit* aims at the representation of the *other* – the experience and affect – by turning it into what Benjamin had labeled "a souvenir", that is, an object in conscious memory that corresponds to an object in the history of events. Once the *other* has achieved the status of an object, the subject can dispose of it. If an experience in the sense of *Erfahrung* is, however, responsible for shaping the self, is part of the self, then it cannot so easily be split off, disposed of, and, in the end, forgotten. The mission of tradition is precisely *not* to make experience into an event or an object because only the power of feeling humbles us, sensitizes us to an *other*, and teaches us to live with what Kant had identified as the monstrosity of the sublime.' 'The broken vessel of tradition', *Representations*, 53 (Winter 1996), p. 90.

[77] Missac, *Benjamin's passages*, p. 10. One might add that, for Adorno in particular, Benjamin's suicide seems to have worked in the way that Heinle's had for Benjamin: as a never-worked-through trauma that came to emblematize the horror of the age. See the discussion in Susan Buck-Morss, *The origin of negative dialectics: Theodor W. Adorno, Walter Benjamin, and the Frankfurt Institute* (New York: Free Press, 1977), p. 165.

Index

Studies in the Social and Cultural History of Modern Warfare

Titles in the series: